MW01054601

The Best Team Over There

The Best Team Over There

The Untold Story of Grover Cleveland Alexander and the Great War

JIM LEEKE

University of Nebraska Press • LINCOLN

Library of Congress Cataloging-in-Publication Data
Names: Leeke, Jim, 1949– author.
Title: The best team over there: the untold story of Grover
Cleveland Alexander and the Great War / Jim Leeke.
Description: Lincoln: University of Nebraska Press, 2021. |
Includes bibliographical references and index.
Identifiers: LCCN 2020029301
ISBN 9781496217165 (Hardback: acid-free paper)
ISBN 9781496226396 (ePub)
ISBN 9781496226402 (mobi)
ISBN 9781496226419 (PDF)
Subjects: LCSH: Alexander, Grover Cleveland, 1887–1950. |
Pitchers (Baseball)—Nebraska—Biography. | Baseball
players—United States—Biography. | Soldiers—United
States—Biography. | Soldiers—Wounds and injuries—United
States. | World War, 1914–1918—Medical care. | War—Medical
aspects—History—20th century. | United States. Army—
Medical care—History—20th century. | Medicine, Military—
United States—History—20th century.
Classification: LCC GV865.A33 L44 2021 | DDC
796.357092/273—dc23
LC record available at https://lccn.loc.gov/2020029301

Set in Arno Pro by Mikala R. Kolander.

For Carol, Dave, Cal, and Jon

The avidity with which American soldiers are entering into the activities of the war on the battle line is astonishing to European armies. In the matter of grenade and bomb throwing the Americans become proficient in but a few days' drill. I attribute this in part to the American games, football and baseball, which makes strategists of them all.

—Gen. John J. Pershing, *Arizona Republican,* 1918

It has been a long, hard pull, this business of warfare, and I am glad it is over.

—Sgt. Grover C. Alexander, *New York Herald,* 1919

CONTENTS

Prologue   1

1. Alexander the Great   3
2. Laddies from Missouri   17
3. Gridiron   25
4. Chicago   32
5. Fast Nine   50
6. Through a Door   59
7. Camp Funston   71
8. Camp Mills   80
9. *Justicia*   89
10. Camp de Souge   100
11. Pauillac   109
12. St. Mihiel   119
13. Euvezin   127
14. Armistice   141
15. The March   151
16. Occupied Germany   160
17. Safe at Home   173
18. Postwar   182
19. The Long, Long Trail   194

Acknowledgments   205
Appendix A: Selected Athletes of the 342nd Field Artillery   207
Appendix B: Composition of the 164th Field Artillery Brigade   209

Notes   211
Bibliography   237
Index   243

The Best Team Over There

Prologue

Shadows of years—ghosts of old days—
Shadows and ghosts—in the grip of fate;
Is it only a dream through the winter haze
When the drill is long where the big guns wait?

—LT. GRANTLAND RICE

Grover Cleveland Alexander, a sixty-three-year-old alcoholic, died alone in a rented room in St. Paul, Nebraska. Once he had been the most dominant pitcher in the National League. He had won 373 games during twenty seasons in the Major Leagues, trailing only Cy Young and Walter Johnson and tied with mighty Christy Mathewson. Schoolboys knew Alexander's record by heart.

The rawboned right-hander and former telephone lineman had been born in tiny nearby Elba but always considered St. Paul home. Half the people in town seemed to own baseballs he'd autographed, many of which he had traded for drinks. Everyone there knew him as Dode, a nickname he otherwise had long since abandoned. Ballplayers had dubbed him Pete and later Ol' Pete. Legions of fans still thought of him as Alexander the Great, even two decades after he'd last thrown a pitch in a big-league park. It was impossible to overstate Alexander's fame. Yet in November 1950 he had died almost a bum.

Branch Rickey, the baseball man whom people called the Mahatma, had worked with Alexander in St. Louis during the 1920s. "I doubt that I ever felt sorrier for any man who ever worked for me than I did for Alexander," Rickey said. "He was a perfectly wonderful fellow and his only enemy was himself."[1]

Alexander hadn't always been a drunk. In another country, during another time, he had been another person. During the First World War the hurler had answered to another nickname, one earned outside baseball. Soldiers in France had called him Sarge—Sgt. G. C. Alexander, Battery F, 342nd Field Artillery, Eighty-Ninth Division, American Expeditionary Forces. His enemies then had been filth, discomfort, and Germans.

Understanding that soldier and his war is crucial to understanding his long, tumultuous decline afterward. Biographer John C. Skipper likens the period to "one bad inning in a ball game."[2] Two veterans from Alexander's old outfit understood that and headed to St. Paul when he died to see Sergeant Alexander to his final rest.

A month earlier the once-renowned pitcher had stood unnoticed in a big baseball crowd watching the Philadelphia Phillies, his first Major League team, play in the 1950 World Series. The *New York Times* had published what now seemed a fitting epitaph. "Sic Transit Gloria," the headline read.[3] *So the glory . . .*

ONE

Alexander the Great

And the story is this—when the hour is due—
And it may be for me and it may be for you—
To-day and to-morrow are one and the same
If we stick to the highway and play out the game. . . .

—GRANTLAND RICE, 1917

The Philadelphia Phillies were in Norfolk, Virginia, barnstorming north after spring training in Florida, when America declared war on Germany. The cool, gray Friday culminated the nation's long slide into the world war that had convulsed most of Europe since August 1914.

The United States initially had stood clear of the conflict between the forces aligned under Great Britain and Germany. Americans had declared independence from England in 1776 and had fought the country again in 1812–14. Millions of Germans had emigrated to America following their own failed revolutions in 1848. During the early twentieth century, King George V wasn't particularly regarded as a friend, nor Kaiser Wilhelm II especially as an enemy. It had seemed best to stay out of the Great War and let American businesses sell to both sides.

Anger at Germany began in May 1915 when a U-boat torpedoed and sank the British passenger liner *Lusitania* taking nearly two thousand lives, including more than a hundred Americans. President Woodrow

Wilson won reelection a year and a half later on the slogan "He Kept Us Out of War," but he couldn't permanently keep the country free of growing entanglements. Yankee anger reignited early in 1917 with the publication of the Zimmermann Telegram, an intercepted German proposal for a military alliance with Mexico if America should enter the conflict. Coupled with resumption of unrestricted submarine warfare aimed at breaking the British sea blockade, the telegram tipped the balance against Germany. At 1:18 p.m. on April 6, 1917, five months after his reelection and one month and a day since his second inauguration, President Wilson signed a war resolution passed by Congress.

"The lamps are going out all over Europe; we shall not see them lit again in our lifetime," British foreign secretary Sir Edward Grey had said mournfully on the eve of war in 1914.[1] Now the lights were dimming across America as well. A headline in the *New York Tribune* proclaimed everything that mattered: "America in Armageddon; Country Is Called to War; All Its Forces Mobilizing."[2]

The Phillies expected to play an interleague exhibition in Norfolk with Clark Griffith's Washington Senators that fateful spring afternoon. Fans were filing into the local Virginia League park for a three o'clock start when Philadelphia suddenly called off the game. The club blamed the cancellation not on the war news, which the teams might not yet have heard, but on soggy field conditions. Even burning gasoline atop the diamond hadn't sufficiently dried it after heavy rain the previous day. "Manager Pat Moran, of the Quakers [Phillies], arrived on the scene, gave the field the once-over, and declared that he would not permit his stars to risk a leg or neck on the slippery, muddy ground. . . . Both teams put in 45 minutes of practice and the fans, to whom the price of admittance was returned, got something for their trip."[3]

Whatever the reason for scrubbing the game, the tough navy town already had cleared its decks for war. A glance toward Hampton Roads confirmed it. "Washington players were considerably disappointed this morning to find that the great fleet of battleships that up to a couple of days ago had been assembled in the waters nearby, had been ordered away for distribution at various points for patrol and guard duty," *Washington Star* sportswriter Denman Thompson wrote.[4] Pat Moran, never fond of barnstorming anyway, was glad to leave Norfolk early and head north for a second planned exhibition with manager Griffith's club in Washington.

The Phillies' spring training in 1917 was Pete Alexander's first since his father's death during the winter. William Alexander had passed away on December 11 in Nebraska after a long illness. Pete was one of his eleven children, eight of whom had lived to adulthood. A married sister had died in 1914, leaving seven surviving brothers. The Alexanders had once been a farming family, but Bill and his wife, Margaret, called Maggie, had given up their unforgiving acres long before he suffered the stroke that ended his life. The local *St. Paul Phonograph* newspaper had recalled the change:

> Some ten years ago they moved down from Elba and took charge of the county poor farm and they continued to make their home here ever since. They were just now arranging to move from the county poor farm and make their future home in this city in a property recently purchased by their son, Grover, for them. . . .
>
> Not many funerals are held where six sons are able to be pall bearers but such was the case yesterday afternoon, when six of the Alexander boys were pall bearers for their father.[5]

Pete was now beginning a new baseball season, his seventh with the Phillies. Traveling by steamboat up from Norfolk, Moran's club reached Washington the morning following the declaration of war. The team prepared to play the second game of a planned three-game series with Washington at three o'clock Saturday afternoon on the Senators' field. "Grover Cleveland Alexander, leading pitcher of the past season, and Walter Johnson's greatest rival on the mound, is expected to exhibit his wares today for two or three innings against the Griffmen at Georgia avenue," sportswriter Louis Dougher wrote in the *Washington Times*. "Undoubtedly many arguments regarding his style will be settled by nightfall."[6]

Alexander started the game for the Phillies, but the Washington fans' hopes for a faceoff with Walter "Big Train" Johnson, their own phenomenal pitcher, were dashed. The Big Train and a second squad of Senators were westbound for an exhibition game with the American Association club in Columbus, Ohio, also called the Senators. Alexander instead pitched four innings against journeyman right-hander Bert Gallia. He surrendered only a single run but the Phillies lost, 3–2. Alexander was tagged with the loss, which counted for nothing and meant as much.

"He came, he saw and he failed to conquer," Thompson wrote in the *Star*. "The mighty Grover Cleveland Alexander, premier pitcher of the Phillies and star par excellence of the National League, showed his wares to a handful of shivering fans at the Georgia avenue grounds yesterday, and when he retired, at the end of the fourth inning, the score was 1 to 0, with Aleck and his Quaker city companions on the 0 end."[7]

The two teams had Sunday free. Every local newspaper the Phillies might have found at a hotel newsstand was filled with war news. The *Times* reported the seizure of scores of suspected German spymasters across the country, with additional arrests anticipated along the volatile southern border with Mexico. The *Herald* warned of an enemy raider off Nantucket and American vessels detained in ports for their own safety. Perhaps the most alarming headline for a young ballplayer ran on the front page of the *Star*: "President Backs Conscription Plan." The article stated that President Wilson, Secretary of War Baker, and the "entire military of the government" believed that America must soon begin conscripting men.

> Secretary Baker solemnly informed the House military affairs committee of this belief yesterday, during a discussion of the War Department bill providing for training an army of a million men, raised by selective conscription during the next year.
>
> There will be opposition to the proposed conscription plan in both the House and Senate, and a bitter fight against this legislation is expected.

But the supporters of universal military service, to be applied through conscription, feel that they will be successful in the end, because, they say, it has been clearly demonstrated in the past, both in this country and abroad, that the volunteer system is not to be relied upon.[8]

Alexander and other Major League ballplayers were whipsawed by conflicting information and opinion. The *Star* reported that the American League president, Byron Bancroft "Ban" Johnson, and the National League president, former Pennsylvania governor John K. Tener, both were "confident that the coming season will be a good one, both as to attendance and competition for the pennant, and that war will not interrupt the sport."[9] But if they had been home in Philadelphia, the Phillies might have read another view in Saturday's *Ledger*: "The rifle is going to take the place of the bat in the hands of many a young ball player in this country within a short time. Baseball will get the hardest blow of its long and stormy career when the War Department starts raising its army by selective conscription."[10] An early plan called for conscripting men of ages nineteen to twenty-five, which would have spared Alexander, along with other established stars such as Ty Cobb, Tris Speaker, and Eddie Collins. But it was too early to know what to expect. All anyone could do was wait.

It was springtime in the East, when skies change quickly. Nature seemed set against baseball as a heavy snow fell on Washington, forcing cancellation of Monday's planned third and final Philadelphia-Washington exhibition. Martial language already had begun infiltrating the sports pages. "Brigadier General Moran . . . issued hurried marching orders," the *Philadelphia Ledger* reported. "Instead of leaving here at 7 o'clock this evening for home, the famous commander in chief in the field (when he can put them there) of the Phillies ordered his light infantry and his heavy artillery to entrain at 3:03 o'clock, and if all goes well they will detrain at North Philadelphia station at 6:10 this evening."[11] Moran could have had no inkling how literally "heavy artillery" would apply later to his star hurler.

The Phillies opened their 1917 season on Wednesday, April 11, on the road in Brooklyn. Alexander strode onto the Ebbets Field mound following pregame ceremonies that included raising an American flag so large that four sailors had to hoist it. He tossed a complete-game, 6–5 victory over Leon Cadore of the Dodgers—or the Superbas, as the Brooklyn club was commonly called (or the Robins, as the Dodgers also were known under manager Wilbert Robinson).

"Whatever was not done at bat had to be discounted by the fact that the Superbas were facing admittedly the best pitcher in the National League, if not the best in the world," sportswriter Tom Rice observed in the *Brooklyn Eagle*. "If Aleck trimmed them, it certainly could not be considered disgraceful. It so happened that Aleck won, but he will not have many games this season in which he will have so many anxious moments." Alexander quashed a Brooklyn rally in the eighth inning by fielding a bunt toward third base, "a $5 lesson furnished free to all the other pitchers in the ball yard."[12]

In Philadelphia the following day, Athletics manager Connie Mack sent one of his young pitchers into his first Major League game. Like Alexander, Winfield "Win" Noyes was a Nebraska native. The rookie appeared in relief during the second inning of a home loss and "pitched impressive ball, despite nervousness on his debut in a major uniform."[13] A year or more later, perhaps, when both wore the same new uniform, Noyes and Alexander would compare memories of taking the mound for the first time in the City of Brotherly Love.

The weeks following America's entry into the war saw a flurry of enlistments among retired players. Former New York Giants teammates Edward Grant and Harry "Moose" McCormick enrolled the first week of May in army officers' training at Plattsburg, New York. The following month little-known Hugh Miller, briefly Alexander's teammate in 1911 and later a first baseman for the St. Louis Terriers in the Federal League, enlisted as a private in the U.S. Marine Corps. Edward "Doc" Lafitte, a former Detroit Tiger and Brooklyn Tip-Top (Federal League), who had earned a dental degree while still playing, enlisted in the army's dental corps during the summer. Harry "Lank

Hank" Gowdy, likeable catcher and World Series hero for Boston's 1914 "Miracle Braves," became the first active Major Leaguer to join the colors. Gowdy enlisted in the Ohio National Guard the second day of June and reported for duty the following month. Sports pages across the country acclaimed these men and would report on their activities in as much detail as censorship permitted throughout the war. It would sometimes make for hard reading.

But the enlistments of McCormick, Grant, Miller, and Gowdy during America's first spring and summer of war were exceptions rather than the rule. Active ballplayers didn't flock to recruiting stations to follow their example, which disappointed the segment of the sports press that believed athletes should serve as role models for American males during wartime. Every ballplayer recognized in 1917 that conscription darkened their horizon. There was no need to march off to join the armed forces. Soon enough, they knew, government notices would order them into khaki.

President Wilson signed the federal Selective Service Act at eight o'clock on the evening of May 18, 1917. The law authorized establishment of a draft system under Provost Marshal General Enoch Crowder, an army general. "The whole nation must be a team in which each man shall play the part for which he is best fitted," Wilson proclaimed. "To this end Congress has provided that the nation shall be organized for war by selection and that each man shall be classified for service in the place to which it shall best serve the general good to call him."[14] With the draft law in place, every American male who had reached his twenty-first birthday but hadn't yet reached his thirty-first was obligated to register with the government on Tuesday, June 5, 1917. Pete Alexander had turned thirty in February and, contrary to early indications, was of draft age after all.

Conscription was generally accepted but not terribly popular; the Selective Service bill had passed in the Senate by a vote of sixty-five to eight. Many communities nonetheless celebrated Registration Day like a national holiday, with flags, bands, and parades in what a Philadelphia newspaper called a "patriotic landslide."[15] General Crowder told the Senate military affairs committee the day before Registration Day that the War Department planned to call 625,000 men into the armed forces from among the ten million men expected to register. "To secure this number, he said, it probably will be necessary to draft at least 900,000 and possibly 1,500,000 because of expected exemptions."[16] Registration Day would prepare the ground for the first draft call, with other calls to follow as needed. America needed conscription to fill the huge new U.S. Army, which would total nearly four million soldiers before the war's end. Eight hundred thousand more men would serve as sailors and marines (coast guardsmen served with the navy for the duration).

The Phillies were one of eight Major League teams scheduled to be away from home on Registration Day. Moran's club was starting a long road trip the last week of May, first traveling to New York for a series with the Giants, then making their first swing through the western circuit. The schedules posed no significant problem, however. Draft-eligible players whose teams would be away on the momentous day could file their forms early. Boston Braves shortstop Walter "Rabbit" Maranville, for instance, strode into city hall in the Hub to register with several teammates on May 25.

Alexander faced the draft in the same way as his peppery little National League opponent, appearing before a registration commissioner in Philadelphia the same day as Maranville in Boston. Alexander probably was accompanied by teammates too. His registration form listed his employer as the Philadelphia National League club at the corner of Broad and Huntingdon Streets. The pitcher stated that he was unmarried and claimed draft exemption as "sole support of mother."[17] Curiously, he also listed two years' military service as a private in the Nebraska National Guard—a claim he didn't repeat on an army form he filled out a year later. Authorities sent the completed registration card to his local draft board in St. Paul. Alexander left the office carrying one of the small blue cards that became familiar to millions of young American men. These documents, a *Wash-*

ington Times article stated, "when properly attested, were given as certificates to those who registered for the draft."[18] A registered man was wise always to carry his card. "A policeman or a provost marshal's guard may at any time demand a view of it," cautioned the *Washington Star*. "Carry it in some protecting envelope or cover to keep it clean, and have it always handy for inspection."[19]

"Eleven members of the Phillies, who are now leading the National League, have registered for the selective draft," a Philadelphia newspaper reported. "The team will be in Chicago on June 5, registration day. Those who registered, all of whom live outside of Philadelphia, are Alexander, Mayer, Burns, Bancroft, Fittery, Killefer, Dugey, Cooper, McGaffigan, Adams and Whitted."[20]

Their duty done, the registered Phillies went out to their ballpark, the oddly named Baker Bowl, and beat the visiting Cincinnati Reds, 5–2. Eppa Rixey, the winning pitcher, filed his registration card the following day. Thirteen of manager John McGraw's Giants, due to entrain for a road trip themselves after facing the Phillies in New York, also registered on May 26, as did various Dodgers in Brooklyn. Nearly all of manager Clark Griffith's American League club registered in Washington on May 31. Throughout the Major Leagues, other managers and owners ensured that all eligible players submitted their paperwork on or before Registration Day. The legal and publicity consequences if they didn't were unthinkable. The situation wasn't much different for ordinary American males.

"So far it is not definitely known whether or not there were any 'slackers,'" the *St. Paul Phonograph* reported from Alexander's hometown in Howard County, Nebraska. "It has been unofficially reported that there are a few instances thru-out the county where men failed to register. The law regarding failure to register does not 'beat around the bush,' and should it be proven that there are any 'slackers' in this county, we all know about what would happen to the delinquent ones. We hope, however, that this county will come thru with a clean sheet."[21] The *Phonograph* later listed Alexander first among the 956 local men who had registered.

The government held the first national draft lottery on July 20. The process was somewhat confusing. Every man's local draft board had written a serial number in red ink on his registration card. Alexander's was 342, which would seem eerily prescient a year later. The lottery determined a man's draft number, which signified the order in which he would be called for military service. "For some it may mean everlasting fame, for Napoleon's saying that every private carries a marshal's baton in his knapsack is still true," the *New York Tribune* observed. "For most it will mean a pulling up of stakes, a breaking of home and business ties, and the entire current of their lives diverted."[22]

Conscripted men would be called before examining boards according to their draft numbers, from 1 to 10,500. Each then would be placed in one of several draft classes and subclasses, according to his marital status, occupation, health, and more. This odd arrangement held for all 4,557 draft districts—even sparsely populated rural districts such as Howard County that had nowhere near the maximum number of eligible men. "In districts where there are fewer than 10,500 men registered, any 'draft numbers' corresponding to a 'red ink number' higher than the number of registrants will be disregarded and the draft number next on the list will be called."[23]

Secretary of War Baker personally began the lottery a little before ten o'clock on Friday morning at the Senate Office Building in Washington. He drew a small capsule from the thousands filling a wide-mouthed glass bowl atop an oak table. Each capsule contained one draft number. "The bowl was large enough to contain three times the number of gelatine capsules which were placed in it. The bits of paper, blackened on the back so that from the outside none could determine the numbers stamped thereon, were curled into the capsules."[24] Blindfolded, Baker drew out the capsule containing number 258. During the long day that followed, other blindfolded men withdrew all the remaining capsules, one at a time, and noted the numbers inside on large chalkboards. It was past two o'clock Saturday morning when they finished. Someone had drawn Alexander's red-ink 342 serial number less than halfway through the process. It was number 4,498 out of 10,500, which meant the pitcher could relax for a while. The army wouldn't call him right away but was unlikely to overlook him entirely.

Newspapers, post offices, and draft boards across the country posted the numbers for anyone to see. Registrants, mothers, fathers, siblings, sweethearts, and friends ran fingers down the long columns, searching for their numbers. In the weeks, months, and seasons ahead, a man's draft number literally might determine his life or death, health or disease, survival or disability. Everything depended on the luck of the draw. Registered men could apply for exemptions in various categories, citing particular occupations or familial obligations, and justifiably receive them. The country assembled over four thousand civilian-led draft boards. "Their most difficult task involved managing the conflicts between family obligations and military ones," a modern history explains. "Local boards gave the first ruling on men's claims for dependency exemptions. Technically speaking, any man could claim exemption from the draft if he had a family member dependent on him for support."[25]

Men had to apply for exemption quickly and follow strict guidelines. "And remember: IT IS UP TO YOU!" an Indiana newspaper warned. "You are not exempt, no matter who or what you are, until you have been examined; . . . You may find yourself suddenly ordered to a training camp or branded as a deserter unless you see to it that you comply with all these legal requirements."[26]

The Selective Service summoned its first active Major Leaguer on August 2 in Philadelphia—not from Alexander's Phillies but from Connie Mack's seventh-place Athletics. Mack's second-year short-stop Lawton "Whitey" Witt (born Ladislaw Waldemar Wittkowski in Massachusetts) had recently returned to the American League club after a month on the injured list. The notice ordered Witt to appear for examination by his local draft board in the Bay State. "Playing with the Athletics," a sports columnist cracked, "should be sufficient cause for rejection."[27]

The draft touched the Athletics again within a week of Witt's notice. Third baseman Ray Bates and pitchers Win Noyes and Alexander "Rube" Schauer (born Dimitri Ivanovich Dimitrihoff in Russia) all received notices. "'Our country is first.' That was the only comment Connie Mack made today to a question whether the draft into the army probably would set at naught his efforts to rebuild the Athletics."[28]

Other Major Leaguers chose to enlist. Chicago White Sox pitcher Jim "Death Valley" Scott applied for officers' training and reported to the army in mid-September. Outfielders William "Baby Doll" Jacobson and Yale "Tod" Sloan of the St. Louis Browns had volunteered for the navy in July during a road trip to New York City, but they hadn't yet been called. Red Sox player-manager Jack Barry had done the same. Pitcher Ernie Shore and outfielders George "Duffy" Lewis and Charles "Chick" Shorten, along with several other Red Sox and Boston Braves, would soon follow Barry; all would report for duty following the 1917 season.

A ballplayer's occupational hazards occasionally worked against his acceptance, as Reds third baseman Henry "Heine" Groh discovered upon reporting for examination in August. "He got away well in the physical test until one of the examiners noted that his fingers were not as straight as they should be," a wire report stated. "At various times during his baseball career Groh had smashed his fingers in finding batted or thrown balls, and they did not 'come back.' As a result, Groh was rejected by the examining board."[29]

The drain on the Major Leagues accelerated as summer faded. Sportswriter Paul Purman captured the anxiety over the anticipated exodus: "The war is already striking hard at baseball and before the 1917 world series is a thing of the past it may be expected that a large number of leaguers will be wearing Uncle Sam's uniforms. . . . From practically every baseball club comes the announcement that men not drawn in the first draft will enlist as soon as the season is finished to avoid being drawn. Many of them are specialists in some line of work and feel they would rather choose their own branch of service."[30]

Ballplayers knew what was at stake but few would say so publicly. Pitcher Bill Doak of the St. Louis Cardinals was among the few who did. "The young player of 25 or 26 is in a quandary under the draft," he said. "He has spent some seven or eight years fitting himself for the position he has, after tremendous effort, obtained. He may reasonably expect three to seven years more of high salary. Then comes the draft and he sees his profession swept away from him. The moment the ballplayer misses the training season or the playing season or gets a cold in his arm or is slightly wounded it is all off with him."[31]

Pete Alexander mostly kept mum. He would never be entirely consistent in speaking of the draft. Perhaps he was unwilling or unable to think the matter through. "I don't believe that ballplayers should be exempted just because they're ballplayers," he would say following the season. "If the government needs me, I'm ready to go. That will be about the last I can do, too, when one comes to think of it. A country not worth fighting for isn't much as a country, and that isn't the kind we have here."[32] Yet on his Selective Service registration card he had affirmed that his mother was dependent on him. If his local draft board agreed, Alexander would be exempted from conscription.

The right-hander continued his 1917 season as if no war raged in Europe. Alexander even won both ends of a Labor Day doubleheader with the Dodgers at Ebbets Field. (He had managed the same feat in September 1916 in Philadelphia versus the Cincinnati Reds.) Tom Rice wrote in the *Brooklyn Eagle* that the "mathematical possibility—although hopelessly huge improbability—that the Phillies might beat out the Giants for the pennant and glory and much money" had induced manager Moran to send Alexander out for the second game.[33] The *Philadelphia Ledger* dubbed the dual complete-game victories—which included twelve straight scoreless innings before twenty thousand fans—Alexander's "Iron Man Act."[34] Rice marveled in the *Eagle*: "The greatest pitcher in the National League, if not in all baseball, was at his greatest, and there you are."[35]

Scribes began running out of superlatives to describe Alexander's season. The Nebraskan ended with thirty victories, his third consecutive season winning thirty games or more. The only man to match the string was Christy Mathewson of the Giants in 1903–5. Matty managed the Reds now and no longer played, so an unparalleled record was Alexander the Great's for the taking in 1918. But if he took it, he would be wearing the uniform of the Chicago Cubs.

TWO

Laddies from Missouri

We know—with all its bleak despair,
With all its phantom exodus,
That somewhere—somewhere Over There
The Great Adventure beckons us.

—GRANTLAND RICE, 1917

The U.S. Army established the 342nd Field Artillery (FA) Regiment on September 5, 1917, at Camp Funston, Kansas. The camp was named for Maj. Gen. Frederick Funston, hero of the Philippine Insurrection following the Spanish-American War, who had died seven months earlier. It was one of sixteen cantonments the government had hastily constructed around the country to house and train its millions of doughboys.

The 342nd FA was organized as a motorized heavy-artillery outfit. "The regiment was recruited from the first draft of men from Green, Polk, Dallas, Stone, Bollinger, and Laclede counties of southern Missouri—men for the most part from farms and rural communities," the regimental history states.[1] More men soon arrived from Barry and Taney counties, which, with Stone County between them, abutted the Arkansas state line to their south. So many doughboys called the Show-Me State home that the 342nd regimental band would adopt as its unofficial theme song a popular regional ditty, "The Laddies from Missouri."[2] (Another Missourian, Harry Truman of Independence, would make a name for himself as a first lieutenant and later captain in another artillery outfit, the 129th FA.)

Most of the 342nd FA's field officers had arrived from the regular army's Coast Artillery Corps. They included the commanding officer, Col. George A. Nugent, as well as Maj. Malcolm P. Andruss, who led the first battalion. Nearly all junior officers were newly commissioned into the National Army—that is, the conscripted army—from the officers training camp at adjacent Fort Riley. Few hailed from the same counties as their men. Small newspapers in southern Missouri were soon publishing letters from "the boys," filled with news and tidbits from Camp Funston. Most of the doughboys seemed to adjust well to their new military lives. One letter came from a group calling itself the Barry County Hard Tack and Hash Eaters: "We are having the 'manual of arms' training this week, which is very interesting but we are officially reminded frequently that we are not carrying a shot-gun hunting Barry county rabbits. . . . Emory Medlin, former Barry county deputy sheriff, is to be on guard duty here, walking a post to keep out skunks who try to harm camps and to see that no one smokes outside the barracks."[3]

Letter writers often mentioned army meals. They marveled at the quantity of food provided in the camp's mess halls (while not always praising its quality) and the weight that many men gained there. Inevitably, some new soldiers had difficulty adjusting. The rural, closely knit Missourians sometimes bemused metropolitan officers from Kansas City or elsewhere. Second Lt. Harold Jacobus wrote home about them to Massachusetts: "We have some very good men and some very poor, the latter coming mostly from the Ozark mountain region. One boy, when asked what his name was, couldn't say it. He possibly was scared out of his wits. Another boy, upon leaving his barracks for his morning ablutions, ran into a line of other men belonging to a different battery and he just followed them, having heard a command from one of the lieutenants guiding the line to follow him. He stayed with that battery a couple of days before he was discovered."[4]

The Ozark lads weren't the only soldiers overwhelmed by the huge National Army cantonments. New York sportswriter and columnist

Grantland Rice, who also became an artillery officer, later recalled a teary young recruit from the Tennessee mountains he had seen at Camp Sevier, South Carolina—"the most homesick pup I ever saw. Looking up at me with a vacant expression, he drawled, 'Is this France?' He'd never been more than ten miles from home before."[5]

The 342nd FA was one of three sequentially numbered units comprising the 164th Field Artillery Brigade, which supplied the big guns for the Eighty-Ninth Division. The 340th and 341st regiments also trained at Camp Funston. The size of the three outfits fluctuated during the war as men transferred in and out and as units were reinforced. The 342nd typically mustered 1,500 to 1,600 men, while the other two regiments generally each had 100 to 300 fewer. Nearly two-thirds of the doughboys in the 340th FA were draftees from Arizona, "the largest body of Arizona troops that participated intact, in the great war."[6] On the way up to Camp Funston, one group had chalked "Phoenix Rattlers" on the side of their railway car.[7] The most diverse outfit was the 341st FA, which had men from thirty-four states plus one wandering Frenchman. The largest contingent (657 men) came from Colorado, which later presented the 341st with its regimental colors.

The 164th Field Artillery Brigade included two additional units: the 314th Trench Mortar Battery, mostly Iowans and South Dakotans, and the 314th Ammunition Train, predominantly Nebraskans. The brigade belonged to the Eighty-Ninth Division, which drew doughboys mainly from Arizona, Colorado, Kansas, Missouri, Nebraska, New Mexico, and South Dakota, with Missouri providing the largest percentage. Troops who later fought beside the Eighty-Ninth overseas called the division the Fighting Farmers, which they meant literally and said with admiration. People stateside often called the Eighty-Ninth the Middle West Division. Its authorized strength was twenty-eight thousand men, but the division usually averaged about twenty-four thousand, since few army units reached or maintained their actual war strength.

What later made the 342nd FA exceptional was its baseball team. Nearly every outfit in the army fielded a ball club, but not one with such an extraordinary roster. The regiment flashed the bat-and-ball talent usually assembled only by an entire division, or even a cantonment. It was no fluke that a mere artillery regiment could assemble perhaps the best team in the U.S. Army, as Major Andruss was quick to point out later.

"When war was declared against Germany and the compulsory service clause was enacted," he wrote, "I at once saw my opportunity to gather under my wing a team composed of 'big leaguers,' my ambition being to organize an outfit the equal of which the Army had never known."[8] One newspaper described Andruss as the "father of the team."[9] The son of a general, Andruss had learned to play ball as a boy in the 1880s at the Presidio in San Francisco. His coach had been Bill "Buck" Lange, a local ballplayer who had gone on to play for the Chicago Colts and Orphans in the National League. Major Andruss was a fifteen-year army veteran by 1917. He outlined three reasons for wanting to build a superior ball club at Camp Funston: "Baseball has a peculiar attraction for the American youth and is a powerful stimulant not only to physical development but to military development as well. . . . A man who has achieved fame on the diamond is a natural leader of men . . . [and] a constellation of these stars of the diamond could be brought together in their new role as soldiers, affording them greater contentment in their new life and incidentally an opportunity to 'bat them out' after hours of arduous work on the drill field."[10]

Andruss was hardly alone in his ambition. Army and navy commanders everywhere embraced sports as a way of providing recreation, building stamina, and boosting morale for soldiers and sailors. Walter Camp embodied this spirit. The former Yale University football star and trainer volunteered his services as a physical instructor for the First Naval District in Boston. By the spring of 1918 he was the navy's commissioner of athletics. The army wasn't far behind in directing men with athletic experience into the cantonments.

The Eighty-Ninth Division's athletic director at Camp Funston was Capt. Paul Withington. He fully supported Andruss's baseball plans. Their connection was key, for although the major held the higher rank, the captain had far greater experience and a national sporting reputation. Withington had been born into a prominent Honolulu family, but he wandered a long way from the islands. The *Atlanta Constitution* had called him "one of America's greatest amateur athletes, . . . a man of fine character and intellectual ability."[11] Withington had earned letters in football, track, crew, wrestling, and swimming as an undergraduate at Harvard University. He had excelled on the gridiron, playing center and guard beside one of his four brothers, Lothrop, at tackle.

After graduation in 1909 Withington had remained in Cambridge as an assistant coach under Percy Haughton. He also completed studies at Harvard Medical School in 1914, the year the First World War began in Europe. One of his uncles, a world-renowned genealogist also named Lothrop, perished in the May 1915 sinking of the British passenger liner *Lusitania* after it was torpedoed off of Ireland. Paul Withington sailed for Europe the next month as a member of the first Harvard Surgical Unit. This group of volunteer doctors and nurses took charge of a Royal Army Medical Corps base hospital in France. The physician-athlete worked there for several months as a contract surgeon.

The University of Wisconsin appointed Withington head football coach in 1916. At Madison he "injected the 'Harvard system' into western football at a great cost and little success," although his own Badgers team went 4-2-1 in the first season and beat Amos Alonzo Stagg's Chicago University team 30–7.[12] Once America entered the world war in 1917, Wisconsin and many other schools decided to abandon athletics for the duration. (At the urging of federal authorities, Wisconsin and most other institutions would later reverse course and restore their sports schedules.) The cancellation was fine with the man from Hawaii, who had other plans.

Withington resigned from his post in Madison. According to newspaper accounts he intended to join the American Red Cross. Instead he entered the army in mid-July as a first lieutenant in the medical corps. Military authorities had their own criteria for deciding personnel assignments. Despite Withington's experience in France, the army prized his expertise on the playing field above what he could do with a scalpel in a base hospital or operating tent. That September the Harvard man's name was among those of uniformed coaches "selected by the commission on training activities for the promotion of the recreative athletics in national army cantonments and other big military camps. . . . Practically all of the coaches are men who have made records in college athletics."[13] Withington reported to Camp Funston and was promoted to captain.

Ironically for an athletics officer who would work closely with Major Leaguers, Withington had little experience with the national pastime. He appeared to have excelled at nearly every sport except baseball. It hardly mattered. The coach-physician understood how to manage and motivate large numbers of young men on a playing field. During his season in Madison he had invited two hundred candidates out for the football squad, an extraordinary number for a time when men normally played on both offense and defense. "There will be so many men fighting for every position on the team that every one on it will have to play high-grade football to hold his place," a Wisconsin newspaper had noted. "That sort of thing is what makes a team. The more men out, the better the team."[14]

It was a useful attitude when working with a group as large as an army division. Captain Withington had strong support from below from Major Andruss. Crucially, he also enjoyed full backing from Camp Funston's top officer, Maj. Gen. Leonard Wood, who commanded the Eighty-Ninth Division. And unlike his athletic director, General Wood did have a strong connection to Organized Baseball.

Wood was an anomaly among the army's officers. He had entered the service not by the traditional route, the U.S. Military Academy at West Point, but via Harvard Medical School. The old school tie alone would have bound him closely to Doctor Withington. Wood had served in the American West during the 1880s, before becoming personal physician to President William McKinley. He had then sought and received a field command in 1898 during the Spanish-American War. Wood had led the First U.S. Volunteer Cavalry, the fabled Rough Riders, with former assistant secretary of the navy and future president of the United States Theodore Roosevelt as his second in command. For their exploits in Cuba, Wood had received the

Medal of Honor. He had held various high positions following the war, including chief of staff and command of the influential Department of the East at Governors Island, New York.

During the years leading up to America's entry into the war, Wood, Roosevelt, and other prominent Americans had championed a military preparedness program known as the Plattsburg Movement. It was named for the town in upstate New York where they established an army-style training camp for civilian volunteers. The Plattsburg enterprise was at cross-purposes with President Woodrow Wilson, however, who had campaigned and won reelection in 1916 for keeping America out of the European war.

T. L. "Cap" Huston, part owner of the New York Yankees and another veteran of the Cuban campaign, had sided with Wood and Roosevelt. The following spring, shortly before America had declared war, Huston and Ban Johnson, president of the American League, had successfully lobbied Wood and the army to assign sergeants as drill instructors to every team in the circuit. The drill program had begun during spring training and continued into the regular season. Huston's Yankees had opened the season at home at the Polo Grounds against the Boston Red Sox, five days after America's war declaration. Wood was on hand to watch the team go through military drills under their sergeant. He then tossed out the ceremonial first pitch to inaugurate the 1917 season.

Within a few weeks middle-aged Cap Huston had talked his way back into the army and was once again indeed a captain. In August he and his regiment of engineers had disembarked for France. In an army shakeup that same month, General Wood had received orders to head west and take command of the Eighty-Ninth Division, which was about to form at Camp Funston. The reassignment was widely seen as a demotion. The general kept mum, followed his orders, and concentrated on training doughboys for combat "over there." Wood reached Kansas in early September as the cantonment readied to accept the first wave of draftees. "The major of each battalion and the colonel of each regiment," the *Omaha Bee* noted, "will be held to account to General Wood for anything that goes wrong."[15]

At least two men in Wood's first troops had played professional baseball. One was Lloyd L. Wait of St. Louis. Wait had caught the eye of Cardinals manager Miller Huggins in 1914 and practiced with the team, but ultimately he had signed with the Pittsburgh Pirates. "Wait is described as a tall, rangy lad with a fine throwing arm, an accurate pegger, and not afraid to take a chance. He is not a strong hitter, but in this respect he is not different from many catchers drawing pay in the majors today."[16] The backstop had never made the club's lineup but had bounced briefly around the Minor Leagues. Wait had then served as an enlisted man in a Missouri National Guard artillery battery during the 1916 emergency on the Mexican border. He was now a commissioned officer, a first lieutenant with valuable gunnery skills.

The other professional ballplayer at Camp Funston was Franklin B. "Dutch" Wetzel. Dutch made his home west of St. Louis in Franklin County, Missouri. Wetzel had spent most of the 1914 baseball season playing left field for the Keokuk (Iowa) Indians in the Class D Central Association. His older brother, Gerald, also played in the league, with the Muscatine Buttonmakers. (Confusingly, Gerald's nickname also was Dutch. When the siblings' teams faced each other, a Keokuk newspaper sometimes differentiated them as Big Dutch and Dutch II.)[17] Frank had knocked around various Minor Leagues and spent the summer of 1917 "playing baseball in the western states."[18] He was drafted into the army that autumn and put into the 164th Depot Brigade, a temporary home for Camp Funston soldiers awaiting permanent assignments. "Arrived fine and dandy and like it here O. K.," Wetzel wrote to his hometown newspaper. "Have been made Corporal and hope to advance soon. Am considering taking over the ball club and if I am here next year can make something out of it."[19]

Wetzel penned his letter October 6, the first day of the 1917 World Series. The Camp Funston ballplayers would have to wait until spring to learn what their athletic futures in the army would be. Captain Withington and the rest of the Eighty-Ninth Division meanwhile turned their attention to football.

THREE

Gridiron

We'll take each day just as it comes
Still shrouded in the mists of Fate,
And move on with calling drums
Without a thought of what may wait.

—LT. GRANTLAND RICE

The Eighty-Ninth Division cobbled together a gridiron schedule for the somewhat chaotic season of 1917. Occasionally the
athletic director was obliged to change plans on short notice—
not unusual for football teams that year. "Doctor Withington has a fine
bunch of athletes for his football team in the army camp," a Topeka
newspaper informed readers. "From Kansas alone he has Assistant
Coach 'Potsy' Clark, Adrian Lindsey and John Fast, three football players of considerable renown. Along with these are players from the larger
schools of the United States, most of whom are officers in the division."[1]

George Clark had starred for the University of Illinois before signing on in 1916 to coach major sports at the University of Kansas (often
referred to then and now as KU). A newspaper in Wisconsin had
recently called him "the greatest quarterback in Illinois history."[2] Nicknamed after a puck or token used in a children's game, Potsy was unusually tough. He had worn an aluminum mask during the 1915 football
season because of an injury—with similarly afflicted teammate George

Halas he had formed what they called the Order of the Broken Jaw—and missed only two games as the Illini amassed a 6-0-2 record. His old coach, Bob Zuppke, would name Potsy and Red Grange to his all-time All-American squad in 1951. Clark had applied for an army commission two days before the United States entered the war; other athletes in major collegiate conferences soon followed his example.

Adrian "Ad" Lindsey joined Clark at fullback in the Camp Funston backfield. Lindsey had captained the Kansas football eleven in 1916 and was playing second base on the baseball team when war was declared. John C. "Jick" Fast was a Jayhawk too. Small for a halfback at five feet four inches tall and 160 pounds, Fast lived up to his name. "That Fast was all his name implied, / And more, can never be denied," a Nebraska newspaper exclaimed after a showy performance by the Kansan.[3] Clark, Lindsey, and Fast all had been accepted for officers' training at Fort Riley in May 1917.

Monroe C. "Poge" Lewis was another new lieutenant on the Eighty-Ninth Division team. He had captained and starred at fullback in 1915 for Washington University in St. Louis. An Iowa newspaper had placed him among "the greatest athletes developed in their respective institutions" at Missouri Valley schools.[4] Clark, Lewis, Lindsey, and Fast all eventually were assigned to Major Andruss's 342nd Field Artillery. (Clark was attached to the 314th Sanitary Train—what today would be called a medical battalion—during the football season.)

Clark shifted to halfback to play behind quarterback Anton Stankowski, the "midget quarter of the Missouri Tigers" the previous season.[5] Weighing but 153 pounds, Stan' was "one of the nerviest, shiftiest and hard working quarters on any of the [Missouri Valley] conference teams."[6] Stankowski also was among the squad's few enlisted men. Nicknamed "the General" at Missouri, he was only a private at Camp Funston, but rank meant nothing on the gridiron or baseball diamond.

Three other former collegiate stars played for Captain Withington's football squad: Capt. F. K. Dennie, an All-American end from Brown University; Lt. F. E. Merrill, tackle and captain from Tufts; and Maj. K. O. Kistler, a Yale fullback. Withington lined up at guard or tackle, while Lloyd Wait occasionally played in the backfield. "Football, the pre-eminent sport at Camp Funston, national army cantonment, nowhere is to be found developed to a higher stage than at this army camp," a Topeka sportswriter declared.[7]

Withington had more than eighty men on his team, which looked impressive on paper. The Eighty-Ninth Division rolled easily to four early victories over small colleges, playing before big doughboy crowds at Camp Funston. The players faced their first real challenge on Saturday, November 24, meeting a powerful eleven from the Great Lakes Naval Training Station outside Chicago. It was an away game for both teams at neutral Kansas City and something of a reunion for the KU men. Their former coach, Herman Olcott, was now directing athletics and physical education at Great Lakes. Interest in the game ran high among servicemen and civilians. The services ran special trains to Kansas City so that two thousand soldiers and several hundred sailors could see the game. "Camp Funston football dopesters believe they have the better team on paper, despite the Great Lakes team's defeat last Saturday of the strong Camp Grant eleven," a Kansas newspaper reported.[8]

With "material for three crack elevens," Withington took a thirty-five-man squad east from Camp Funston, along with the 341st Field Artillery band.[9] "A general order, issued when the first of the drafted men went into training, forbids gambling, else many months' pay of many a man in olive drab would be wagered on next Saturday afternoon's contest," a Topeka newspaper reported. "Hundreds of soldiers have applied for leaves of absence for that day, with the intention of occupying seats in the Camp Funston section of the rooters' bleachers at Association park."[10] Withington had one problem: quarterback Stankowski's company was quarantined for measles, "and every afternoon when he goes out to play he must be fumigated, but he gets there just the same, and will be in the game Saturday."[11] In the end Stankowski didn't go to Kansas City. Instead, Sgt. Gordon Beck, a 1913 All–Missouri Valley end and sometimes quarterback at the University of Nebraska, played behind center for the doughboys. The game became an interservice classic, the hero no surprise to anyone:

On a slippery field that gave the weighty army team a shade advantage the foot ball representatives from Camp Funston defeated the Great Lakes training school team, 7 to 0, yesterday. The one touchdown was made by "Potsy" Clark, former Illinois university star, now a lieutenant, after a thrilling 35-yard dash through a broken field. Clark put the ball on Navy's 3-yard line, where the sailors braced and held for two downs, the army being penalized for holding on the third down. Clark then dropped back for a punt formation, but instead ploughed through for a touchdown and Beck kicked goal.[12]

The *Chicago Tribune* declared the game a "great scrap." Proceeds went into the two installations' athletic funds. "The cold weather and an occasional gust of snow," the *Tribune* added, "seemed to have no effect on Kansas City's desire to see football players of the service in action and 15,000 attended the game."[13]

Camp Funston's next contest came at home five days later on November 29, Thanksgiving Day. Clark faced the team on which he'd starred at the University of Illinois. "Bob Zuppke and his Illini are asking themselves a curious question: 'Can we stop Potsy Clark?'" an Illinois newspaper reported. "It doesn't seem long since Potsy Clark, the greatest all around football star in Illinois history, was piloting the Illini to championships. Now the Illini have to figure out some way to halt the little man when they meet the army team at Camp Funston."[14]

Perhaps overly confident, the Eighty-Ninth Division scheduled two games on the holiday. The second opponent was the Thirty-Fifth Division, largely national guardsmen from Missouri and Kansas who were training at Camp Doniphan, Oklahoma. Withington dispatched a twenty-two-man squad that included Stankowski and Fast to meet the Doniphan team at Joplin, Missouri. Splitting his squads put him at a disadvantage against the strong Illinois eleven. "Today, for the first time in ten years, the Illini squad will compete on Thanksgiving Day," the Illinois student newspaper reported. "Camp Funston's soldier boy eleven is to serve as the holiday host. They say they have a number of entertaining features in store for the boys. . . . Of course the center of interest for the Indians is Potsy Clark, erstwhile terror to conference elevens of a couple of years past."[15]

The army crowd at Camp Funston was impressive. "An hour before the game 10,000 men in olive drab already had filled the makeshift grand stands and covered the stony hills just north of the field. It was such a day that patrons of football might have ordered." The entire 342nd Field Artillery sat or stood among the thirty thousand soldiers swarming the hillsides like khaki-colored ants. Once the game began, however, the doughboys had little to set them cheering. Potsy Clark never got going as the Illini "split the army line like so much paper" and kept Camp Funston scoreless.[16] The final tally was 28–0. It was little consolation that the division's second team under Stankowski had defeated Camp Doniphan 11–0 at Joplin.

The Eighty-Ninth Division swung back into action two days later on Saturday, December 1. "The treat of the 1917 foot ball season is in store for Omaha fans tomorrow afternoon," the *Omaha Bee* reported, "when the gridiron elevens representing Camp Funston, Kansas, and Camp Dodge, Iowa, the two largest army cantonments in the United States, clash on Creighton field."[17] Proceeds were earmarked for the gymnasium fund at each camp. On Friday a special Union Pacific train conveyed the Camp Funston team, military band, and rooters the two hundred miles from Kansas City to Omaha. Ad Lindsey wasn't among them, too badly injured during the navy game to make the trip. The second squad traveled twice as far from Joplin to reunite with their teammates.

The Camp Dodge team arrived on Saturday morning after a stop at Council Bluffs. The Iowa cantonment was loaded with football talent and hadn't played Thanksgiving Day, while both Camp Funston squads were surely exhausted from their holiday contests. With Beck again at quarterback, their exhaustion showed during what a *Chicago Tribune* correspondent described as "about the hardest fought gridiron battle ever witnessed in this city."[18]

"More than 9,000 cheering Omahans saw Camp Dodge return triumphant over Camp Funston by the narrow margin of 3 to 0 at Creighton field yesterday afternoon," a *Bee* sportswriter wrote. "A 40-yard drop kick, which was so doubtful that even the officials disagreed over it at first, gave the Iowans the victory in the last quarter."[19] A sports historian writes that Withington committed "a rookie coaching mistake" during the game; Camp Dodge's center had played for him at Wisconsin and Withington was still using the same old signals.[20] The *Bee* noted that Clark, "the muchly-heralded halfback . . . couldn't even get started. According to the dopesters, Potsy was scheduled for long runs, but five yards seemed to be his limit." The newspaper added of the hard-fought contest: "There is a prevailing suspicion that some of the athletes took advantage of the situation, yesterday. Toward the latter part of the game, Kistler, former Yale player, went into the Funston lineup. Now Kistler is a major. Some private evidently had been tipped off to the fact, for after a couple of plays, Kistler was among those on the hospital list."[21]

The Eighty-Ninth Division had one more game during the odd 1917 season. The University of Nebraska, its roster depleted by war and injury, decided not to play postseason contests, which ended long-held hopes for a game on December 8. Another game slated with KU at Camp Funston on December 12 was similarly canceled on short notice. That left only Camp MacArthur at Waco, Texas, on December 17, after the nation's colleges and universities had finished their campaigns.

"Some of the best men on the [Camp Funston] team were badly crippled up after the recent game with the Camp Dodge team but careful attention has put the eleven in good shape for the clash with the McArthur aggregation."[22] Withington's crew lost again, 13–6. "The game was full of thrills and brilliant gridiron work on both sides, but in the last half the strong Camp MacArthur team seemed to rally in response to the weakening of the visitors and piled up a winning score."[23] The Eighty-Ninth Division's former Illini star made it close in the final minutes. "Potsy Clark, who made Funston's score, smashed the line repeatedly for 10- and 15-yard gains until the last quarter, when he got the ball on the three-yard line and went over."[24]

The division footballers returned to Kansas with winter now fully upon the plains. There they buckled down to the much more serious business of preparing to join the war raging in France.

FOUR

Chicago

Perhaps when we are called to go we'll find the game is tough;
But what of it?
We'll find out dreams are shattered where the hand of Fate is rough;
But what of it?

—GRANTLAND RICE, 1917

Few National League fans in Philadelphia likely noticed or cared about an army football score from out West. They were still reeling from a hefty lump of coal they'd discovered in their holiday stockings two weeks before Christmas. The Phillies had abruptly sold Pete Alexander and catcher Bill Killefer—"the greatest battery in either big league today"—to the Chicago Cubs.[1] The deal gutted the Phillies. A local headline reflected the mood in the Quaker City: "With Alex and Bill Gone, In Order to Draw Crowd, the Phils Will Need a Lead Pencil."[2]

Killefer had worked with the star pitcher more than any other Phillies catcher, and the two were frequent companions during the off-seasons. Killefer was "a great backstop and a splendid character," Alexander wrote years later. "He was my pal and friend."[3] Although slightly younger, Killefer had played in the Major Leagues a full season longer than the pitcher, breaking in with the St. Louis Browns near the end of the 1909 season. Both had played with the Phillies since 1911. Unlike Alexander, Killefer possessed a strong baseball pedigree; his big brother Wade had played seven seasons in the Major Leagues and was now a player-manager in the Pacific Coast League.

The Killefer brothers had a genius for acquiring and bestowing nicknames. Bill's was Reindeer, Wade's Red or Lollypop. (Imagine the introductions: "Hi, I'm Reindeer Bill. This is my brother Lollypop. We play ball.") Bill had anointed Alexander with his baseball moniker. The Phillies already had an outfielder named Dode Paskert when Alexander arrived in 1911. The tale of the new nickname varied in the telling, but it generally involved an off-season ramble across bare Nebraska plains. As Alexander related it years later, his catcher and their teammate Oscar Dugey had knocked the pitcher from a mule-drawn wagon, then leapt off themselves when the mules bolted. Once dusty Alexander caught up with the pair, Killefer had exclaimed, "Take a look at Alkali Pete!" The name was common for dusty cowboys in western novels, movies, and stage shows.

"When the season opened, they kept calling me 'Alkali Pete,' and soon everybody on the club started calling me 'Pete,'" Alexander recalled. "It spread around the league and everybody got it after a while."[4] "Alkali Pete" turned gradually into "Pete" and in time would become "Ol' Pete." Ballplayers rarely called Alexander anything else.

Reports that Pete and Reindeer Bill were both bound for the Windy City echoed like thundersnow across Philadelphia. The first bulletin came late December 11, exactly a year after the pitcher's father had died. A sportswriter likened the news to the Liberty Bell ringing in 1776: "We are bringing in this historic stuff because there has been nothing in Philadelphia, to our mind, that can compare with the recent baseball developments since the good old bell cracked under the strain."[5] In exchange for their star battery, the Phillies received $50,000 plus Cubs pitcher Mike Prendergast and catcher William "Pickles" Dilhoefer. "Oh, boy! Grover Cleveland Alexander was just sold for the price of a day's battling in Europe," the United Press exclaimed.[6]

The comparison was apt if inaccurate, since the deal was entirely a wartime transaction. The sale hinged on the draft status of the two stars, Alexander and Killefer both being of eligible age. Many fans believed that the draft was the impetus for Phillies president William Baker to deal Alexander in the first place—the club could cash in now or risk losing the star battery to conscription later. Stung by such criticism, Baker went on the offensive. Alexander, he said, was "one of the boys who do not keep themselves in the best of condition."

> Alexander, according to President Baker, was sold for just that reason. Baker does not believe Alexander's effectiveness will be so pronounced next season and declares he sees a beginning of the end for the power that lurks in the famous pitcher's right arm. . . . Alexander's habits, according to Baker, are rapidly cutting the star's worth and soon will lay him among the has beens. . . .
>
> The case of Killefer, who goes to Chicago with Alexander, according to Baker, is considerably different. There is a distinct peeve existing in Philadelphia over the way Killefer has acted. . . . According to Baker, Killefer was on the market and would have been traded to some club without Alexander being included had the Chicago offer not come along.[7]

Alexander later wrote that he didn't blame Baker for making a business decision, but fans and many baseball men considered the magnate's arguments baloney. "I was thunderstruck when I read the news," raged Charles "Red" Dooin, the Phillies' player-manager from 1910 through 1914. Dooin had helped to make Alexander a star and didn't hesitate to compare the Chicago deal to wartime atrocities in Europe. "Money can never replace wonders like Alexander and Killefer," Dooin said. "Alexander is the greatest pitcher in the history of the game and it is a matter of much personal pride to me that I was responsible for his development. Selling Alexander, to my mind, is something like the practice of the Germans in demolishing a cathedral or destroying priceless works of art."[8]

The Philadelphia-Chicago deal smells little better today. Although a troubled man following the war, Alexander would pitch effectively in the Major Leagues until 1930. Historian Jan Finkel writes that "the Philadelphia front office carried off one of the most cynical acts in baseball history."[9]

The alcoholism that Alexander would exhibit over subsequent seasons wasn't an obvious concern for the Chicago club in 1917. In hindsight a few sportswriters would write decades later about early indications of his heavy drinking. Alexander's teammate Hans Lobert, however, remembered to the contrary that the pitcher hadn't been a serious drinker when he joined the Phillies in 1911. "I've had my beer ever since I was knee high to a duck," Alexander acknowledged years later. But before the war he apparently didn't frequently over-imbibe or drink hard liquor.[10] He would be among several Major League players whom evangelist and former ballplayer Billy Sunday would cite as good examples in May 1918: "Ask Grover Cleveland Alexander how much booze has helped to make him the best pitcher that Charles Weeghman could buy to give the Cubs a pennant."[11]

A little over a month after the sale's announcement the Philadelphia-Chicago deal suddenly was in danger of collapsing over an entirely unrelated issue. Alexander had told Cubs president Charles N. Weeghman that he expected to be placed in Class 3 of the draft because his mother was dependent on him. But the big right-hander learned January 15 that his draft board had listed him instead in Class 1-A, the first group to be called. Alexander spoke to a journalist by phone from Omaha, where he spent the winter:

> Yes, sir, I'm drafted. I just got my card from St. Paul and I've been placed in class 1 division A. Don't know when they will call me up for examination. I wired Weeghman this afternoon and haven't heard anything yet, so I can't say what this will do with the deal which transferred me from the Phillies to the Cubs. I didn't intend to play this summer anyhow unless I got my part of the purchase money. I don't know what my chances were for getting that money, so I don't know what difference the draft will make. Ready to go. Sure, I'm no slacker.[12]

"I shall ask no exemption," Alexander told another reporter. "I don't know what they will do about transferring me from Philadelphia to Chicago. That's up to the baseball people, not to me."[13] The pitcher added a day later, "Plans, hopes, ambitions? Yes, I had and have all of them. But they cannot interfere with Uncle Sam. I can only say that I am ready if I am called, which now seems soon, according to the classification I have received."[14]

Alexander was among 109 Howard County men classified 1-A who passed their draft physicals in Nebraska during the last week of January. Their exam results made them all eligible for military service. If the pitcher had spoken up about his complete medical history, he might well have failed the exam and been clear of conscription. Such candor might also have damaged his baseball career. Therein lay the conundrum and the likely reason Alexander kept silent.

The pitcher had been badly injured while playing with the Class D Galesburg Boosters in 1909. A shortstop's wide throw struck him in the head as he ran toward first base at Pekin, Illinois. Many biographers have written that Alexander was rushed unconscious to a hospital, but Pekin had no hospital until 1913. A contemporary account has him regaining consciousness after ten or fifteen minutes. "Alexander was removed from the field and taken down town where Manager Wagner and another player stayed up all night with him."[15] Alexander's later recollections differed. "I woke up 48 hours later, and my first question was, 'Who won the game?'" he said. "'Oh, that was two days ago,' they told me. I couldn't believe it."[16]

A week after the beaning a Saint Paul newspaper reported that "while he seems to be conscious, he is not exactly right."[17] The blow to his left temple affected the vision in Alexander's right eye. This seeming contradiction can be explained by human anatomy, since the optic nerves crisscross inside the brain, although the vision problem may have been neurological in nature rather than ophthalmic. Alexander saw double for a while, which nearly ended his playing days right there.

"The big pitcher, who has been confined to his bed continuously since the accident, appears but a shadow of his former husky self, and he is still weak and unable to be about much," a Galesburg newspaper reported in mid-August.[18] Alexander tried to bunt a few practice balls a week or so later but "found that he couldn't get the wood against the ball at all." The paper wished him a full recovery, "as he is a steady, sober, industrious, and capable young fellow."[19] His vision later improved and he was able to play again the next season.

A blow to the head like Alexander's would be classified as a traumatic brain injury (TBI) today. TBIs can affect what doctors call executive functions, the cognitive processes that determine a person's ability to make decisions and carry out everyday tasks. It's possible that following his injury Alexander's motor skills—including his ability to throw a baseball with amazing accuracy—remained intact while his executive functions were to some degree impaired. That would help to explain various poor decisions, actions, and inactions later.

The Nebraskan also began suffering from seizures, which many modern writers and physicians attribute to epilepsy brought on by his TBI. When the seizures began remains unclear. Hans Lobert remembered Alexander having two or three episodes a season in Philadelphia. Teammates held him down to prevent him from choking or accidentally injuring himself, according to the third baseman, then administered a little brandy to help revive him. "It always happened on the bench, though, never on the pitching mound," Lobert said decades later. "We always kept a bottle of brandy handy because there never was any warning."[20]

Alexander biographer Jack Kavanagh contended that Lobert concocted the story and that the pitcher hadn't been afflicted with epilepsy while with the Phillies—that is, through the 1917 season. Kavanagh believed that St. Paul, Alexander's hometown, "was small enough, and its native son famous to a point where, if he had been epileptic, the neighbors would have known it."[21] The argument isn't entirely convincing. Alexander certainly would have endeavored to keep his condition private, and his neighbors, friends, and family might not have spoken of it even had they known. He unquestionably experienced an epileptic episode in 1918. "Whether he had any beforehand is not known," author and sportswriter Tom Meany wrote.[22]

Current medical literature suggests that Alexander was far more likely to have experienced his first seizures within a year or two of suffering the TBI in 1909 than to have developed full-blown epilepsy nine years later at age thirty-one. No matter when he first exhibited signs of the condition, the relative privacy of a Major League dugout let players keep knowledge of Alexander's epilepsy among themselves. A code of silence surrounded him for years.

The draft-board physicians who examined Alexander and his Howard County neighbors in 1918 surely would have been interested in knowing the pitcher's complete medical history: the terrible blow to his head, the double vision, the seizures if they had begun. There's no indication that Alexander shared any such information, despite every opportunity to do so on a government form that he completed and signed. "Have you found that your health and habits in any way interfere with your ability to earn a livelihood?" No. "Do you consider that you are now sound and well?" Yes. "Have you ever been under treatment in any hospital or asylum?" No.[23] And while unlikely, it's conceivable that Alexander also suffered from a condition called anosognosia, which is a lack of personal awareness of an illness or disability. Anosognosia is why some people don't perceive, for instance, that they're struggling with conditions such as schizophrenia, bipolar disorder, or the effects of a stroke.

Local draft boards had considerable leeway in determining which young men they selected. The loss of a finger, blindness in one eye, slight muscular tremors, and many other physical features didn't automatically disqualify a registrant for limited army service. Epilepsy, however, likely would have exempted Alexander from conscription. A government guideline explained the situation this way:

Local boards and medical advisory boards should be especially careful in the selection of registrants who suffer from defects of vision, defects of hearing and with chronic discharge from the ear or ears; toxic conditions associated with abnormal conditions of the thyroid gland; valvular disease of the heart; tuberculosis, epilepsy, mental disease or deficiency and irremedial defects of the feet. In other words, to make a good soldier the registrant must be able to see well, have comparatively good hearing, his heart must be able to stand the stress of physical exertion, he must be intelligent enough to understand and execute military maneuvers, obey commands, and protect himself, and must be able to transport himself by walking as the exigencies of military life may demand.[24]

But how would the Chicago Cubs have taken news of their new star pitcher receiving a medical exemption on such grounds? What would have happened to the Philadelphia-Chicago deal? How would fans and other Major League clubs have reacted to a sudden revelation of epilepsy? The condition could be profoundly frightening both for the afflicted and for witnesses. In earlier, darker times, epileptic seizures often were associated with demons or occult forces. The condition stigmatized sufferers even well into the twentieth century. Alexander always would strive to keep his condition private, no matter when he had first noticed it. He may well have accepted a high draft classification rather than reveal it. The results of his medical examination by the local board practically ensured that soon he would be bound for military service.

Alexander's draft status was still fuzzy three weeks after his notice. He said on February 6 that "he had heard nothing of his claim for exemption from the draft and said he would not press the claim."[25] The mistake he and other interested parties made was to assume that the army would call him quickly, as it had called so many young American males. The date on which a fellow reported for duty, however, depended both on his draft number and on the quota that his local draft board was required to send to the nearest cantonment during a particular month. The St. Paul board didn't yet require the presence of Alexander the Great during early 1918. "Grover Cleveland Alexander will not be called to the colors for a while yet and will be permitted to wear the baseball uniform instead of the army uniform this coming summer," a sports column predicted with middling accuracy.[26] Alexander began prepping for the 1918 baseball season as weeks passed without a notice to report.

Although not publicly unhappy with the Philadelphia-Chicago deal, the hurler did want a piece of the action. Alexander announced that he was holding out for a bonus and in February began working out by himself in Hot Springs, Arkansas. The Cubs meanwhile readied for spring training in Pasadena, California. Relations between the hurler and the Chicago club nonetheless remained cordial—suspiciously so, to some minds. "It is said that Alexander's unreasonable demands were prompted by the Cubs' desire for widespread publicity, and that the star boxman had a thorough understanding with his new employers all along," the *Washington Herald* reported.[27] Weeghman assured Cubs fans, "Nothing but war will keep Alexander out of the game. Bonus, salary and any other matters will be ironed out to his satisfaction."[28]

The impasse ended in mid-March. "G. C. Alexander received a wire from President Weeghman of the Chicago National League team, instructing him to join the Chicago team at Kansas City, and inform-ing him that Manager Mitchell had authority to close the deal that will 'let loose' all strings and yarns making 'Dode' a hold-out for a bonus," the *St. Paul Phonograph* reported. "In plain words, it means that the Chicago club has decided to concede everything which 'Dode' asks for in demanding a bonus."[29] Alexander told friends in Kansas City he wouldn't sign unless he got a $10,000 bonus, the *Kansas City Star* reported. "Manager Mitchell of the Cubs told friends here that he had absolute power to deal with 'Alec,' so the guessing is now on as to what station along the route will flash the news that Grover Cleveland has ornamented a contract with his own peculiar style of hieroglyphics."[30]

The pitcher compromised on a $5,000 bonus and a two-year, $12,000 contract—hefty sums for the day. Fans and sportswriters were relieved, although some eyebrows rose as well. "Grover Cleveland Alexander is suffering of a swollen head. . . . Mr. Alexander is also in Class A 1 of the selective draft. Will he demand a bonus from the government in case of a call to the colors?" an Arizona newspaper asked.[31]

Alexander first stepped onto a diamond wearing a Chicago uniform on March 20, his "apparent satisfaction" evident to the scribes covering the club in Pasadena.[32] Only two days later he received the sort of news no player wants to get in camp. His eldest brother, the popular manager of a farmers' elevator, had died of blood poisoning (septicemia) in Elba at age forty-five. George Alexander's death made front-page news in nearby St. Paul. Since there wasn't time enough for the pitcher to reach Nebraska to attend the burial, Alexander stayed in California as his new teammates rallied around him. Among the "many beautiful floral offerings" at his brother's funeral "was a fine and very expensive wreath from the management of the Chicago National League ball club."[33]

Remaining with the team also gave Alexander two opportunities to investigate life in the armed forces. The U.S. Navy had an excellent baseball team less than thirty-five miles from Pasadena at the submarine base in San Pedro. "Aleck, with William Wrigley, went to the home of Douglas Fairbanks to appear with the movie star in some pictures for the benefit of the submarine base at San Pedro," *Tribune* sportswriter James Crusinberry reported.[34] The Cubs played and lost to the bluejackets' team the next day. "With Howard Ehmke, the former Detroit star hurler, on the slab and backed by several big leaguers and Coast league players, the Jackies were too much for the Cubs, who were caught unprepared for such a fight."[35]

The Cubs broke camp and headed east to Chicago, providing Alexander a firsthand look at army life during exhibition games in New Mexico. The Cubs first faced a strong industrial team from the state's Copper League at Santa Rita on Friday, April 5. They played Santa Rita again and the Thirty-Fourth "Sunshine" Division team over the weekend at Camp Cody outside Deming. Alexander pitched two innings of the initial Santa Rita game, yielding his first run of the spring as the Cubs fell 6–5 in ten innings. "Every one in the town, which has about 2,500 persons, was present."[36] Chicago then beat the copper miners 7–0 at the army post on Saturday, with Alexander slated to go again on Sunday versus the soldiers.

The army had gone all out in preparation for the games, expanding the stadium to seat eight thousand, ordering new uniforms, and opening the base to civilians for the first time in months. Some twenty-five thousand soldiers trained at Camp Cody, mostly national guardsmen from Iowa, Minnesota, Nebraska, and North and South Dakota. Maj. H. M. Nelly was head of athletics for the Thirty-Fourth Division. "If Alexander is taken for army service he is likely to be placed in this camp," the *Tribune* reported (incorrectly, since guardsmen and draftees generally trained at separate installations). "Maj. Nelly today told the big hurler he would be most welcome at any time."[37] Neither Camp Cody nor its ballpark held much appeal for the Cubs, however. "The stadium is inside the camp, simply dug out of the sand," Jim Crusinberry wrote. "The sand terrace surrounding it made the bleachers."[38]

Major Nelly sent two army trucks to ferry the Chicagoans to the camp's YMCA building (invariably called a hut, no matter its size), where the players dressed for the game. Outfielder Les Mann had a brother training at Camp Cody; the *Tribune* didn't mention whether they managed a reunion. The Cubs toured the camp before the game and spent time at the base hospital. They also watched a bayonet drill by four squads of infantry, led by a British army sergeant major who reputedly had killed thirty-four Germans in hand-to-hand combat.

"He had learned all the tricks of 'getting' his man, even after his gun, bayonet, pistol, and knife had been lost, and he was showing the American boys those tricks," Crusinberry wrote. "But the main thing he taught was 'fighting spirit.' This, he declared, was more important than bayonets or knives and he had the soldiers so wrought up that they actually barked like fighting dogs. Every man wore an expression so intense, it made one shudder. It was then that Manager Mitchell was heard to say: 'That's what I call "punch." It isn't possible to beat a bunch like that.'"[39]

About seven thousand people clustered in the stadium for the 2:30 p.m. first pitch, a thousand fewer than Saturday after the departure of the Santa Rita team and its followers. The game got off to an awful start when Dode Paskert broke the army third baseman's leg with a first-inning slide; fans sitting fifty feet away heard the snap. The weather didn't improve the dismal mood. "Before the game had gone two

innings clouds of dust and sand began rolling over the field," Crusinberry wrote. "At times one couldn't see to second base."[40] Matt Foley
of the *Chicago Examiner* added that the swirling sands "had the Cubs
longing for gas masks."[41]

Alexander started for the Cubs and pitched five innings, surrendering only a Texas leaguer to right. "After that, although Alex put
none of his famous smoke on the ball and apparently was only taking a light workout the home guard couldn't find him at all," a local
weekly newspaper reported.[42]

Manager Mitchell sent infielder Fred Lear into the game after Alexander's departure. Just back from a Cubs rookies' game in Arizona,
Lear promptly got booted for "kicking" (complaining) about a called
third strike. "The King had just reached the town from Douglas at
noon and had entered the game only half an inning previously, so he
was not quite inoculated by the military spirit that pervaded," Foley
wrote.[43] The other Cubs shouldn't have been surprised by the swift
display of military discipline. Major Nelly had gone onto the field
during Saturday's game when first baseman Fred Merkle objected
to the Santa Rita catcher's tipping his bat. Nelly ordered the umpire
to eject anyone else who kicked. "The umpires they encountered at
Camp Cody, N. M., wore silver bars, gold leaves and silver eagles on
their shoulders and those ornaments completely discounted the chips
worn in the same positions by the Cubs," a United Press correspondent wrote.[44] Crusinberry described "King" Lear's sudden downfall:

> No one knows exactly what happened, because it was done so quickly.
> Lear had struck out and kicked, but not one-quarter as long as they kick
> in the big league parks. He started for third base to take his position
> when Major Nelly, in charge of athletics here, rose from his chair near
> third base and called for the officer of the day. The officer appeared and
> was commanded to escort Lear off the playing field.
>
> Lear was as much surprised as any one, but offered no objections.
> Manager Mitchell simply sat down and said not a word, but he won-
> dered what it was all about.[45]

The army team's manager, Maj. T. C. Crimmins, won no friends among the Cubs either. "Crimmins appeared to be a stern soldier," Crusinberry added, "and removed several men, one for striking out and another for making an error, and others for similar reasons."[46]

The afternoon ended in a disappointing 8–0 loss for the dough-boys. The Major Leaguers wanted only to get off the field and back onto their train. "The Cubs did not score after the fifth, a wind that whipped up at about that point filling the air with dust, and as big leaguers never want to risk their eyes, they made little effort to hit the ball except when the air was clear," the local paper explained. "This robbed the game of most of its interest and a good part of the crowd went home before it was finished."[47]

A report that Alexander had been called to the army clacked into American newsrooms the second Friday of April, four days before the Cubs' season opener. The *Brooklyn Eagle* ran a bulletin below the fold on the front page: "St. Paul, Neb., April 12—Grover Cleveland Alexander, pitcher of the Chicago National League Baseball team, has been selected by the draft board of Howard county, Nebraska, as one of twelve men to go to Camp Funston, Kansas, during the five days beginning April 26."[48]

"What's that?" Charles Weeghman exclaimed when someone tele-phoned the news to Chicago. "Read it again!" The Cubs' president needed a moment to absorb the news. "That certainly is a wallop—a serious shock for the Chicago club," Weeghman said. "It means that we shall lose $50,000. There was a stipulation in the deal with the Phil-adelphia club that if either Alexander or Killefer was called into the army thirty days before the opening of the season the deal could be called off. That time, of course, has passed. While we are sorry to lose him, especially at this time, we are glad to help the government in any way and, of course, will do nothing to obtain his release."[49]

"President Weeghman realized the chances he was taking when he purchased Alexander," columnist Jack Keene wrote. "With the big pitcher on his team the Cubs immediately loomed up as pennant contender. Without him their chances of making a successful fight were very gloomy. So Weeghman decided to flip a coin with the government and the government won."[50]

"It's a tough blow for the Cubs," manager Fred Mitchell said. "However, that's something all the ball clubs have to expect at any time this season and nothing can be done to help it. Of course, it's especially hard when it takes a star like Aleck. I'm hoping the call is not for immediate service and he will be able to go along with baseball for the greater part of the season. If he has to go it will hurt the Cubs a lot, but we'll have to do the best we can."[51]

Weeghman tried to sound optimistic, perhaps unintentionally misled by his big pitcher. "Recently I talked to Alex and he was of the impression he wouldn't be called until late in the Fall, if at all," the club owner said. "I believe the board of his home town gave him to understand that inasmuch as he had a mother and brothers to support, that he would be among the last to go."[52] Alexander himself took the draft news calmly. "If they want me to join the army at once, of course I shall go and go most willingly," he said.[53] The pitcher also injected a note of uncertainty. "I know nothing about the order, but I presume it is in the mails," he said. "I am ready to go. No one will have a chance to call me a slacker."[54]

The problem was that his draft order *wasn't* in the mail. A local sheriff who doubled as chairman of the exemption board at St. Paul had been mistaken in saying the matter was decided. "The question as to whether Alexander will go to Camp Funston this month depends upon the number of men the board exempts because of agricultural reasons," another board member explained that night. "Some of these claims for exemption by farmers are still pending, but will be decided by the board within a few days. Alexander is now the thirteenth man in the list of the month's quota and there are twelve to be selected." He added, "We will not send out the official notification until after we know for a certainty that Alexander is to go."[55]

Few fans or sportswriters were naïve enough to believe that Alexander would pitch for long on Chicago's north side in 1918. Weeghman's pricy gamble clearly hadn't paid off during this second season of wartime baseball. After the Cubs' dusty weekend at Camp Cody, it's not surprising that Alexander thought he'd rather don navy blues than army khakis. Many Major Leaguers had already enlisted in the navy. Player-manager Jack Barry of the 1917 Boston Red Sox was now Chief Yeoman Barry, running a fine baseball team composed largely of former Red Sox and Braves players at the Charlestown Navy Yard. Several players served as yeomen at other naval stations. Alexander likely also knew about Whitey Witt, the Athletics' shortstop; drafted for the army in August, Witt had landed instead on Barry's navy squad in Boston.

Alexander already had two offers from the navy. Red Sox outfielder Duffy Lewis, like Barry, was a chief yeoman, stationed at Mare Island near San Francisco. Lewis, too, managed a good ball team. He wired Alexander in care of the *Chicago Tribune* sports editor: "Will pay transportation to San Francisco and will guarantee to take good care of you. Same for Elliott and Kilduff. Answer immediately."[56] The *Chicago Examiner* added, "Alex has told Mitchell that he prefers the navy to the army and that he would enlist at the station near Chicago rather than become a doughboy. Mitchell confided this information to an aviation officer who asked him about the chances of having Aleck join an aero squadron. It is known that the San Pedro submarine station near Los Angeles also was in hopes of landing Alex as slab mate to Howard Ehmke, former Tiger, because of Alexander's statement that he preferred life on the rolling deep to land service."[57]

The Cubs' hurler arrived April 15 for a meeting with Weeghman in Chicago. "He feels that the Cub management has been on the square with him and that he should let Weeghman in on his future plans," the *Examiner* reported.[58] "If the Kaiser were a baseball fan he would call off the war until October," columnist George E. Phair wrote. "In fact, if the Kaiser had been a baseball fan there wouldn't have been a war."[59]

Many sports pages reported that Alexander met that same day with the navy commandant at the Great Lakes training station north of the city. These articles were wrong. "They were waiting for him at Great

Lakes with photographers and press agents all in shape to fix up a fine story, but Aleck didn't appear," the *Tribune* reported. "There is no doubt Alexander would prefer naval service to entering the national army, but he made no effort to enlist here."[60] The paper added that Howard County would send eight drafted men to the army during May. "This, it was said, makes certain Alexander's call to the colors at an early date even should he be eliminated from the April quota."[61]

The navy quickly announced that if Alexander did enlist at Great Lakes, he would be "called into service immediately, put through the preliminary training course and at its completion sent to sea."[62] The pitcher wired his draft board asking for permission to join the blue-jackets. "He believes he will be able to get this permission without any difficulty," the *Examiner* reported.[63] If that was so, however, Alexander was deceiving himself. Local boards normally allowed such a switch only when a man wasn't part of the immediate quota, and Alexander hadn't acted as quickly as Whitey Witt the previous autumn. "Alexander had all winter to join the navy if he wanted to," Nebraska's representative to Provost Marshal General Crowder said. "Our general orders are to release no registrants to the navy after they have been called for duty in the army, and there is no reason why Alexander should be taken out of his present quota."[64] Unless the pitcher somehow got permission from the War Department, he would go to Camp Funston with a St. Paul contingent.

In the meantime the right-hander pitched in the Cubs' season opener on April 16 in St. Louis. The Cardinals pounded out nine hits in a 4–2 victory. "Grover Cleveland Alexander is wondering tonight if even the army wants him now," Crusinberry quipped in the *Tribune*. He followed with an explanation: "It is hardly right to expect Alexander to be in his best style after his experience of the last two weeks, trailing over the desert, spending sleepless nights in a sleepless sleeper, and then, just before opening, being compelled to chase over the country to Chicago and back to find out his standing for army service. Arriving this morning, Alex tried to snatch a nap at the hotel, but went to the ball park pretty well worn out."[65]

A thunderstorm and damp grounds forced a rainout the next afternoon. "Having nothing else to do, the Cubs spent the day speculating what the team would look like after Uncle Sam gets through drafting men for his big league affair on the other side of the ocean," Crusinberry reported. "With prospects of losing Alexander and Killefer, the star battery, along with Rowdy Elliott and Pete Kilduff, and the possibility of losing another man or two, it didn't look bright for baseball on the north side in Chicago, but it does look bad for the kaiser."[66]

Alexander also drilled informally with several teammates in preparation for military service. "The Cub cadets were organized this morning by Bill Killefer, one of the latest national army prospects," the *Chicago Examiner* reported. "He is the manager of the army, which includes Alexander, Rowdy Elliott, Pete Kilduff and [Harry] Weaver, all Class 1 men. The army drilled in Bill's room before breakfast until George Tyler let it out."[67] Reindeer Bill had gotten pointers on military drill from outfielder Leslie Mann, who had spent the winter as a YMCA athletic instructor at Camp Logan, Texas.

Chicago Tribune columnist Ring Lardner offered a unique take on Alexander's situation. "It is to be hoped that the moral of the Alexander case will not be lost on our young men," Lardner wrote. "The great pitcher's present plight is a convincing argument in favor of early marriage. If Aleck had taken unto himself a wife at the beginning of his big league career or shortly thereafter, he would now be in a position to continue earning his $12,000 per annum for five, six, or possibly ten years, and the Giants would be assured of a little healthy competition for the National league championship."[68]

"There has been great excitement because Grover Cleveland Alexander, the Chicago National league pitcher, was called in the draft," the army newspaper *Stars and Stripes* reported in Paris, "but after studying many heated columns we know only that maybe Alexander will be drafted and maybe he won't."[69] Alexander and his countrymen knew the resolution before the piece appeared on April 19. "Aleck Called!" screamed a headline in the *Tribune*. "St. Paul, Neb., April 18.—Official notice summoning Grover C. Alexander, star pitcher of the Chicago Cubs, to go with the draft quota from Howard county, Nebraska, to Camp Funston April 30 was sent to Chicago by Alexander's draft board today."[70]

The headlines finally were correct. Nebraska guardsmen training at Camp Cody fired off a telegram to their governor, urging him to do what he could to have Alexander assigned with them. "They need him on the ball club," the *Omaha Bee* reported. "Six thousand wishes was the best they could do, but a ball player never was known to consider wishes as a consideration when signing a contract, and this time the big pitcher will probably have little to say besides."[71]

The cornhuskers' request had no chance of fulfillment. The 342nd Field Artillery already had plans for the Cubs' hurler in Kansas.

FIVE

Fast Nine

This game is not the game they knew before they faced the guns;
The game that called for tackle drives,
    Or cracking in the runs;
The game they played on friendly sod
    Beneath a friendly sky.
To poke a double down the line,
    Or snag the winging fly.

—LT. GRANTLAND RICE

Gen. Leonard Wood's reassignment to the Eighty-Ninth Division at Camp Funston had remained controversial. A congressman had said that even David Lloyd George, the British prime minister, had expressed "wonderment over what had become of Gen. Wood."[1] The general had dutifully trained the doughboys until late November 1917, when the army sent him to France as an observer.

Wood's Own, as the division's men called themselves, had given the departing commander a stirring sendoff from the Kansas cantonment. "Without the knowledge of General Wood, orders were issued that the Division be assembled and the troops formed in line on both sides of the road through which he would pass on his way to the station," the division history states. "The kindly secret had been well kept, and the formation was an agreeable and affecting surprise to the General."[2]

Two months later Wood visited a French "school of fire" near Soissons with a major and his chief of staff, Lt. Col. Charles Kilbourne. A shell stuck in the barrel of a trench mortar during a live-fire demonstration and exploded. Shrapnel killed five poilus (French soldiers) and wounded the three Americans. American headquarters announced that Wood had received a slight arm wound, but Kilbourne later recounted the real horror. "A piece of the trench mortar went through Gen. Wood's trench coat, tore away the breast of his uniform, grazed the flesh of his breast and lodged in the biceps of his left arm," the lieutenant colonel said. "He was hurried to a hospital, put under an anesthetic at 3 o'clock, the steel removed and he was assigned to a room an hour later."[3] Wood noted in his diary that a Frenchman's brains had splattered his overcoat and another man had been disemboweled. The three wounded Americans eventually recovered.

Military and sports training continued at Camp Funston despite the shocking news. A three-sport athlete at Illinois, Lt. Potsy Clark had taken over coaching the division basketball team. He compiled a winning record with a squad of former collegiate players assembled from the cantonment's huge manpower pool. Clark named Lt. Karl Hodge of Williams College his captain. Although it included "some of the best basket tossers west of the Mississippi river," the team wasn't as strong as it appeared on paper.[4] Camp Funston lost four times, all on the road, to the University of Kansas, Schmelzer's sporting goods, Creighton University, and Ottawa University.

The victory column was nonetheless substantial, Clark's quintet winning at least ten games. Camp Funston crushed the University of Nebraska, twice beat Camp Dodge, and cruised past Camp Doniphan and several lesser opponents. While attracting much less attention than the gridiron season, the hoops campaign exerted "a great moral effect on the people who have relatives at Funston," a Topeka newspaper opined. "It settles their minds to see rugged soldiers from the cantonment—samples of what their own relatives are or may be."[5] With basketball over and baseball about to begin, Potsy Clark exchanged his coach's whistle for a player's set of flannels.

Major Andruss wouldn't be officially assigned as director of the 342nd Field Artillery baseball team in mid-March, but by January he already had five key players: Lloyd Wait; Ad Lindsey; a former third baseman for the Kansas City Red Sox; a one-time star of the St. Louis municipal league; and Poge Lewis, once offered a Cardinals contract and now Camp Funston's top grenade thrower with a record of fifty-four yards. Andruss then spent five weeks poring through records in the Eighty-Ninth Division's personnel office. His eye-straining effort led to the reassignment of Win Noyes, Frank Wetzel, Potsy Clark, a former Texas Leaguer, and another ballplayer from the St. Louis municipal league.

Clark was an especially good acquisition. He and teammate George Halas had starred on the University of Illinois baseball team as well as the football squad. Their athletics director had declared that the Illini had never assembled another outfield equaling the one in 1916 with Clark and Halas. "Clark is a wonderful athlete—a man who always made good in a pinch," the athletic director said. "He never gets excited. He jokes around before a big game as if he were getting ready for afternoon practice. He was a great hitter, too."[6] Now Potsy would play for Andruss's extraordinary army team. "I could never have effected the transfer of these men," the major later wrote, "had it not been for the good sportsmanship of their respective organization commanders who were with me from start to finish and who helped to make my efforts a success."[7]

The parent Eighty-Ninth Division assembled a team of its own that appeared at least as strong as the regimental squad. "Ten promising big leaguers are already listed as material in the athletic office," the camp newspaper reported in mid-March, stretching the term *big leaguers* to embrace men who had played in the Minor Leagues or in college.[8] The list included several of Andruss's men, plus Captain Withington, who had pitched for Harvard, and Hodge, of Williams, who once had received a Major League tryout. The article was correct that the Eighty-Ninth Division nine would be loaded with talent. But most of it would come from the 342nd Field Artillery, which belonged to the division's artillery brigade.

The only true Major Leaguer yet in camp was Win Noyes, Connie Mack's rookie pitcher in Philadelphia a year earlier. Noyes had received his draft notice in August and entered the army after the season. Being first into camp may have helped him. Noyes would rise to sergeant major, the highest enlisted rank, placing him above every Major Leaguer who arrived afterward. "I remember him telling me when he reported for duty that he had joined the Army with the firm determination to become an efficient soldier," Andruss later wrote.[9]

Minor League outfielder Dutch Wetzel was the best of the remaining ballplayers at Camp Funston. Andruss didn't stand pat. "Plans are laid far in advance for noted players and many weeks before the men arrive in camp the request has been made that he be assigned to the 342d," the *Omaha Bee* reported. "Since January this well known organization has been working to add Grover Cleveland Alexander to its already large number of base ball players."[10] Three Major Leaguers would reach Camp Funston during the coming weeks and quickly be snapped up by Major Andruss for the 342nd. These were Charles Ward, Otis "Otie" Lambeth, and Clarence Mitchell.

Infielder Ward had been a rookie in 1917 at Pittsburgh, where he had taken over at shortstop from the legendary Honus Wagner. Called Chuck or Chick, he'd gone to Brooklyn over the winter in a trade that sent popular outfielder Casey Stengel to the Pirates. Ward was "the apple of my eye so far as this year's team was concerned," Dodgers manager Wilbert Robinson said upon losing him to the army. "I had figured confidently on him filling the hole at third base."[11]

Pitcher Lambeth of the Cleveland Indians had been in touch with Col. George Nugent since January. Lambeth had been born in the hamlet of Berlin, Kansas, but his family now worked a farm near Moran. Otie had thrown a no-hitter for Topeka in the Western League in 1916 before reaching the Major Leagues later that year. He had dazzled in a thirteen-inning, 4–3 loss that August to Yankees freshman hurler Urban Shocker. "Lambeth is likely to be heard from often before he is a year older," the *New York Tribune* had declared. "He has a very deceptive delivery. Though a sidearm pitcher he can throw either overhand or underhand and at any of the three styles he is capable of a marked change of pace."[12] Lambeth was considered one of Cleveland's most dependable pitchers.

Pitcher Clarence Mitchell had more Major League experience than either Ward or Lambeth. Teammates called the journeyman Mitch or Clarey. Mitchell had been born in a sod house in Nebraska. As a Minor Leaguer he had once beaten Pete Alexander's brother Raymond while hurling for Denver in the Western League. Throwing a spitball was legal during the Deadball Era, but Mitchell was a rarity: a left-handed spitballer. Hughie Jennings of the Tigers, his first Major League manager, hadn't believed him. "There ain't no such animal," Jennings roared. "Get out of here!"[13]

Mitchell, like Ward, was a new Dodger, claimed on waivers from Cincinnati before the 1918 season. He got saliva for his spitballs by chewing bark from a slippery elm tree that grew on his farm in Franklin, Nebraska. He supplied bark to Burleigh Grimes, Urban "Red" Faber, and other Major League spitballers too. Mitchell also was "a left-handed son of Old Man Swat, as pitchers go," according to Brooklyn Eagle sportswriter Tom Rice. The glowering Nebraskan had been so good at wielding a bat for the Reds that he'd often taken the field as a position player. "Our new bold athlete pitched in thirty-two games . . . but he batted in forty-seven, and had a batting average of .278," Rice noted.[14] The southpaw would report to Camp Funston a few days after Lambeth.

Andruss kept track of the draft status of players by reading The Sporting News. "Much to my gratification I found that these men were all acquainted with one another," he wrote, "and those already under arms helped beyond measure by writing to their friends explaining the conditions they would face upon entering the service and the manner in which they were to proceed in joining our outfit." The regiment built a ballpark that it dubbed Nugent Field in honor of the colonel. Andruss would describe it as "the finest field I have ever seen on any military reservation."[15]

Up at the divisional level, Captain Withington had help running the Eighty-Ninth's team, from civilian Johnny "Noisy" Kling of Kansas City. Kling had played with the Chicago Cubs in 1910–11 and afterward with the Reds and Braves. "No official coach has as yet been appointed, but Johnny Kling, former premier catcher, was here today giving the soldiers the benefit of his experience," a Kansas newspaper reported in late March.[16] As powerful as their team was, the doughboys still needed Kling's help. The Eighty-Ninth Division's first opponent would be the St. Louis Cardinals, who had finished third in the National League in 1917. The Cards were set to visit the cantonment for two exhibition games after breaking their spring training camp.

About a hundred ballplayers turned out for the division baseball team, but Major Andruss already had nabbed the best talent for his regimental squad. Coincidentally, the artillerymen received their new baseball flannels on the morning of the first Cardinals game, Saturday, March 30. The division players, in contrast, showed up in whatever baseball togs they could throw together.

"Major, those men of yours certainly look nifty—can they play ball as well as they look?" Withington asked. Andruss assured the captain they could. "Very well, then—go in and play St. Louis." Andruss considered this order from a junior officer "one of the toughest assignments in my thirty years on the baseball diamond and it made me sort of weak in the mid-section."[17]

With Nugent Field not yet finished, the Cards and the soldiers met on a diamond built by an entrepreneur in an adjacent wartime boomtown called Army City. The spacious park had five thousand reserved seats and bleachers accommodating fifteen thousand more. Most of the doughboy ballplayers were familiar from the football and basketball seasons. Poge Lewis was the starting pitcher, with Karl Hodge appearing in relief. Andruss put himself into the lineup at first base, Ad Lindsey at second, and Lloyd Wait behind the plate; Potsy Clark was in right field and Dutch Wetzel roamed center. Cardinals manager Jack Hendricks started his second string and sent pitcher Óscar Tuero to the mound. The camp newspaper reported the result:

It took ten innings to decide the battle between the St Louis Cardinals and the 89th division of Funston in the first baseball game of the season on the Army City diamond Saturday when the Funston team defeated the Cardinals by a score of 9 to 8.

Major Andruss who covered first for the Funston team was proclaimed the hero of the day when with two down and two on he connected with a swift one which was the deciding score of the game.[18]

Funston fielded the same team except for Andruss and Lewis for the second game Sunday afternoon. Hodge took the mound for the soldiers and Oscar Horstmann for St. Louis, both later giving way to relievers. The Major Leaguers staged an eighth-inning rally to win 13–10. An immodest soldier-journalist wrote:

We of the 342 like to feel that the absence of our major and lieutenant considerably weakened the division team and that the regular 342 lineup of the day before would have witnessed such a victory as that of the previous game. . . .

We prophesy that the 342 team will clean up anything in baseball togs in Camp Funston this season. Valuable players are being added daily from the new men just coming in, and among the lineup will be a few veterans of the game, several of whom have already made their name in baseball.[19]

One of the newly arriving players was Chuck Ward, who reached Camp Funston with other draftees from his hometown of St. Louis. "Ward has been assigned as acting sergeant to a squad from his own political ward," the New York Tribune reported on April 7. "A large crowd of Ward's friends gathered at Union Station, St. Louis, on the occasion of his start for the training camp last week, and presented him with a jewelled watch."[20]

Ward wouldn't reach the 342nd Field Artillery in time to play for the Eighty-Ninth Division against its next Major League opponent, the champion Chicago White Sox. During the interim Captain Withington directed Andruss to send his regimental team to division headquarters to be measured for baseball flannels. "So my ball players instead of having one uniform sported three—battery, regimental and divisional,"[21] Andruss later recalled. Withington wired Chicago manager Clarence "Pants" Rowland and urged him to use his best players. The division wanted a good showing because the game at Army City on Friday, April 12, marked the return of General Wood. "The big boss wired back that all the regulars would be in the game, barring accident between here and there," the *Chicago Tribune* reported.[22]

Potsy Clark greeted Rowland and "showed him about the camp when the team arrived about noon, after a 14-mile auto ride from Manhattan [Kansas]. The players had to make the same dusty trip over a rocky road after the game." General Wood reached Camp Funston late that afternoon. "When the general stepped off the train a band struck up 'Hail to the Chief,' and the tune was picked up along the line as the general, escorted by headquarters staff, passed down a long lane between thousands of soldiers standing at attention. The game was started immediately after the welcome to Wood was completed."[23]

Despite missing his second baseman Eddie Collins and pitcher Eddie Cicotte, the Chicago skipper kept his promise to field a good team at Army City. "Manager Rowland played as many as possible of the world's champions so as to give the boys in khaki a final look at them before going away from here," *Tribune* sportswriter I. E. Sanborn wrote.[24] Ten thousand doughboys watched Win Noyes pitch for the division. They had little to cheer about except the return of General Wood as the doughboys lost, 13–1.

Andruss, Withington, and their ballplayers had no time to stew about the walloping. They hit the road for games the next two days with the Western League club in Topeka. "The soldiers looked like they had a fast team in the warming up period before the umpire took his place," the *Topeka State Journal* reported. "The 'O. D.'s' [olive drabs] were a husky, clean looking bunch of fighting men."[25] The soldiers won both games, 5–4 and 7–2. The winning pitchers went unrecorded, but Hodge started again for the division. The *State Journal* expressed surprise at what it called the "democratic equality" of the doughboys on the diamond. "There was no saluting by Private Pitcher before he made a delivery to Officer Catcher, no orderlies were in evidence, and the privates along the coaching line did not click their heels and say 'sir' when they were calling to Lieutenant Lindsey and Lieutenant Clark for a hit or to take a longer lead. They used language something like this: 'Hey, Potsy, come on and give a push, hit it out! He's easy Swede, lay on and make the outfielders wake up!'"[26]

Rematches were scheduled for the Eighty-Ninth Division and Topeka clubs the following week at Army City, but a twenty-eight-hour snowstorm forced cancellation of both games. Snow and rain also erased a game with the Western League club in Wichita. The 342nd team finally took the field again on Friday, April 26, at Army City, beating visiting University of Missouri, 2–1. Rain washed out a second game on Saturday, along with a separate Eighty-Ninth Division game scheduled at Kansas City with the Blues of the American Association.

The division team then played in Kansas City on Sunday, April 28, losing 5–4 to the Blues. Chuck Ward and Win Noyes both appeared for the army club. The Athletics pitcher took the loss despite a strong complete-game performance. Veteran Major League pitcher Charles "Babe" Adams tossed the first three innings for the Blues. "Win Noyes was hard to solve. The Blues could nick him, but every threatened assault was short lived. . . . The soldiers played a clean, stiff game. They tried to the last and the 1,200 present were for them to a man. The fans passed up their otherwise favorites to boost the men in their service."[27]

The Eighty-Ninth Division team defeated a Salina club 2–1 at home on May 5, its last game for a while. Four games scheduled for mid-May—two with Camp Dodge at Army City and a pair with Camp Grant at Galesburg, Illinois—were abruptly canceled. Terse announcements first stated that Camp Dodge was unable to travel, then that Camp Funston couldn't fulfill the commitment. Both statements likely reflected the quickening pace of preparation to ship out for Europe. The ballplayers of the 342nd Field Artillery meanwhile learned that Otis Lambeth, Clarence Mitchell, and Alexander the Great were on their way to Kansas to join them.

SIX

Through a Door

When it comes to crabbing in the good old fashioned way;
When it comes to knocking with the accent on the K,
My bet is on the army when the gales begin to blow
And a fellow has to slush around in rain and wind and snow.

—LT. GRANTLAND RICE

Some fans concluded that Pete Alexander was sent to the army because he no longer worked a farm back in Nebraska. An Associated Press dispatch from St. Paul attributed his conscription to "Uncle Sam's urgent need for greater food production to help win the war. . . . Alexander's call to the colors, members of the draft board figured, meant just one more man for work on nearby farms. It was clearly their patriotic duty, they concluded, to carry out the provisions of a recent selective service bulletin, calling upon exemption boards to keep the farmers at work on the farms, where they are most needed. As a result, the famous ball player, who stood eighteenth in the list of men in class 1, suddenly was placed as the ninth man in a quota of twelve."[1]

"If Grover Cleveland Alexander had only been a farmer," the *Omaha Bee* opined, "he might have escaped the draft at this time, thus showing that agriculture has something on art when it comes to a pinch."[2] Cynics expected him to return to the soil to keep from going to war.

Jack Veiock, sporting editor of the International News Service, banged out a dour little ditty that read in part:

> While the Cubs fight on alone,
> Aleck will be staying home,
> Raising corn and wheat and hay—
> Aleck's in the draft today.[3]

Alexander disproved such sentiments by sticking with the Cubs and making no further effort to change his draft status. He won his first game for his new club April 21 in front of a small crowd in Cincinnati. "Alexander won the game easily, his mates supporting him with some bang up hitting," the *Chicago Tribune* reported. "The score was 9 to 1, and the one Cincinnati tally came in the ninth, when no one cared a whoop."[4] The pitcher then briefly visited St. Paul and missed the Cubs' home opener, but he returned to Chicago for his third and final appearance of the season. "A telegram from the great pitcher arrived yesterday from his home in Nebraska, where he was attending to business matters before joining the colors," the *Tribune* reported on April 26. "It said he would arrive in Chicago this morning ready to pitch. He intends to leave tonight to begin training for the bigger game with Uncle Sam's great team."[5]

The departing Cub said he wasn't going into the army to play baseball but nonetheless would keep his arm in condition. "I will take a bunch of baseballs with me into camp, will go equipped with my own glove and a catcher's mitt and if I find a pal who will act as my backstop I shall be greatly delighted." Alexander added of the army, "I am going in with the same determination, the same spirit that I carried into baseball. I'm going to succeed as a soldier and it shall never be said of me that as a soldier I'm a good pitcher."[6]

Alexander likely was stung by calculations that he was costing his club $16,666.67 per game during his war-shortened season. When the Cubs subscribed for $12,000 in Liberty war bonds before his last appearance, the pitcher paid for $5,000 of it and manager Mitchell paid for the same amount. Alexander in effect spent his entire signing bonus on the bonds, "declaring the Chicago club was not getting its money's worth on its investment."[7]

The afternoon that Ol' Pete pitched his first and last game of the season in Chicago was "damp and cold and awful for baseball." Back from St. Paul, he "hadn't touched a ball for several days, and went to the hill 'cold,'" the *Chicago Examiner* reported, but he pitched a game that would "go into the records as one of the greatest of the season."[8] His pal Reindeer Bill Killefer caught him versus the Cardinals. Six thousand chilled but wildly enthusiastic fans cheered Alexander, who surrendered a run in the first inning and then settled down to beat Frank "Jakie" May, 3–2. He threw a complete game while giving up two hits, both to Rogers Hornsby. After St. Louis tied the game in the top of the ninth, the Cubs pushed across a walk-off run at the bottom.

"Veni, Vidi, Vici" read the headline in the *Chicago Tribune*. "Alexander the Great has come and gone!" James Crusinberry wrote. "In the space of about one hour and fifty minutes yesterday, Chicago's baseball fans enjoyed the presence of Mr. Grover Cleveland Alexander as pitcher de luxe of the Cubs." The crowd rooted "better than in years" until the victory was complete. "Several hundred small boys and grown men jumped upon the field and surrounded Aleck, but he escaped to the clubhouse. A half hour later, when he came out in street clothes, there still were more than a hundred boys and men, who swarmed around him and practically carried him to the front entrance, where he again escaped into President Weeghman's office."[9]

In the clubhouse before the game the Cubs had given Alexander a handsome wristwatch inscribed "To Alkali Pete from the Cubs." Weeghman now offered him a toast at a gathering of stockholders, fans, and a few friends. The pitcher's eyes were damp as he stammered a reply. "I am sorry to leave such good friends as I have found you to be during our short acquaintance," Alexander said, "but Uncle Sam has called me and I am going gladly, because he wants me to help make this country safe so that the rest of us can play ball or do any lawful act in peace. And if I don't come back from over there there'll be a lot of other holes dug besides the one for me."[10]

That same afternoon Clarence Mitchell made his only 1918 appearance for the Dodgers. The southpaw spitballer's start versus the Giants was brief and disastrous. Mitchell threw eleven pitches for four hits before manager Wilbert Robinson relieved him in what became an 11–5 shellacking. "Uncle Robbie couldn't be blamed for trying to get an extra day's work out of Mitchell," W. J. Macbeth wrote in the *New York Tribune*. "The army is calling his trained athletes so fast these days that Robinson, the Ebbetses and McKeevers [the Dodgers' co-owners] may all have to get into uniform before the end of next week."[11]

Mitchell headed for the army immediately afterward. "Grover Alexander and Clarence Mitchell—two Nebraskans, were heroes of yesterday," the *Lincoln State Journal* observed. "Both left one National league to enter another. But there is a sad contrast in the departure of Alex, of St. Paul and Clarence of Franklin, Neb. Alexander pitched one of the greatest games of his career—a two-hitter. Mitchell was yanked from the Brooklyn mound—yanked on his last appearance. Both hurlers are to join the colors at Funston."[12]

Otis Lambeth of the Indians reported to Camp Funston the same day. The young Kansan had pitched his second and final game of the season five days earlier versus the St. Louis Browns in Cleveland and had been lifted without a decision in the fifth inning of an 11–7 loss. "Lambeth will make one more splendid addition to the Camp Funston nine's pitching corps," newspapers reported.[13]

Alexander and eleven other drafted men assembled in St. Paul on Monday, April 29, their official enlistment date. The contingent left town early the next morning on a Chicago, Burlington & Quincy passenger train. "Grover Alexander because a draft board thought that war was more important than baseball left this week with his draft contingent from St. Paul, Howard county, after trying his best to get away from his duty to his country," sniped the *Weekly Journal* in Ord, Nebraska. The loyal *St. Paul Phonograph* was having none of it. The newspaper acknowledged that the pitcher had applied for an exemption but added: "The district board overruled the claim, wisely no doubt, but

Alexander was 'every inch a man,' and was satisfied to take his turn on the firing line for Uncle Sam. . . . Alexander left St. Paul with the remark that 'too "darn" much' had been said about his case that was not due him. Aside from his perfect willingness to go to war, Alexander's biggest single piece of patriotism was shown in Chicago on Friday, April 26, when he invested $5,000 in Third Liberty Loan Bonds."[14]

Each Howard County draftee boarded the train carrying a soldier's kit presented by a local entertainment committee. One man likely carried the orders for all twelve. "This is a husky bunch of young fellows and will materially add to the already splendid fighting forces that Uncle Sam has received from Howard county," the *St. Paul Republican* reported.[15] The rail trip to Camp Funston was long and indirect, about 265 miles altogether. The group first went east to Lincoln, there boarding a southbound Union Pacific train at three o'clock. They crossed into Kansas that evening, turned briefly west, and reached the depot at Camp Funston about one-thirty in the morning on May 1. Alexander may have looked about and wondered what sort of place it was. "At first, as one peered through the window, the station seemed a tiny islet of light in an ocean of darkness," a visiting civilian had written. "All beyond lay in such silence and night that it was hard to believe 25,000 men were close at hand."[16]

Walking exhausted into a darkened military camp doesn't fill a new soldier's heart with hope or inspiration. Camp Funston and other cantonments were "primarily great centers for sorting of men into the supplies of human raw material which headquarters used in building a completely rounded army with a combat force in France," a contemporary history states.[17] The St. Paul men likely looked around in bewilderment and stupefaction. "The Nebraskans were first sent to detention camp No. 1 on Pawnee flats, where Alexander bunked with eight other men. Later in the day they were moved to barracks near the receiving station ready for their call when their turn comes."[18]

Nebraskans got little or no sleep that first short night as reveille sounded at five thirty. The Camp Funston receiving station consisted of two barracks with an enclosed passageway to a latrine and bath.

Signs affixed to the walls read: "This way to Berlin" and "Make it snappy, 1-2-3-4-."[19] It's unclear how Alexander and the others passed their first day in the army; they may simply have waited for the station to make room for them. The earliest entries stamped into Alexander's surviving army records are dated the following day.

The draftees' first job was to pack their civilian clothes for shipment home. "The men then proceeded to the bathhouse and took hot baths, the quartermaster furnishing soap and towels. All examinations were made on one floor of the second barracks. If a man was accepted, he was furnished with a complete equipment by the quartermaster."[20] Doughboys called their initial processing "shooting the chutes" because of the "chutelike arrangement of the station."[21] Alexander stood out even amid this shuffling mass of anonymous men.

"Grover Cleveland Alexander," a sergeant called out, prompting other prospective soldiers to break into applause when the pitcher stepped out of line. Can you imagine that, a rookie getting a hand? The sergeant, however, never batted an eye. The Cubs' $50,000 pitcher was nothing in the young life of this veteran of six months' training. Either he was no fan or else he was wedded to army discipline. "Come along," was all he said, and with his fellows from Howard county, Alexander started on his way through the mill that takes in civilians at one end and turns out soldiers at the other.[22]

Like the doughboys in line ahead of and behind him, Alexander moved from point to point through the receiving station for about three hours. He underwent medical checks that likely reminded him of his Selective Service examination back home in Nebraska. The process was identical for each man.

He goes before the "nut" board which examines his mentality. Then, much to his surprise, he gets by, he goes from one examiner to another, has his finger prints taken, gets his vaccination and anti-typhoid shot and is poked, prodded and tested out from head to foot. If the regular examiners suspect that he needs an especial survey, there are specialists in all lines, heart, nerve, in fact all kinds of boards to whom him he might be sent. Emerging from one of these a rookie is usually covered with cabalistic signs, for the doctors keep books and mark their reports on human pages. He arrives at the desk of Major O'Donnell, brigade surgeon, with his record on his sheet, literally, where that officer reads it off, looks over the medical record card he has carried through the process, accepts or rejects him and down the chute he goes.[23]

The report of his physical exam reveals that Alexander was sent to a "special venereal examiner" because he acknowledged past treatment for the social disease soldiers called the clap.[24] A neuropsychiatric board—"the nut board"—also examined and passed him. There's no mention of epilepsy or seizures. Alexander may have hoped that his flat feet, poor teeth, and color blindness would prompt his rejection instead. None did. "I got into that Army in 1918 like walking through a door," he said with a laugh nearly a quarter-century later.[25]

Soldiers from across the camp clustered in doorways for a peek at the famous hurler. "In the medical examination Alexander was given his 'shot' in the left arm, as the divisional baseball club is taking no chances with his famous right wing."[26] Doughboys during this era didn't receive the swift, buzzed haircut familiar to later generations of inductees; news photos of the pitcher in his new army khakis showed Alexander still sporting his reddish-brown pompadour. The St. Paul draftees left by truck after shooting the chutes and receiving their uniforms and equipment. Their next temporary home was Detention Camp No. 2, six miles from Camp Funston on the other side of Fort Riley and within sight of Junction City to the south. There 620 tents sheltered five men apiece.

The army had erected the camp in February to prevent draftees who were ill when they arrived from infecting men who were already in training. Diseases could easily sweep through a group the size an army division. The precaution wasn't always effective. Mumps and measles were still dangerous in 1918; the latter had put quarterback Stankowski's whole company into quarantine during the football season. Sometimes the threat was deadlier. Camp Funston had experienced a meningitis outbreak during the fall and a football player from visiting Iowa State Teachers College had died after his team played the Eighty-Ninth Division eleven. The 342nd Field Artillery later became the first unit in the army to receive an experimental meningitis inoculation.

In some cases the effects of disease were catastrophic. Fourteen doughboys from the 342nd Field Artillery had died at Camp Funston in December, mostly from pneumonia. Far worse, many modern researchers believe that the great influenza pandemic of 1918 and 1919, which would kill tens of millions of people around the world, began among Kansas draftees stationed at the crowded camp that spring. Alexander therefore began his army training essentially in quarantine at Detention Camp No. 2. The Union Pacific Railroad press bureau offered a long description that read in part as follows:

> "Detention Camp No. 2" is an unlovely name, and it has just been changed to "Camp Wood." There on a flat between the low hills and the river, it presents the site of acres of tents, laid out in trim rows. Headquarters, the post exchange, and the infirmary are housed in the only wooden buildings in camp, excepting those of the kitchens. . . .
>
> Instead of the heartbreaking days of drill, drill, drill, that have made the first weeks of army life hard for many, the newly arrived man will find the days at the detention camp divided into fourteen half-hour periods in which drills, lectures and other duties alternate.[27]

Army records show that in addition to his diamond work Alexander was an expert lineman with three years' experience working for a telephone company. Ordinarily an army detailer might have directed such a man into the Signal Corps. Not so with Alexander the Great. The hurler was only two days at Camp Funston before newspapers began reporting he would be snapped up by the 342nd Field Artillery. The *Chicago Tribune* reported—inaccurately, as it turned out—that he would "probably be assigned to the clerical work to save his strength for athletics."[28] An Arizona newspaper added, "His induction into the service is hailed with joy by Funston baseball fans who are already planning additional conquests for the 89th division team with Alexander on the mound."[29]

Soldiers played ball in the detention camp, too, which no doubt pleased Private Alexander. "Between anti-typhoid inoculation 'shots' and vaccination unpleasantness, Grover Cleveland Alexander, premier twirler, late of the Chicago Cubs, is keeping his pitching arm in form," a Topeka newspaper reported. With Clarence Mitchell in the camp as well, a National League rivalry soon emerged. The Cub and Dodger assembled teams to play during late afternoons, when baseball was allowed. Mitchell had the better nine in the tent city. "They've walloped the tar out of us thus far," Alexander conceded with a smile, "but wait until this inoculation siege is over. This dope they shoot into a fellow sort of takes the pep out of him for a while."[30]

Although confined there for only a short time, new doughboys learned a few useful lessons at the detention camp. They learned, for example, "the mysteries of 'right dress,' 'attention,' 'squads right,' and 'forward march.' This is the kindergarten of the army, so to speak."[31] If they didn't yet curse when they arrived, they surely did by the time they left. Everyone also quickly picked up the army's distinctive slang— *shavetail* for a second lieutenant; *Holy Joe* for the chaplain; *guard house lawyer* for a company know-it-all; *hardtack* for a hard unappetizing cracker; *windy* for a bugler.[32] Alexander and Mitchell learned the meaning of the bugle calls they heard throughout the day, especially the chow call summoning them to meals. Soldiers had put words to the tune:

Soup-y, soup-y-, soup
    Without a single bean;
Pork-y, pork-y-, pork
    Without a streak of lean;
Coffee, coffee, coffee
    Without any cream.[33]

Alexander performed well during his first weeks in khaki. "At the detention camp he has been promoted to an acting first sergeancy, and as he bosses his company around in their various camp duties, he would hardly be recognized as the former idol of the diamond," the Union Pacific news bureau reported. (The report was slightly inaccurate; the pitcher had been appointed an acting corporal.) "Alexander has taken to army life like the proverbial duck to water, is popular with both officers and men and is working hard to make the best possible soldier out of himself."[34] His permanent duty assignment wasn't in doubt. In a letter to General Wood, penned the same day the pitcher had boarded the train for Camp Funston, Colonel Nugent had requested that Alexander and Mitchell both be assigned to the 342nd Field Artillery. "These men are professional ball players. They have friends among the other professional ball players now in the regiment, with whom they have been in correspondence for some time. They both have expressed a desire to be assigned to the regiment, and their assignment to the regiment will be a most valuable incentive in its physical training and the building up of esprit. Therefore it is earnestly requested that if practicable the above assignment be made."[35]

Doughboys normally spent two or three weeks assigned to the 164th Depot Brigade in the detention camp. Records show, however, that Alexander transferred into the Eighty-Ninth Division's Headquarters Troop after a mere six days. It's not clear what he did there, or whether he remained in the detention camp. Alexander officially reported to Colonel Nugent's regiment on May 29. "On his transfer to the 342d field artillery, his temporary ranking did not hold, of course, and he is now a full fledged 'buck private,'" a wire service reported. "He has made a very good impression by the manner in which he has taken to army life, however, and is looked upon as excellent future 'non-com' material."[36] Clarence Mitchell reported to the regiment at about the same time.

The two arriving Major Leaguers brought the regiment's total to five—Alexander, Mitchell, Noyes, Ward, and Lambeth. Dutch Wetzel, too, would reach the big leagues following the war, giving the outfit an even half-dozen. Ward had played briefly with Mitchell on the Dodgers and with Noyes on the Portland Beavers in the Pacific

Coast League. All now wore the khaki of Uncle Sam's gunners. "It was a great day for the regiment when the blue [infantry] hat cords of the Depot Brigade were replaced by the red insignia of the Artillery," Major Andruss later wrote. "Incidentally, this coup d'état completed the classiest baseball aggregation the Army has ever known."[37]

Hopes that Alexander might soon play army baseball were unrealistic. The Eighty-Ninth Division was preparing to leave Camp Funston for the East Coast and then France. After cancellation of its series with Camp Dodge and Camp Grant, the division team didn't play another game in the United States. The 342nd regimental nine—essentially the same squad in different flannels—played only two more games. These came May 17 and 18 versus the University of Missouri at Columbia. Alexander appeared in neither, despite a hopeful newspaper ad placed by a local restaurant: "See Grover Cleveland Alexander pitch for the Camp Funston baseball team and stop in at the Palms after the game. 'Atta boy, Tigers!'"[38] Otis Lambeth won the first game, 6–3, striking out eight. The Tigers won the second game, 5–4, with a rally in the ninth. Despite the loss, the artillerymen got a strong pitching performance from Win Noyes, who struck out a dozen collegians.

Plans for Alexander and Noyes to pitch a Fourth of July doubleheader versus a semipro team in Lincoln proved premature. The regiment would be gone long before the holiday arrived. Newspaper reports that Bill Killefer would be drafted and sent to Camp Funston to catch for Alexander also were wrong. The Michigan native would enter the army only after the 1918 season ended and report to Camp Custer outside Battle Creek.

Newspapers likewise reported the hope of Alexander pitching occasionally for the Cubs in Chicago, "providing it can be arranged with the government and Alexander. It is intended to have Alexander make overnight jumps from the cantonment, when possible."[39] Numerous Major Leaguers, especially pitchers, did briefly don their civilian uniforms and return to the diamond during the season and even the World Series. War Department regulations permitted a ballplayer to perform for his old team during a normal leave or furlough. None, however, was granted extended time away from his unit or ship simply to play baseball, despite a request from at least one Major League owner for exactly that kind of special treatment.

Conditions never aligned for Alexander. "The army has a rule of some sort that a private cannot obtain a furlough until he has been in camp a certain length of time," the *Chicago Tribune* reported. "If that is strictly applied to Alexander he may not be seen on the north side until late in the season."[40] Whether due to this guideline or to what the army and navy called "exigencies of the service," Alexander didn't pitch again in the Major Leagues in 1918.

SEVEN

Camp Funston

When the drill somehow seems longer
    Than it ever was before;
When my back feels halfway broken
    And my aching feet are sore . . .
Then it is I pause a second
    In the long day's rushing pace
And I cuss the bally Kaiser
    Till I'm purple in the face.

—LT. GRANTLAND RICE

L ike most cantonments Camp Funston was still under construction when draftees began arriving in late 1917. "There are seven thousand workmen here besides the soldier boys," Pvt. Emory Medlin of the 342nd Field Artillery's (FA's) Battery B had written after reaching the camp that September.[1] Calling Camp Funston a finished installation would have been charitable even late the following spring. *National Geographic* magazine described the camp for parents and families:

> It devolves on Camp Funston, located at Fort Riley, Kansas, which stands at the confluence of the Republican and the Kansas rivers, to accommodate the National Army forces from seven States. . . . The men who will train at this camp may well feel that they are closer to the heart of

the United States than any of the other military forces of the nation, for at Fort Riley stands the Ogden Monument, proclaiming the exact geographic center of the United States. . . .

Camp Funston can accommodate 41,000 people—a city as populous as the State capital. To the south of the camp runs the Kansas River and to the north are grass-covered hills. It would be difficult to imagine a more striking location for a camp. The fertile valley of Kansas' middle river sweeps eastward, and one gets the feeling of the boundless reaches of America as he surveys the scene from the green hills to the north.[2]

What the magazine omitted was how uncomfortable the doughboys usually were, living and training on twenty thousand acres of prairie. "The dust out here has sure been awful since the large number of men have been here and the grass which was about a foot high has been worn down in less than a week and now it is nothing short of a desert when the wind blows," a private in the 342nd FA's medical detachment wrote. "On one day the wind blows the dust to one end of the camp and the next day it blows back. . . . [I]f we have a nice clear day and the wind does not blow we are lost without it."[3] One soldier thought only a poet could adequately describe the wind, especially when it blew during a Saturday morning inspection. "That wind can blow loose flaps in cartridge belts, or unbutton buttons that should be closed, misplace packs and hatcords, turn up collars, tickle the nostrils of the poor, unhappy soldier boy so he simply has to sneeze in the face of his commanding officer."[4]

Extreme seasonal changes compounded the misery. Doughboys found Camp Funston too hot in the summer, too cold in the winter, and too unpredictable in between. The camp mud at least provided realistic training for French battlefields. "We have had some pretty cold, disagreeable weather lately," Lt. Harold Jacobus wrote in September. "The streets in the camp not being graded are very similar to the streets of Venice—whenever there is a slight depression a miniature lake forms. Just outside our present quarters we have quite some pond, about 40 yards square. There is nothing like this Kansas mud to trudge around in—unless it be the mud in the trenches. It just clings to your shoes in successive layers until your foot looks and feels like that of a full-grown elephant."[5]

One positive was that draftees from small towns or farming communities often served alongside their neighbors. Several men from Pete Alexander's contingent were assigned to the Eighty-Ninth Division's 355th Infantry Regiment, which was made up largely of Nebraska men. Familiarity helped to pull such units together, particularly at the company level. Many draftees nonetheless found Camp Funston enormous and intimidating. The cantonment's 250 identical, two-story wooden barracks stood aligned on the prairie in precise rows like troopers on parade. Their sheer number could confuse and frighten men accustomed only to lonely farms or mountain ridges. An Arizonan in the 340th FA penned a description: "Camp Funston is so laid out that every regiment is like a ward in a big city. For instance, the men in the 340th have their own central steam plant, barracks, bathing establishments, regimental exchange, hospital, officers' headquarters, and post office; in fact [they] form a complete, well organized community—organized for just one thing—efficient military service."[6]

The Union Pacific Railroad bisected the cantonment. A dozen depots along its main line handled the immense amount of freight needed to keep the camp humming. Camp Funston had fourteen miles of steam railway, twenty-eight miles of paved roads, a base hospital and fourteen infirmaries, a fire department, a library, recreational facilities, a hostess house for visitors and families, fourteen YMCA facilities, and three facilities for the Knights of Columbus. There also was "the only city ever built within an army camp," a four-block area officially designated the Zone of Camp Activities and Amusements but generally simply called the Zone.[7] "Fifty-five firms are represented in The Zone and every line of business is to be found," the camp newspaper explained. "It is a place where the soldiers may do their trading and where they can be furnished with high class, clean and moral amusement without leaving the cantonment."[8]

What publications could only hint at, however, was how ill prepared the new citizen army was for fighting. General Wood had trained the Eighty-Ninth Division since autumn and his infantrymen were reasonably ready for frontline duty; most at least were familiar with their weapons and tactics. The same wasn't true of the 342nd FA or the rest of the 164th Field Artillery Brigade. The artillerymen were to support the infantry on the battlefield, but they had only a few outdated guns on which to train. Men sent to a motor school in nearby Manhattan learned how to operate the tractors for a mechanized brigade, but the brigade's machines never reached Camp Funston. The gunners instead maneuvered teams of horses, much as their grandfathers had during the Civil War a half-century earlier. A doughboy in the 341st FA shared his difficulties in a letter home:

> While grooming the horses Friday morning, I picked me out an old dead plow horse. He looked like he could hardly get out of his tracks, but I found he could get his hind feet up. I was grooming him so nicely and handling him like a pet and all at once he groomed me in the face, knocked me about 10 feet, but as luck would have it it did not hurt me in the least. But never again do I want to groom him; if I do I sure won't handle him like a pet. . . . We also have one we call Kaiser Bill. If the Kaiser is that mean I don't care to meet him.[9]

Proficiency naturally lagged without modern equipment or realistic training. The history of the 340th FA's Battery A later offered an appalling recollection from late 1917: "The men who were with the Battery in the early days of training at Camp Funston will readily recall the difficulties encountered; the wooden pieces made of running gears of escort wagons and butts of telephone poles; the cannoners' drilaround stakes driven in the ground to represent wheels of carriages; the men tied on ropes to represent teams, and various other devices to simulate actual conditions."[10]

The division's artillerymen had few illusions about their readiness even once training improved. "We are not near ready to start to France as an organization," Cpl. Carey J. Maupin of Battery E, 342nd

FA, wrote at the end of March 1918.[11] He still struggled to catch up a month later:

> In the school of fire, I am learning much about artillery. But we attempt to cover so much in so short a length of time that the work is strenuous. This morning we had the usual weekly test and it was long and difficult. In the last weekly test I had a grade of 79. Not what I should have made owing to such hurried work that we do not grasp it all. But I led the 342nd Regiment even at that. A little consolation. We study the gun, its parts, the kinds of shells, their use, how and why used and their effect. We work problems and compute reflection, angles, ranges, etc., that the Battery Commander must know and do. I hope to be of more value to my battery, to my officers and to myself after the completion of this course.[12]

The brigade conducted its first live-fire exercise in mid-April, when it finally got to fire at dummy barbed wire, pill boxes, and trenches. The three regiments weren't nearly ready for a real battlefield and wouldn't be for some time. Few artillery outfits in the army were much better.

Perhaps it was some small consolation within the brigade that the 342nd FA fielded such a terrific baseball team. The regiment had the finest players and best equipment in the army. Newly arrived Pvt. Pete Alexander, however, had little time in which to learn his far more important duties with the artillery before his regiment shipped out. He may also have found it ironic that the three men most responsible for landing the best pitcher in the army were themselves moving on to other duties.

Major Andruss was promoted to lieutenant colonel and given command of the 317th Ammunition Train, attached to the African American Ninety-Second Infantry Division. Andruss was among the white officers who would lead the buffalo soldiers in France. Captain Withington likewise received new orders to Camp Devens, Massachusetts, where he was to take charge of athletics. The former Harvard star somehow remained with the Eighty-Ninth Division, however, possibly by pulling strings within Wood's Own. Withington instead was appointed medical officer for the 354th Infantry Regiment's first battalion.

General Wood was the last of Camp Funston's baseball magnates to depart. The first elements of his Eighty-Ninth Division entrained for the East Coast on May 21, leaving behind the 164th Field Artillery Brigade. The weather was dramatic: three tornadoes touched down in Kansas that day, one only fifty miles away. More troops left the following day, including several men from Alexander's draft contingent now assigned to the 355th Infantry Regiment. The hurler was fortunate not to be among them. "Many of the new men had just come from the detention camps," the unit's history states. "More than half of them had had no drill of any kind and had only just felt of a rifle without knowing the use of bayonet or grenades or any of the other weapons used by infantry. Most of them had been in the service either two or four weeks."[13]

Articles published at the time were far more optimistic. "The Funston boys are going over there," the *Omaha Bee* reported in an upbeat, censored dispatch. "Where they go from here or when and how they leave are points of information that cannot be made public. The men themselves know little about it and care less. . . . The few civilians who are seeing the sight of a lifetime can never tell what they saw. Words would not describe it."[14]

The division reached Camp Mills, Long Island, and was preparing to cross the Atlantic when the army announced on May 27 that General Wood had been relieved of command. Wood neither expected nor wanted reassignment. Historians generally cite two reasons for the order: The general had long publicly disagreed with President Wilson on war policies; and Gen. John J. "Black Jack" Pershing, commanding the American Expeditionary Forces, didn't much want Wood in France. The War Department offered Wood command of the Western Department at San Francisco. He declined, preferring to train more troops at Camp Funston. The news stunned the country. "Friends of General Wood in Congress when told of the department's refusal to permit him to serve with American forces in France were indignant," the *New York Tribune* reported. "The shelving of the distinguished army officer generally was attributed to politics. It has been no secret that General Wood has been under the displeasure of the President and Secretary Baker since the beginning of the war."[15]

Wood said nothing and went to Washington to meet with Wilson at the White House. Editorial pages railed against what many considered mistreatment of America's most talented and experienced soldier. "The news that General Leonard Wood is to be kept in this country while the division whose training he is completing will go abroad under his second in command will give every fair-minded man a bad taste in the mouth," the *New York World* grumbled in a widely reprinted editorial.[16] The president and War Department stood firm. General Wood met with his staff officers on June 2 at Camp Mills.

> "I will not say good-bye," he told them, and those who heard him said his voice trembled with emotion, "but consider it a temporary separation—at least I hope so. I have worked hard with you and you have done excellent work. I had hoped very much to take you over to the other side. In fact, I had no intimation, direct or indirect, of any change of orders until we reached here the other night. . . .
>
> "There isn't anything to be said. The orders stand and the only thing to do is to do the best we can—all of us—to win the war. That's what we are here for, that's what you have been trained for. I shall follow your career with the deepest interest, with just as much interest as though I were with you. Good luck and God bless you."[17]

Brig. Gen. Frank L. Winn assumed command of the infantrymen General Wood had trained so well and diligently. They sailed away in convoy on June 4. Winn was later promoted and the command next passed to Maj. Gen. William W. Wright. The names of the division's three generals would inspire a battle cry among the Fighting Farmers overseas: Wright-Wood-Winn. *Right would win.*

Momentous but more pleasant changes were in store for Alexander back in Kansas. The pitcher had little opportunity at Camp Funston to

learn much about soldiering; that would have to wait until the 342nd
FA and the laddies from Missouri got "over there." He did barely have
time for a quick wartime wedding. The bride was Amy Marie Arrant.

Amy was a petite, pretty, vivacious twenty-five-year-old with bright
blue eyes. The pair shared a birthday, February 26, although Amy
was six years younger than the hurler. Both soon had outgrown rural
Nebraska. Amy had started school in St. Paul, left when her family
relocated elsewhere in the state, later returned, and left again. In recent
years she'd begun spelling her name *Aimee.*

Newspapers called them school sweethearts, but Aimee had met the
pitcher in 1914 at a Thanksgiving dance in St. Paul. She always remembered him as a good hoofer. The next summer she participated in a
stage play that benefited the town baseball team. The *St. Paul Phonograph* gushed that she and two other lively young women in the play
would "ever have a warm spot in the hearts of the local ball boys, and the
management as well."[18] Aimee went east in August 1915 to watch Alexander play ball for the Phillies. "While in Philadelphia she visited with
all the ball players' wives and she is loud in her praise of the good time
they showed her."[19] The *Phonograph* was disappointed later when Alexander denied marriage reports somewhat too vociferously. "We believe
he needs the care and attention of some good young lady and we will
be more than anxious to give the good news to our readers that he has
taken our advice and taken unto himself a wife, when the time comes."[20]

Aimee left Nebraska for a while to study costume design at the
McDowell School in New York City. She and Alexander's mother
traveled together in August 1917 to watch the pitcher face the Cubs in
Chicago. Aimee now worked in Omaha, which explained Alexander's
presence there over the winter. For the past year she had lived with
the family of Otto Merz, a pitcher for Omaha's Western League team.
She had visited St. Paul in the last days before Alexander entered the
army, returning home the day he left. Nobody was much surprised
by their whirlwind marriage.

The bride-to-be was preparing to catch a train for Kansas when she
got a long-distance telephone call on Tuesday, May 28. "I expect to

be placed in 342d field artillery this afternoon," Alexander told her. "Better wait and come Friday instead, as my possible short furlough may be longer then." His regiment was a flurry of activity as the brigade prepared to leave Camp Funston and follow the division overseas. Aimee told the *Omaha Bee* she liked not knowing exactly when she would wed. "Of course, I'm very proud of Grover and want him to serve his country," she said. "I will return to Omaha to make my home until the war is over."[21]

The pitcher almost certainly received special treatment from the 342nd FA. Few buck privates with a month in the army received forty-eight-hour furloughs to marry or even got permission to leave their cantonments. A county probate judge married Alexander and Aimee on Saturday afternoon, June 1, in his office in Manhattan, Kansas. Clarence Mitchell and Mrs. Georgia Merz stood up with the couple. Alexander flashed a rare smile for a photographer outside. "That man has a mighty big heart, and his wife is certainly a good looking girl," the judge said.[22] "The marriage was a quiet one," the *Chicago Tribune* added in a front-page article, "but is one of interest to thousands of people who have followed the great pitcher through his successful baseball career with the Philadelphia Nationals the last few years. . . . Miss Arrant is a beautiful girl and will remain in Manhattan close to her husband until he is called to overseas duty."[23]

Had the couple fulfilled the *Phonograph*'s hopes and wed a year or two earlier, Alexander's name would have been lower on Howard County's draft list and he wouldn't yet have been in uniform. Had they begun a family it would have been far lower, perhaps never to be called. As it was, he left Camp Funston with his regiment two days after their wedding. Aimee had taken a local business course, an Omaha newspaper reported, "and expects to work while her husband is swatting the Hun overseas."[24]

EIGHT

Camp Mills

I called them from their ancient homes
  To meet the battle's brunt;
I took them in from ship and boat
  To face the Western front. . . .

—LT. GRANTLAND RICE

The 342nd Field Artillery (FA) distributed its athletes throughout the six batteries and headquarters company. Pvt. Pete Alexander's new home was Battery F, in which Potsy Clark and Jick Fast were lieutenants. Their battery commander was Capt. John J. O'Fallon of St. Louis, considered by some "the best captain in the whole reservation."[1] Alexander had been in the army only about long enough to know how to speak the lingo, pack his barracks bag, and march in step to the depot. He already understood teamwork. He would pick up a soldier's other skills across the water in France.

Many of his half-trained comrades were eager to go. "The boys are all anxious to go to France, England or even right into Germany just to get away from this place for this is one of the hottest, coldest, and also the dryest places I have ever been in," T. B. Thompson of Battery E wrote home. The Missourian added, "I heard a man say the other day that we boys were all 'Jewelers.' I asked him why, and this was his answer: 'Because you are going to put a new set of works in the 'watch on the Rhine.'"[2] Other doughboys in the regiment echoed the sentiment. One lieutenant canceled a subscription to his home-town newspaper by writing, "I am going to Berlin for the summer."[3]

The French would reequip the batteries overseas, so the 164th Field Artillery Brigade left all its guns and horses at Camp Funston. The three regiments left the cantonment separately. The 340th FA and 341st FA departed on June 2. The 342nd FA left the next day, a Mon-day. With 75 officers and 1,336 enlisted men the regiment was some-what understrength, having sent about a hundred men a month to replacement detachments since January. Heeding the ancient military axiom to hurry up and wait, Alexander and his barracks mates rose from their bunks at three o'clock in the morning, then didn't board at the depot until afternoon. A YMCA worker described the dough-boys' last few hours in camp:

"Well, on a certain day I heard they were to leave, so I got busy tell-ing my friends good-bye," the worker wrote. "All of them were anx-ious to go and I want to say they were the best looking soldiers that have left this camp. The band played 'Over There' as they left the bar-rack. . . . It was with heavy hearts that the staff of this building told the men good-bye, and we think of them each day, but at the same time we were proud of them for the spirit they showed."[4]

Battery F clambered into the last of the regiment's three trains, which consisted of sixteen coaches and five box cars, the one in the middle serving as a kitchen car. Barrels on the car platforms supplied fresh drinking water. "A guard was placed at each end of the coach with orders to prevent any one from leaving the cars. This order was passed merely to protect the female population along the route from the too gracious farewells of the boys."[5] The train pulled out of Camp Funston bound for Kansas City, St. Louis, and cities farther east.

Unlike many of the young Missourians around him Alexander had traveled extensively by rail before entering the army. He had traversed the Northeast and the Midwest with the Phillies and gone to Califor-nia for spring training with the Cubs. Alexander had even gone to sea while barnstorming to Hawaii in 1914. A crowded troop train wasn't the Major Leaguer's usual mode of transport. Walter Maranville could have told him about travel in the armed forces; the Braves' quick little shortstop was now serving on a navy battleship. "The Rabbit has been across to the other side as convoy to transports twice," *The Sporting News* reported, "and says it's [a] great life and that he thinks it would do some ball players who kick on Pullman berths and $5 a day hotels good if they would take a swing at it."[6]

The army rushed troops to the Atlantic embarkation ports from cantonments all over the country. The Germans had launched a series of dangerous spring offensives and could still win the war. Over half a million doughboys headed for the seaports during June alone. Their journeys were long, tedious, and meticulously planned. "What road the train would traverse from a junction point on through the next stage of its journey was not left to chance or to the state of traffic," a World War I history records. "Every arrangement had been made in advance for the progress of that train from point of origin to terminal."[7]

Alexander's regiment attracted a good deal of comment once the coaches had rattled through a city or town. "Grover Cleveland Alexander, the famous pitcher, now a member of Battery F, 342d Field Artillery, 89th Division, passed through St. Louis last night on his way from Camp Funston to an eastern camp," the *St. Louis Star* reported. "'Chuck' Ward of St. Louis, formerly shortstop of the Brooklyn Dodgers, and Lieut. Lloyd Wait, a local boy, were also members of the battery that passed through."[8]

The train chugged across the Mississippi River before curving northward. It stopped briefly in Kewanee, Illinois, at eleven thirty on Tuesday morning. The 342nd FA stepped wearily down from the cars "and marched over the main streets of the city for exercise," a local newspaper reported. "A large crowd gathered to see the artillerymen. A good delegation went from here to view the soldiers. They were given treats of all kinds by the people of Kewanee and the short visit there was greatly enjoyed by the soldiers." The paper noted the presence of Potsy Clark and all five current Major Leaguers, adding, "The soldiers were a fine looking lot of fellows."[9]

The *Pittsburgh Press* observed wartime security and censorship in its later account of the ballplayers: "Alexander and Ward both were with a certain battery that is moving from one of the western camps to an Atlantic port of embarkation. Both have arranged for short leave at the port, and it is their hope that they will get to participate in one more game at home before starting on the journey that eventually will take them to Berlin."[10]

Cpl. Carey Maupin of Battery E was also aboard the train. The preacher's son had fought to get into the army and make this journey, overcoming pleas from his father to have him exempted from the draft to work on the family farm. Maupin later penned a long letter to his mother about his three-day journey. "We passed along the southern shore of Lake Michigan, making northern Indiana, Ohio, Pennsylvania and Buffalo, N. Y. We passed through Syracuse (where we had a parade without arms for exercise), through Rochester, and Utica. From Utica we were routed into the hills of western New York into southern New York City last Thursday noon. . . . The Red Cross met us at almost every stop and their work and service is certainly appreciated by the soldier on board the troop train."[11]

The last stop was Hoboken, New Jersey, across the Hudson River from Manhattan. The doughboys then boarded a ferry for Brooklyn, many marveling at the water traffic and other unfamiliar sights. "Here we saw the skyscrapers of New York City, most of us for the first time, and the Statue of Liberty; also [the] Brooklyn Bridge," the Battery F history states. "We again placed our equipment on board a train, and proceeded to Camp Mills."[12] Crossing Brooklyn, doughboys no doubt asked the Major Leaguers how to get to Ebbets Field, in hopes of seeing the Dodgers while on weekend passes.

The 342nd FA reached Camp Mills late that evening. The army had erected the canvas city on Hempstead Plains in central Long Island the previous summer, "entirely for concentration rather than for training."[13] Corporal Maupin wrote that on the day after the regiment's arrival "the camp was visited by some heavy showers of rain and we were properly initiated into the uncomfortableness of army life in a tent."[14] Camp Mills likely reminded Alexander and Mitchell of their recent experience at Detention Camp No. 2. Doughboys would have found this *New York Sun* description of the place at night overly romantic:

> Now and then the flare of a match lighting a cigarette would pierce the night and the dull red of the burning end add another glowing firefly to the scores sprinkled about. It was dark—the black bowl of night had clamped down over the great camp near Hempstead. To the north where the aviation men were playing at the game of war an arm of light would shoot into the sky—cutting the dark dome and darting, dancing, striving, would finally pick up the attacking enemy aeroplane a mile up. Then it would be dark again, with only the glow of cigarettes to take the place of the tired stars.[15]

The army did its hard work during the daytime. Clerks typed up records, doughboys picked up equipment, and three hundred replacements—mostly New Yorkers and men from the East—arrived to fill out the thinned ranks. These newcomers began intensive training to become artillerymen. Regimental and battery histories don't indicate whether Alexander and Mitchell joined them, but the sessions would have benefited both privates.

Sportswriters speculated that Alexander might briefly rejoin the visiting Cubs while the regiment waited to ship out. Army lieutenant and Dodger pitcher Leon Cadore recently had won a game at Ebbets Field while on furlough. Navy chief petty officer Bob Shawkey would pitch twice for the Yankees during the summer. Other ballplayers likewise would play in a game or two for other clubs. It was possible that Alexander, too, might stand on a Major League mound again in 1918.

Alexander said nothing to dampen Cubs fans' hopes of seeing him face manager John McGraw's National League club at the Polo Grounds. Aimee meanwhile had followed him east to New York and reached him by phone out at Camp Mills. Alexander told her he would be right over and asked her to order him cold beer and something to eat; decades later she remembered his "$37.50 cab fare from the camp into the Big City"—an enormous tab at the time.[16] "Grover Cleveland Alexander and his bride were at a New York hotel last night awaiting the arrival in town of the Chicago Cubs," the *New York Tribune* reported on June 11. "Alex came to New York on a furlough with the expectation of pitching one or two more games against the Giants, in the series between the Giants and the Chicago team, being scheduled to start at the Polo Grounds this afternoon."[17]

But the Cubs had no room on their roster, which already was at the league's war-reduced player limit. Why the club didn't send someone down to the Minor Leagues temporarily to make room for Alexander was never explained. The hurler merely sat on the Chicago bench in his khaki uniform Tuesday afternoon and looked on as the Cubs downed the Giants, 5–3. "This was the ninth straight victory for the Cubs, who have not been defeated since the morning game of Memorial Day," the *New York Herald* noted, "and which record they offer as evidence that there is no accident about them being at the top of the league."[18]

"Alexander has become a fine looking soldier and will no doubt be a credit to baseball on the other side," *New York Herald* columnist Fred van Ness wrote.[19] The pitcher said his army team "had accepted a challenge from the Princess Pat [regimental] team of Canadians now in England to play a game in London in the presence of the king on July 4."[20] The 342nd FA would be at sea on the holiday, however, and George V instead would attend a historic U.S. Army–U.S. Navy baseball game at Stamford Bridge, Chelsea.

The Cubs left the Polo Grounds without a mound appearance by their expensive pitcher. Alexander did have a memorable moment out on Long Island, however. *The Sporting News* reported that one day he "wandered over to the aviation field at Mineola, where a couple of service teams were playing a game of ball. Grover naturally drifted toward one of the players' benches and a member of the aviators' team, recognizing him, invited him to sit down." Their shortstop raced around the bases for a home run and returned panting to the bench to find an unfamiliar doughboy sitting there. "Here you, why don't you get off there," the man barked, "this bench is for ball players."

> Alex stood up hastily, with a funny look on his face, but before he could move away he was caught and the aviation team member who had ordered him to vamoose was introduced.
>
> The aviator took it so to heart and was so fearful he had made a mess of things that he was upset for the rest of the game, but Alex tells it as a good joke on himself and says he supposes an aviator has a right to think the men in the flying services are the only ones who can play ball.[21]

Alexander may have been visiting the flying field to scout one of the teams. A member of Battery E would recall years later that the 342nd FA nine had played a game with an aero squadron shortly before leaving Camp Mills.

Chuck Ward and Clarence Mitchell both hoped to don home whites again and play a few innings with the Dodgers while on Long Island. A Brooklyn-Cincinnati game scheduled for June 11—the same day that Alexander sat in the stands watching the Cubs and Giants—would have been the perfect occasion.

Ebbets Field and the Polo Grounds were each slated to host a Bat and Ball Fund game that afternoon. The fund was a brainchild of Senators manager Clark Griffith, who had begun to collect small donations the previous year to buy baseball gear for American troops at home and overseas. (The official name was Ball and Bat Fund, but fans and writers usually reversed it.) Dodgers owner Charles Ebbets and several other Major League magnates strongly supported Griffith's charity. Unlike the Giants, however, the Dodgers didn't play that day. Rain twice forced postponement of the game and the soldiers' return. When the contest was first called off, Reds manager Christy Mathewson went to the Polo Grounds instead and watched the Cubs and Giants, who did manage to play.

Ward and Mitchell were on furlough and had time to wait. "They will both receive complete baseball outfits for their comrades before the game starts," the *New York Times* reported. "Twenty-eight other complete outfits of baseball paraphernalia will be distributed to representatives of various other nearby camps before game time."[22] Ebbets Field was finally dry enough for play on June 13. "Eight or ten packages of baseball equipment of the twenty-eight on hand were distributed to military units at the plate," the *Brooklyn Eagle* reported. The two postponements had caused "some of the other representatives of soldiers and sailors to be missing. They will get theirs later."[23]

Ward stood at third base as southpaw Richard "Rube" Marquard took the mound for the Dodgers. Mitchell would go in later as a pinch hitter and first baseman. Ward was a soldier in Brooklyn home whites; Marquard would wear the navy's uniform before the season ended. A thousand or so sailors, a detachment of soldiers from Fort Hamilton, and several hundred school kids contributed to the crowd of about two thousand people. The afternoon was chilly for June, but Brooklyn fans got their money's worth.

> It was a toss-up yesterday at Ebbets Field whether Chuck Ward or Rube Marquard should be decorated with the High Sign of Efficiency in the bout between Brooklyn and Cincinnati. It was Bat and Ball Day, and Brooklyn won by a score of 6 to 0. . . . Chuck was responsible for a trio of the tallies that came across the plate by the use of his bludgeon . . . and he has evidently learned to shoot some since he left the diamond for the trail to the trenches.
>
> Clarence Mitchell, another boy from the same division, batted for Dauert in the seventh inning, which should be considered quite an honor, inasmuch as Jake used to be the king pin of the National league batters, but Clarence gave evidence that he needs a little more intensive training in gunnery for he struck out.[24]

Reds pitcher Horace "Hod" Eller, a former teammate, fooled Mitchell into believing he might have an easy time at the plate. "Hello, Clarry, how's the Army treating you?" the hurler asked.[25] "Eller greeted me most chummily," Mitchell remembered. "'You poor boob,' says he to me, 'you haven't had your eye on the ball and your team has a big lead.

I will slip you three fast ones that you can murder,' says he. Right on top of that he slipped me three curves in succession and I never got the bat off my shoulder."[26] The chagrined doughboy put on "a neat exhibition in the closing innings at first base" and fielded a grounder for the last out.[27] Mitchell said afterward, "If he [Eller] joins the Army and the Huns don't get him, I will."[28]

After their series with the Giants, the Cubs next swung down to Ebbets Field. Hopes rose that Alexander, Mitchell, and Ward might all appear in the Brooklyn-Chicago game on June 15. Mitchell suited up that Saturday, with much less fanfare than during the earlier Bat and Ball Fund game. He hit for Otto Miller in the seventh and flied out. Ward had hoped to play but reached the park too late to start and never got into the lineup. The pitcher everyone hoped to see was a no-show. "Grover Cleveland Alexander had an engagement with Manager Mitchell of the Chicago Cubs yesterday morning, but failed to keep it," the *Brooklyn Eagle* reported. "He may be used by Chicago against Brooklyn tomorrow or in the last game of the series next Tuesday."[29]

Alexander didn't pitch again before sailing. Neither Mitchell nor Ward played again for the Dodgers. Their 342nd FA squad had scheduled a final game June 29 versus a team of aviators from Mineola. The fliers would play the Brooklyn Navy Yard marines instead, for by then the artillerymen would be crossing the blue Atlantic. Pvt. Emory Medlin of Battery B wrote a quick note home to his brother in Missouri: "Just a few words in my closing hours here, to say good bye to all through you. I am fine and dandy. Don't write me at Camp Mills any more. Just A. E. F., 89th Division."[30]

NINE

Justicia

Here's the jumping-off place now, ready for the charge;
Ready when the signal comes with the next barrage;
Now the mighty thunder rolls where the flashes wait,
As they swing to meet again the final gift of fate.

—LT. GRANTLAND RICE

The regiments of the 164th Field Artillery Brigade, Eighty-Ninth Division, departed Camp Mills separately in numerical order. The 340th Field Artillery (FA) boarded a British transport ship June 13 in New York to head across the Atlantic in convoy via Halifax, Nova Scotia. The 341st FA entrained for Boston on June 21, then likewise sailed in convoy via Halifax. The 342nd rolled packs for departure late on Wednesday, June 26.

Pvt. Pete Alexander and mates in Battery F huddled together around a fire, "spending the night listening to the various tales, authentic and otherwise," from their bugler. At three o'clock in the morning they heard the shrill blast of a whistle and a command to fall in. "Having marched to the entraining platform and loading on," the battery history records, "we went to Brooklyn and boarded a ferry which took us down East River, and around the City of New York, and landed us on the pier of the White Star Line."[1]

YMCA and Red Cross workers passed out "safe arrival" postcards.

Printed atop each card was a single sentence: "THE SHIP ON WHICH I SAILED HAS ARRIVED SAFELY OVERSEAS." Below were spaces for name and organization; below that was "American Expeditionary Forces." "The soldier signed and addressed as many of these cards as he chose, and kept them on his person to deposit in the military mail bag which he would later pass at the head of the gangplank. Just before the ship sailed, the mail bags were taken off."[2] The undated cards would be mailed once the army post office had received a cablegram stating that the ship had arrived in Europe.

The regiment filed on board His Majesty's Transport F-8261, a 740-foot vessel launched in July 1914 as the liner *Statendam* for the Holland-America Line. The builder was Harland & Wolff, the same Belfast yard that had built *Titanic*. Great Britain had requisitioned the ship once war began and completed it in 1917 as a troop transport. The government rechristened the vessel *Justicia* and turned it over to the White Star Line. The Latin name meant "justice," which might have pleased Alexander and the others bound for France. *Justicia* grossed over thirty-two thousand tons and could crowd on board four thousand or more troops. The 342nd FA shared the space with other army units plus soldiers traveling independently as what the army called casuals.

Justicia's three raked smokestacks would have looked elegant wearing the White Star's peacetime livery. But like thousands of other transports and warships plying the dangerous seaways, the vessel instead wore an imaginative camouflage scheme called dazzle paint. Since hiding a ship at sea was impossible, artist Norman Wilkinson of the Royal Naval Reserve had devised the dazzle scheme to confuse a U-boat captain gazing through his periscope. "The purpose is to paint a ship with large patches of strong colour in a carefully thought out pattern and colour scheme," Wilkinson had written, "which will so distort the form of the vessel that chances of successful aim by attacking Submarines will be greatly reduced."[3] *Justicia*'s bright harlequin patterns and colors look deceivingly drab in black-and-white photos. A convoy of dazzle ships was "all aglow with colors that gave them an air of hastening across the ocean to some gigantic carnival

of joy and merry-making."[4] Military authorities were divided, however, as to whether dazzle painting was effective.

The 342nd FA swarmed aboard the transport single file. The sight may
have reminded Alexander of capacity crowds filling the Baker Bowl
when he pitched home games for the Phillies. Each soldier received
another small card, assigning him to a particular compartment or
hold where the men would sleep side-by-side in hammocks slung
from hooks. While normal for a British crew, the accommodations
were "anything but pleasant" for the landlubbers.[5] "These sections
were filled to war time capacity, which means 'sardine' style," Battery
F's history reports. "At night June 27, we received our first meal concocted from an issue of the British ration. This meal, and others, are
indescribable; they were merely a conglomeration of carrots, spuds
with the overcoat on, and over-ripe fish, with an occasional smear of
jam. Jam sandwiches were really numerous—ingredients: two slices
of bread jammed together. The first day aboard ship was taken up by
an exploration of the ship which was easily noted the next morning
by many bruises, said bruises being caused by hobnails [boots] and
iron staircases not working in unison."[6]

Justicia stayed dockside overnight before sailing on June 28. The
cruiser USS *Huntington*, destroyers, and small sub chasers escorted the
convoy of a dozen ships. Some convoys steamed directly to France.
Others, including *Justicia's*, headed for England, where troops disembarked and traversed the countryside by train before crossing the
English Channel. The 342nd FA was kept below deck during departure, disappointing the men who had hoped to see the Statue of Liberty as the ship left the harbor. Airplanes and a dirigible hovered above
the convoy for a while near the coast, added protection from U-boats
that might have prowled offshore.

Once safely at sea the soldiers exercised on deck and stood guard
around the ship. Progress was slow to match the speed of the slowest
vessel. "The voyage was favored with ideal weather, only one or two
days being at all stormy," Pvt. Walter Kuelper of the headquarters com-

pany wrote home. "Even then, our ship being quite a large one, we did not experience any serious discomfort, though we pitched and rolled about considerably."[7] The soldiers fretted about submarines and held lifeboat drills twice daily. "The atmosphere of mystery surrounding our course, occasional sudden changes of direction, active rumors, and the strict regulation of lights at night, made the trip somewhat adventurous," the regimental history reports.[8] Otis Lambeth, the Indians' pitcher whose nickname in Battery D was Grandma, penned a brief account of the voyage: "Had quite a nice trip coming over, only we could not find any 'subs' to play with. Yet two were sighted by our convoy. Good times aplenty on the boat—for we had all kinds of sporting contests. A daily bulletin was sent by wireless of news, including the scores of major league clubs. So we had the news almost before the game was finished. Some class!"[9]

The troops celebrated the Fourth of July at sea with a speech from a general, boxing and wrestling matches, and a concert by the regimental band. Four days later eight British destroyers appeared to escort them the rest of the way as USS *Huntington* turned back for the United States. The doughboys awakened July 9 to see the high cliffs of Scotland on the horizon. Ireland and the Isle of Man came into view later as the transport steamed southeasterly across the Irish Sea. Someone, perhaps one of the British crew, "told us of the reputation of the localities for lurking submarines. During the morning, one of the destroyers furnished some excitement by blowing some mines that were picked up. In the meanwhile, the serious concern of the powers on the bridge was beginning to give way to a solid look of satisfaction."[10]

Justicia arrived off Liverpool early on July 10. The doughboys climbed out of their hammocks at four thirty and saw the sun rise over the city. The transport tied up at one of the city's stone wharves at five o'clock that afternoon. "We had a dandy trip on the water," Alexander later wrote to Bill Killefer. "I did not get sick at all, and very few of the boys did. It was a splendid journey."[11]

The 342nd FA disembarked and marched up Parliament Street under full packs. The soldiers received friendly shouts from Liverpudlians and waves from British troops wearing the distinctive blue uniforms of convalescents. They reached a camp called Knotty Ash, a former brewery near a small railway station outside the city. "Knotty Ash of unsavory memory," *Stars and Stripes* later described it. "Knotty Ash, where some thousands of Americans spent their first nights on foreign soil and did not like it."[12] The men slept in small round tents and entrained the following morning for Winchester. Many found the British train compartments small and old-fashioned. Missing the comparative luxury of American passenger cars, they reached their destination after a full day on the rails. "Winchester was shuttered, muffled, lifeless—playing possum to escape the Hun marauders in the air," states the history of a regiment that came through a few days later.[13]

The doughboys spent their second night in England at a camp called Winnal Down. They rose July 12 to ride another train the few remaining miles to the busy port city of Southampton. Here the regiment encountered the 134th FA of the Sixty-Second Field Artillery Brigade, Thirty-Seventh Division, mostly Ohio national guardsmen.[14] Early that evening Buckeyes and Missourians boarded three narrow side-wheel steamers for the overnight passage across the English Channel. The 342nd FA took *Marguerite* and *Mona's Queen*; the 134th boarded *Mona's Queen* and *Prince George*.

The little ships were jammed far beyond normal capacity. Once out on the water the doughboys were seasick almost to a man. "Crossing the English channel is about as bad as crossing the Atlantic; it isn't as far across, but it is just as far up and down," one Missourian wrote home.[15] Private Kuelper hoped never to experience another night like it. "The water was so rough that the boat plunged and rolled and pitched as though every minute might be our last," he wrote. "Wave after wave was dashing spray everywhere and the wind was blowing cold. By sitting on deck all night I managed to keep my supper to myself, but the chilling I got and the loss of sleep took several days on shore to restore me to myself again."[16]

Pete Alexander claimed later that he had never actually been seasick during his army travels, but admitted to "one tough time in the

English channel. . . . The water was the roughest I ever saw." Conditions grew so wild that Clarence Mitchell couldn't muster a dozen men to relieve the guards at the pumps and gangways on *Marguerite*. "He reported to his captain and the captain said he didn't give a so-so if they never did have any guard again," Alexander related. "'I'm the sickest man on this ship myself,' the captain complained."[17] The history of Battery F provides another grim picture: "Any day or night at the front never equaled in misery that night of horror on the steamer. Private Luther L. Muse very unconsciously voiced the sentiments of every one aboard when he so earnestly and incessantly pleaded for some lurking sub to plant a torpedo amid ships. The pit of a shark's stomach, or the rocky bottom, would have been his, and others', preference at that time."[18]

The doughboys stumbled ashore at Le Havre the next morning. They roused themselves to march through the city to a rest camp, where they collapsed into small tents for twenty-four hours. "We heard the rumble of the big guns the first night in this country just like the faint roll of thunder far, far away," Kuelper wrote. The next morning was Bastille Day, the great French national holiday. The men reassembled and marched back through falling rain to a railyard in the city. French interpreters told them they were bound four hundred miles south to the city of Bordeaux. "This time we came down even a greater step in regard to transportation, finding ourselves loaded into queer little box cars," Kuelper remembered.[19]

Each car bore the war's famous stenciled label: "40 Hommes, 8 Chevaux." Forty men, eight horses. The regiment's history states that the 342nd FA "again appreciated the luxury of American travel."[20] The train crept through the French countryside for three days and two nights before arriving at St. Medard, a few miles northwest of Bordeaux. Private Alexander, Cpl. Chuck Ward, and all the other artillerymen climbed down from what they jokingly called side-door Pullmans and shouldered their packs. Ward described the final leg of the journey in a letter to Charles Ebbets Jr., secretary of his father's Dodgers ball club. "After arriving at our destination we had to hike seven miles with a 90 pound pack on our backs. The day was one of the warmest I've ever experienced. I had the opinion before taking some of the many hikes that the Cincinnati Ball Park was the warmest place of all, particularly when a double header was played. But, to tell the truth, the Cincinnati Ball Park was like an ice box compared with that day."[21]

The men at last reached the village of Le Taillan. Here they would remain until the regiment entered the nearby training center at Camp de Souge, which was already filled with doughboys. Maj. Gen. Ernest Hinds, chief of American Expeditionary Forces artillery, later wrote that American artillery units had been sent to France faster than the camps could accept them, so that "a number of brigades had to be sent into training areas, in the vicinity of the camps as far as practicable, until those in training could be gotten out of the way."[22] The 164th Field Artillery Brigade's other two regiments were quartered in nearby villages, as was the 314th Ammunition Train.

The 342nd FA dispersed into billets throughout Le Taillan. Ward lived in a stable with seven other men. "I do believe the ground felt like a feather bed beside the hard floor of those box cars," he wrote. "We were told that our stay in that village would be two weeks of rest. . . . I found Webster's definition for the word 'rest' does not mean what he defines it. Instead we had gun drills, road marches and squads East and West."[23]

The regiment received only a single battery of Schneider 155-millimeter howitzers, the gun it would fire in combat. Such stinginess was the norm during the mad rush to train American artillery units in France in 1918. General Hinds wrote that deficiencies in matériel among the howitzer regiments were well known. "Seventy-five millimetre guns were usually available but, as a rule, after July 15th only about four 155-mm. howitzers were available for the entire regiment during the greater part of the training period." This wasn't the only deficiency. The 342nd FA still lacked the tractors and vehicles it was due as a mechanized regiment. And according to General Hinds, the outfit wouldn't have had enough literal horsepower to pull the guns, caissons, and limbers the old-fashioned way either. "After June 15th horses were not available in sufficient numbers to give proper instruction in problems involving mobile warfare methods. In one brigade, at least, in a problem involving movement the guns were dragged 600 or 800 yards by the men, horses not being available. Mobile warfare methods cannot be properly taught with immobile guns."[24]

The 342nd FA set about training with its few guns at Le Taillan. Despite its German-sounding name, the Schneider 155-millimeter howitzer was manufactured in France. The brigade's other two regiments would be equipped with smaller 75-millimeter guns, also French made. A gun's caliber indicated the size of the shell it fired. A 75-millimeter gun took a shell about three inches in diameter; a 155-millimeter howitzer fired one more than twice that size.

The British Army arrayed its firepower somewhat differently than the Yanks. An American officer recalled that the artillery for a British division in France or Belgium "comprised three battalions of light guns (18 pounders, practically equivalent to the 75 mm). Heavier metal, such as the howitzers, the 60 pounder, etc., were attached as circumstances required." Howitzers made up a larger proportion of General Pershing's firepower than they did in the British Army. "Our American divisions then had, as a permanent component, a regiment (24 guns) of 155 mm howitzers in addition to two regiments (48 guns) of 75 mm."[25] The army's Coast Artillery Corps regiments, charged with guarding against coastal raiders in America, in France fired even bigger guns than the field artillery and from farther behind the lines.

Once fully equipped, the 342nd FA would provide heavy firepower for the Eighty-Ninth Division at the front. The six four-gun, company-sized batteries were designated A through F. Until all three regiments had completed advanced training and rejoined the division, the brigade would contribute little more to the war effort in France than it had back at Camp Funston. The division prepared for combat separately from its artillery units, five hundred miles away in the Haute-Marne department east of Paris. "Though not in the most picturesque or the most prosperous part of France, the Division was now hardly more than sixty kilometers [thirty-seven miles] from the front, and therefore available for use against the rumored fourth German Drive."[26]

Officers from Camp de Souge supervised the 342nd FA's training at Le Taillan, the doughboys drilling while awaiting orders to move into the bigger nearby camp. Alexander enjoyed mingling with the locals while off duty, although many in the brigade considered them quaint and old-fashioned. "And now, Bill, we are away over here, where we used to sing about," Ol' Pete wrote to catcher Killefer in America.

> It is like our country, only we can't talk to any of the people, so the best we can do is to make signs. We had some swell signs, Bill, but they don't go here, because they don't know what they mean. But that hit and run sign is working swell on the Germans, eh, Bill?
>
> It is not what the old life was, and yet it is not so bad, only the getting used to it. I don't know if you have gone [into the army] yet or not. If not, I hope it is over before you do, and if you are in camp you will know the worst of it by now, for the first hundred years are the hardest.[27]

Doughboys received occasional passes into Bordeaux. Clarence Mitchell stopped by a photographer's studio wearing his steel helmet and sidearm. He sent a copy of the photo to Dodgers owner Charles Ebbets with a note, "Notice that I am carrying a gas mask and an armed pistol."[28] Mitchell, Alexander, and other artillerymen all carried .45-caliber pistols rather than rifles.

Bordeaux was known for its statues, museums, and cathedrals. "Last Sunday I went down to Bordeaux on a tour or rather an educational sight seeing trip and I sure had a dandy [time]," a sergeant in brigade headquarters wrote to friends. "The 'Y' there has instituted a tour and one of the members takes you around and explains all of the things to you."[29] There were other diversions the YMCA didn't recommend. Lt. Harold Jacobus got himself restricted to the regimental area for the remainder of training after being "reported as having been drinking champagne with two girls—inmates of a house of prostitution."[30] (His letter of reprimand misspelled the lieutenant's last name.)

Many doughboys surveyed the grape-growing region that surrounded Bordeaux with farmers' eyes. "The country here is very much like our section of the United States," wrote a Missourian in the medical detachment. "There are hills, rocks, trees, but very few streams. About all the French farmer does is to raise grapes—I have seen hundreds of acres of the land in nothing but vineyards."[31]

"Wine is about the cheapest thing that we can buy here," an Arizonan in the 340th FA wrote home. "It costs about 27 cents per quart."[32] The history of Alexander's Battery F declares, "While billeted here, the boys seemed to be under the impression that they were duly charged with the duty of consuming the sole output of French wine."[33] Alexander also noted the abundance. "This is the land of wine, but as yet I have not found any Paul Rogers [Pol Roget champagne], although I know it is made over here some place," he wrote to Killefer. "As soon as I find the place I'll drink some to the memories of last summer."[34] In hindsight it was a disturbing promise.

SS *Justicia* hadn't immediately returned to America after delivering the regiment to Liverpool. The transport was bound from Belfast back to New York City, steaming through the Straits of Moyle between Ireland and Scotland, when the first German torpedo struck. Three more torpedoes detonated later against the dazzle-painted hull. *Justicia* somehow survived the night and was under a tug's tow when two additional torpedoes struck the next morning. Wire services sent breathless dispatches, somewhat inaccurate from the fog of war. "London, July 21.—The great White Star liner Justicia was sunk Saturday [the 20th] off the west coast of Ireland after a desperate battle between a group of German submarines and a number of destroyers, which continued for eighteen hours until the big ship went down."[35]

Modern historians generally agree that two U-boats had attacked, one Friday and the other Saturday. The pair hit the liner six times and escaped before British escorts sank yet a third German submarine. Nearly all *Justicia*'s crew survived and were taken off as the ship sank near Rathlin Island. "The Justicia and more like her may be lost," the *New York World* observed. "None the less will the great overseas march of Americans go on in swelling volume."[36] The 342nd FA dough-boys counted themselves fortunate when news of the sinking soon reached Le Taillan. "Mamma, the ship I came over on while it was turning back to the United States was sunk by the Germans," a man in Battery B wrote home. "It was lucky it was going instead of coming, but nevertheless we are here and had a fine trip; but it will be a better one when we start back."[37]

The doughboys had survived the submarine-infested Atlantic, storm-tossed English Channel, and cramped and uncomfortable British and French railway systems. Now the postcards Alexander had filled out dockside in New York had arrived. "It is only about three months since 'Dode' left here and it is almost unbelievable that he is over there so soon," the hometown *Phonograph* reported.[38] Lacking details, newspapers sometimes went overboard in speculating what Alexander and his fellow Major Leaguers might do in the war. "The artillery unit which includes Grover Alexander, Clarence Mitchell, Charley Ward, Otis Lambeth and William [*sic*] Noyes landed in France some time back, according to word received last week by relatives of Mitchell, and the presumption is that they are pretty well toward the front by this time, as artillery has been taking a big part in the recent allied advance. When things quiet down, however, the regiment to which these players belong will be heard from on one of the diamonds back of the lines."[39]

Fans only vaguely knew what lay ahead for Alexander and the others. A headline across the top of a *Philadelphia Public Ledger* sports page would have cheered the rangy right-hander: "Huns Had Better Beware, for Grover Cleveland Alexander Is Somewhere in France."[40]

TEN

Camp de Souge

Tilt up your long, black, ugly snout
And let it lift against the sky,
For when you bark your message out
We hear the roar of Freedom's cry. . . .

—LT. GRANTLAND RICE

Pvt. Pete Alexander and the 342nd Field Artillery (FA) passed beneath a wooden archway into Camp de Souge. Their first glimpse of the training center on August 3 was discouraging.

A long line of brown barracks stretched along the road. Windows had no glass and rows of double-deck bunks lined the walls inside. Out on the range, observation platforms rose on wooden legs like ancient guard towers. Tethered sausage-shaped bags filled with gas floated above the Balloon School, curiosities soon familiar in the barren landscape. Ears buzzed from the boom of guns on the firing range. The historian of another regiment further described the scene:

> Camp De Souge, we soon found, was very fittingly called "The Little Sahara." It had a late-summer sun that shone down every day in true Sahara form. Everywhere there was sand—black, fine stuff that rose above our ankles, filtered into our shoes and exacted double the amount of energy for ordinary walking. This the wind shifted through the chinks in our doors and cheese-cloth windows, filming bunks, blankets, and mess-tables

with grit. The water supply was scant at all times. It ran but a few hours each day through tiny faucets fitfully emitting a puny three-sixteenths inch stream. Returning from long marches that enveloped our sweating bodies in clouds of black dust, we often found no water with which to wash. Flies increased so rapidly that the "Swatting Detail" became as regular and more popular than guard duty. There were no shade trees for a mile around.[1]

Here Alexander and his companions set out to learn their deadly business. "We were issued the French 155 m. m. howitzers, with horses and equipment," the Battery F history reports. "We received several days' firing practice."[2] But becoming combat-ready entailed much more; the brigade consequently began a strenuous regimen at the camp's School of Fire. When not training, the men often wielded picks and shovels to help extinguish brush and forest fires ignited by the firing in dry countryside. The 342nd FA history records the routine: "The crowded curriculum of this six weeks included the final and basic training for the front. Telephone, radio, machine gun and reconnaissance officers and details took practical courses and drivers and cannoneers had their first actual experience in handling a battery. After two weeks, firing was begun on the sandy range to the south of the cantonment, applying the theoretical work under the school instructors. Such excellent progress was made by the Brigade during this training that we completed the final big problem a week in advance and received official commendation from the Director of the School."[3]

Doughboys also learned how to don gas masks instantly, seal them properly, and work in them for long periods. These skills were critical, for the regiment would face gas attacks at the front and likewise hurl American gas shells back at the Germans. Shells might contain anything from nonlethal but highly irritating sneezing and tear gasses to deadly mustard or chlorine gasses. "Of all the helpless, suffocating, strangling sensations known to man, there are few to be compared with the first attempts to wear a gas mask," the chronicler of a New York regiment wrote.[4] A battery historian in the same brigade recounted a captain's graphic lecture. "Well can it be remembered how he raised his hand in warning as he told us that we must learn to be quick, for, if we were a second late, we would be subject to the 'horrible death' of 'drowning in our own blood.'"[5]

"There were gas masks for the horses, too, which some drivers have been known to wear in a pinch," an artillery officer recalled after the war. "We usually got them on the 'animules' once, but—never again."[6]

The main job for Battery F was learning to handle the 155-millimeter howitzers. It took a gunner and seven cannoneers (numbered one through seven) to man each gun under the orders of a chief of section. Doughboy T. B. Thompson had explained the workings of Battery E shortly before leaving Camp Funston.

"Each man has a different position on the gun and a different duty to perform," Thompson wrote. "I act as No. 6. My duty is loading the gun, or pushing the shells into the breech after the range is given and the fuse timed. Each shell weighs 85 pounds and it is no small days' work to handle them all day long." He explained that some were shrapnel shells designed to mow down troops, while others were "made to explode upon coming in contact or striking some object strong enough to offer resistance to the shell. These kinds are used to blow up trenches or breast works."[7]

Thompson's battery had trained in Kansas on old American 4.7-inch guns. In France they learned to fire the 155-millimeter howitzer, which was slightly larger than a 6-inch gun. It weighed close to four tons when fully equipped in its carriage. The rifled barrel extended more than seven and a half feet long but looked shorter in profile. The crew rammed a fused project into the breech when preparing to fire, then a powder charge behind it. The howitzer hurled a ninety-five-pound projectile seven miles or more at nearly 1,500 feet per second. The manufacturer described the Schneider 155-millimeter howitzer as "a medium caliber weapon which could be charged with the destruction of the normal enemy defences and with counter battery work."[8] It was designed "for indirect, high-angled-plunging fire," a regimental history adds. "On account of its high trajectory, it can be used to drop shell into deep ravines and well-defiladed positions, which a rifle with a flat trajectory could not reach. Because of the same advantages, the Howitzer itself can be hidden in deep valleys and behind steep slopes."[9]

Alexander and the others learned how to fire a battery's four guns simultaneously. The history of another regiment at Camp de Souge recounted how this was done with 75-millimeter guns; the process wasn't greatly different from what Battery F learned:

> There was a moment of quick activity on the part of the cannoneers as they carried out the directions and slammed the shells into the breeches.
>
> "Ready to fire, sir," reported the telephone operator.
>
> "Fire!" ordered the Captain.
>
> "Fire!" repeated the operator.
>
> There were four flashes and four loud reports.
>
> "On their way!" called the man at the "phone."[10]

The 164th Field Artillery Brigade suffered its first fatality in France during a practice barrage, a mishap that was eerily similar to the accident that had nearly killed General Wood the previous winter. One of the 341st FA's 75-millimeter guns burst, killing Pfc. Felix Miller of Battery C and wounding the sergeant who was working as chief of section. "The battery was firing and the men were wearing gas masks," the regimental history recounts. "The squad of the exploded gun remained at their posts, without removing masks, and continued to act in a most cool and collected manner until the barrage was completed."[11] The regiment buried Miller the next day, his comrades forming an honor guard with the brigade commander standing graveside. The unit history recalled him in a poem about the war.

> We camped at Mills, came 'cross the sea, and trained at Camp de Souge,
> Where we lost our "Number One Man"—damn the luck....[12]

The 342nd FA learned at Camp de Souge that it wouldn't become mechanized after all, at least not soon. Nor would its two companion regiments receive vehicles either. Doughboys who had trained to steer tractors found themselves instead driving teams of horses across the sandy range. The 314th Ammunition Train, which would supply the entire brigade, was an exception; it would have one motor battalion and a horse battalion.

Mechanization early on had led some observers to dub the European conflict the gasoline war. The U.S. Army's Billets and Remounts Division strongly disagreed. It later declared to the *Stars and Stripes* "that the horse and its hybrid offspring, the mule, have played a highly important part in this war, and . . . that this was still very much a horse war."[13] Allied forces would have 1.5 million horses and mules in France by November 1918, about half with artillery units. Even this extraordinary number was insufficient. Too few animals were available during the summer to serve all six of the 342nd FA's batteries in training. The same was true throughout the American army.

"The French had furnished us 130,000 horses, but they were of inferior quality and were rapidly used up," General Pershing wrote.[14] Many animals succumbed at Camp de Souge. "Wagons loaded with dead horses continually passed along the dusty roads," states a regimental history.[15] The animals that Alexander's regiment received weren't docile plow horses but big draft horses impatient with anyone who didn't know how to control them. "They were desperate characters," an artillery sergeant in another outfit recalled of the animals. "Some of us who fed, watered, and manicured them at imminent peril of our lives, will never forget them. Nor the long plow through the hot sand from the stables to the watering troughs. Let them boast of our dangers and conquests on the Vesle [River] and in the Argonne— the scene of our greatest dangers and most heroic deeds was the stable at Souge."[16]

To make life even tougher for the laddies from Missouri, some lessons the brigade had learned at Camp Funston didn't apply here in France. "The drivers at Camp de Souge, previously having learned the nomenclature and fitting of the American harness, found that French harness was to be used, which fact meant hard work," the 341st FA regimental history reports.[17] Chuck Ward, the Dodger infielder who hailed from St. Louis, wrote that "instead of a supposed motorized outfit we had a couple of hundred head of horses to take care of. Just imagine me around horses. I had never ridden a horse before in my life."[18]

Some men in the regiment were more experienced than Ward. "I ain't done nothing all my life, only drive mules," a Missouri farmer said.[19] Alexander joked that Clarence Mitchell, Dodger spitballer and Nebraska farmer, "had the banker's job of being stable sergeant."[20] But these sergeants had a huge, unenviable task—feeding, stabling, and tending to all the horses that pulled the guns, plus the mules that hauled the regiment's hundreds of wagons and carts in support of the howitzers. White-haired veterans of heavy artillery regiments during the Civil War would have well understood the challenges. The history of a 75-millimeter regiment that also trained at Camp de Souge described the unsettling experience of learning to manage big artillery horses with a colonel looking on.

> It is no small task for inexperienced men to get a team of six horses, with gun and limber, around a sharp turn, and for the first few miles it looked as if some of the guns might be ditched. [The Colonel], himself an expert in all that pertains to horses, waited at every corner to watch the batteries go by, and to make suggestions to the drivers. With the faults at the head of the column he would be very patient.
>
> "Let go your off horse, my man. Just drive the horse you're on; the other will follow along. That's it. Don't touch him!"
>
> But by the time the sixth battery came past and the drivers were still making the same mistakes as the first, he would be ready to commit murder.
>
> "*Let go that off horse!*" he would roar. The poor driver, terrified by this sudden command from some one he had not noticed beside the road, would promptly do the wrong thing, and dropping the reins of his own horse, would begin to belabor the other.
>
> "*Do you hear what I say?* LEAVE THAT OFF HORSE ALONE! You've got enough to do to drive your own. DROP THAT REIN!"

After a few experiences of this kind, however, the drivers began to learn, and on the return trip, two days later, the guns rounded the corners as if they had been running on tracks.[21]

The ceremonial caisson platoon used for funerals at Arlington National Cemetery is the only similar team today. Handling such animals was far more challenging for the 342nd FA. Howitzers were much bigger and heavier than 75-millimeter guns and required more literal horsepower to pull them. "The gun carriage and its limber (a limber serves the same purpose that a front axle and wheels serve on a wagon) are drawn by eight horses," the history of another 155-millimeter regiment explains. "The gun usually goes forward at a walk, except with the best roads, or in great emergencies, when a trot is sometimes taken up, but only for a short distance. Hurrying the guns out of a shelled road-area is an example. The gun and caisson are supposed to cross any country suitable for other field artillery."[22] Teams sometimes would be reduced to six horses in the field. The ability to move batteries across shell-pocked roads would be crucial once the British, French, and American armies finally broke the German lines and ended the bloody four-year-long stalemate.

Gone now were the broad-brimmed campaign hats with the red cord denoting artillery that the 342nd FA had worn in Kansas. Doughboys wore angular overseas caps in France. Soon they would sew the Eighty-Ninth Division's new insignia onto the left shoulder of their uniforms and paint it onto the side of their steel helmets. The design was a *W* inside a circle, which upside down became an *M*; together they signified the Middle West division. Sideways the letter could be seen as sigma, the Greek symbol of summation, the circle implying the ability to exert force in any direction or rest in any position. "Notwithstanding the official explanation," the division history states, "there is ground for the suspicion that the symbol has another and esoteric meaning. The *W* in the circle might serve to recall to memory an old general pining in inaction in the states and be read as 'Wood's Own.'"[23]

Each unit filled in the *W*'s central arch with the color of its own branch of service. The arch of the 342nd FA insignia resembled a red artillery shell. The rush of their training at Camp de Souge was arduous for officers and men alike. "The last two weeks were to be spent in firing, but the brigade was pronounced ready for action one week before the course was completed, the most efficient brigade having attended the school," a brigade history states.[24]

This account was somewhat misleading or perhaps merely indicative of a low bar for success during the scramble to send batteries to the front. Lloyd Wait and Potsy Clark were among ten 342nd FA officers ordered to retake an examination on firing data such as deflection, range, and height of burst. Wait, the former Pirates prospect, had served as a first sergeant in the National Guard before the war, with duty on the Mexican border. He had more military experience than most officers, but he grew so discouraged over his performance once in France that he requested a transfer to work with horses in the remount service of the Quartermaster Corps. "Lieut. Wait is an energetic officer and capable along some lines, but lacks ability to handle firing data," Colonel Nugent wrote. "It is believed that the transfer he requests would be in the best interests of the service."[25]

Wait ultimately failed his artillery course and faced a court martial for skipping an exam; an adjutant later recommended his removal from the field artillery. But with the regiment soon to move toward the front the 342nd FA needed every officer. Wait didn't get his transfer. He retained his rank and proved to be a popular officer once the regiment left camp and went into action. "Lieutenant Wait is the best manager we ever worked for," a St. Louis semipro ballplayer in Battery E later said at the front, "and the men follow him in battle as they'd follow John McGraw on the ball field."[26]

Alexander meanwhile had been promoted to corporal. He probably received the two stripes more for his ability to mold men into an effective team than for any military knowhow he might have acquired. He also suffered at least one epileptic seizure while in France. It's unclear whether it happened at Camp de Souge or in the field later; his pals in the regiment, like Major League teammates before and after, kept quiet about the episode. Aimee Alexander wouldn't know about her husband's seizures until after the war, the revelation coming during a dinner for army buddies at their Chicago apartment. "During the party one of his pals said, 'Say, Pete, what kind of a spell was that you had in France?'" she told *The Sporting News* decades later.[27] She believed, perhaps naively, that this was his first seizure. According to Aimee, Bill Killefer told her he hadn't known of any earlier episodes.

Despite intensive training at Camp de Souge and indications that the regiment was preparing to move forward, Alexander and Battery F concluded that the war situation was improving. He even began to think he might wear a Cubs uniform again in 1919.

"The way things are going over here now, Bill, I hope to be back to open the season with you next Spring," he wrote to Killefer. "We are full of 'pep' about finishing the war before next Spring. Of course one never knows how soon it will end, but the boys certainly have the spirit to go right through to Berlin without a stop. There are a lot of interesting things to write about the war, but we are not permitted to say anything, and we can't even tell where we are, but maybe they'll let me say we can hear the big guns booming on a still night."[28]

ELEVEN

Pauillac

Fate is a party who ducks from the fighter
That laces him squarely and grins,
But, oh, what a wallop he takes at the blighter
Who trembles when trouble begins.

—LT. GRANTLAND RICE

Pete Alexander received bad news while training at Camp de Souge. His niece Esther Elizabeth Alexander, toddler daughter of brother Alva, had died in St. Paul on the Fourth of July of septicemia following a skin infection. Alexander wrote home August 14 to raise his mother's spirits and share what little he was allowed to say about his life in the army. It may have been his only letter to anyone other than Bill Killefer published during the war:

> Dear Mother: A few lines once more to say that I am still fine and dandy, and never felt any better in my life. I am awfully glad my card had reached you telling of my safe arrival and by now some of my letters surely have reached you. I try to write once a week and I write often to Amy and she can let you know that I am well. I only get mail once in a while, but I generally get quite a bunch of it and believe me, it sure is welcome. I got your letter yesterday and as you know I had Alice B's' letter, so knew all about the sadness you were having. It certainly is hard to stand, but we must be brave and do our best. I am glad Alva has such a good position

and hope it keeps up all along. The [draft] reclassification sure did get a lot of the boys from there. Which camp did most of them go [to]? Most all the young fellows must be gone from there now. But never fear, we will soon put old Kaiser Bill out of his misery and then all come marching home. When you write I want you to be sure to tell me all the news and how everyone is getting along. It is impossible for me to write to everyone, so you will just have to keep them posted. I go to school now. I am studying gas and it sure is interesting and is all new to me. I am allowed to tell you where I am at, so get out your map and look it up. We are about 20 miles from Bordeaux, France. There is no use of telling the name of the camp for it is not on the map. You will see we are down towards Spain and are about due east of New York City. I think we will be here for a while yet getting well trained and then, well Old Kaiser, better get a move on for he sure will get it. Our climate here is about like you have, only the nights are cooler, which makes it fine for sleeping. But they get us up at five o'clock, so what's the use of the cool nights. On the other hand they put us to bed early, so it is even all the way around and one feels just as good as if he slept late. I would like to hear from [brother] Ray, but I suppose he is too busy to write, so let me know what you hear from him.

We play ball every Sunday and have not been beat yet, so I think we are the best team over here and are willing to play any of them. You see I figure on being able to play again when we get back. Night has come so I must ring off. Be sure and let all the folks know that I am well and tell me how they are all getting along. I will write again in a few days.

With lots of love to all, I am your loving son. G. C. ALEXANDER.

P.S.—Tell all the children that Uncle Dode sends his love to them all.[1]

Contrary to his reassuring letter, the pitcher couldn't play all that much ball while in camp. "Alexander is now a corporal and he has little or no time to devote to baseball," Chuck Ward wrote to a friend.[2] None of the Major Leaguers had much time beyond their regular Sunday games. "Since leaving the United States Ward says none of the boys in the battery who were former ball players has received any word from here as to what the big leagues are doing in the states, and night after night while in the trenches [*sic*] they tell some of their former experiences while playing baseball here."[3]

The sport was wildly popular among Yanks serving in France. The *New York Times* and other papers at home dubbed the baseball-mad troops "Uncle Sam's League."[4] Doughboys played ball whenever they had time and a safe place in which to toss around the horsehide. The YMCA, American Red Cross, Knights of Columbus, Clark Griffith's Ball and Bat Fund, and other groups all provided equipment for games in rest areas behind the trenches. Military leagues also flourished in cities and ports in the rear areas; Paris alone had thirty teams. African American units fielded independent teams that often trounced challengers in a racially segregated army.

The *Stars and Stripes* provided as much local coverage as space and wartime censorship allowed. (Alexander likened his battery's censor to a famous umpire: "That guy is like Bill Klem," he wrote. "He never misses anything.")[5] The army paper had described one game between navy aviation and dirigible units under the poetic headline "Sea and Sky Men Meet on Diamond."[6] Lloyd Wait later related a story—funny and illustrative but surely apocryphal—about another game played close behind the trenches.

> Lieut. Lloyd Wait, formerly a Pirate [prospect], now an officer in France, says that the German troops know a lot more about baseball than generally is supposed. On several occasions, when American soldiers were playing games in dangerously exposed positions, Germans within good firing distance not only let them alone, but stood up in their trenches and hooted derisively when anybody made a fielding error, struck out, or boneheaded on a play. "And," says the lieutenant, "maybe you think it wouldn't get a fellow hot under the collar, after muffing a fly with bases full, to get the raspberry from a whole Bavarian regiment across the way!"[7]

During the war and afterward sportswriters often wrote that Alexander and the 342nd Field Artillery (FA) team were never beaten. This was inaccurate. The team was unbeaten only after Alexander joined the squad and began pitching in France. The sporting press fawned over the big Nebraskan once he arrived overseas, in sharp contrast with complaints military ballplayers sometimes heard in the United States. Writers and editors who believed that athletes should serve as role models were quick to toss around insults like "slacker." For such scribes, the only proper place for Major Leaguers was in the front lines, hurling bullets and grenades at the enemy Boche (German soldiers).

Writers and fans overlooked the facts that might have dulled Alexander's shiny new image—that he had dithered over his draft status, for example, and entered the army only after attempting to join the navy. No matter. His assignment to a combat unit erased all negativity. A naïve fan might well have believed that Alexander had enlisted specifically to join the artillery, rather than being pulled into it by officers eager to build a fast baseball team.

America needed the millions of young men like Alexander—the men who sensibly waited until called, then did their duty simply because it *was* their duty. No country could win a war without them. But in dangerous times people also needed heroes, even if they were inventions or exaggerations. Alexander the Great had to live up to his grand nickname and to the expectations of the writers and fans who had bestowed it. Through no act or intention of his own, the big-time pitcher and reluctant soldier became in the public's mind a lion-hearted cannoneer, hurling high-explosive shells instead of baseballs. Perhaps in reality Alexander was an amalgam of both.

The country had other baseball heroes, of course. Color Sergeant Hank "Hankus Pankus" Gowdy of the Boston Braves, the first active Major Leaguer to join the colors in 1917, now fought with the hard-charging Forty-Second Division. Hankus Pankus was far and away Organized Baseball's most popular soldier, surpassing even Alexander. Others justly earned praise for their battlefield service. But the 342nd FA nine were America's team "over there" and Alexander was its star. *The Sporting News* would splash a panoramic photo of the team taken at Camp Funston across five columns of an inside page. "Others May Have Class, but Look at This One," the headline demanded.

"If there are any service ball clubs in France that can beat this lineup they will have to go some," the caption stated.[8]

Despite Chuck Ward's complaint, Alexander and other Major Leaguers in France did manage to keep abreast of the league standings back home. "While in camp here we get the daily papers—so we keep in touch with what is happening in the good U. S. A. Not papers from home, but others edited in Paris," Otis Lambeth wrote.[9] They also might pick up military newspapers published at American bases and air stations. No matter the source, Alexander knew that the Cubs were in the heat of the National League pennant race.

"The last ball scores I saw made me feel better, for the boys were leading and I am pulling for them to win and only wish I could be there to do my part," he wrote to Bill Killefer. "If you are still with them, give all of the boys my best and tell them I think of the game quite often. We work out nearly every evening, and the old arm still feels pretty good." The new corporal added, "Have hopes of getting back before the start next year as I think the Germans will be well whipped by that time. If not, by —— we will know the reason why."[10]

The 342nd FA team began playing games while billeted in Le Taillan, possibly on a diamond at Camp de Souge. "I am keeping the arm in good shape by working out every day," Alexander wrote to Killefer. "We play quite a few games every week, and surely do have lots of fun. It is wonderful recreation for the boys. You cannot imagine the enthusiasm that they show. They have the fans at the parks backed off the boards, and the French and English who are mingled with us are as interested as our boys are. I think baseball will be the national sport over here after the war, judging from the way the soldiers are playing it. Some of them are crude, but they learn in a hurry."[11]

By "quite a few games," he probably meant pickup contests within the regiment. If the 342nd FA team had games with other units only on Sundays, then it played no more than nine times while training in France. Alexander later said he had pitched in five. Ward was the captain. "The pitching staff was as follows: Alexander, our ace; Noyes,

Philadelphia Americans; Lambeth, Cleveland Americans, and Mitchell, at different times," he wrote. "Mitchell was our first baseman and he sure showed some class, hitting 'em high and far away, and stepping about the sack like a two-year-old."[12]

American newspapers carried accounts of at least six games, all won by the 342nd FA. The team first played five days after stepping down from the French boxcars. "Last Sunday afternoon [July 21] I was out to see a baseball game that Otis Lambeth, of Moran, pitched," a Kansan in the Signal Corps wrote to his mother. "He is the first fellow from Allen county that I have met yet." (The homesick soldier also mentioned meeting an African American doughboy "who used to play baseball with the Iola colored baseball team. I knew him well. He sure was glad to see me and I guess I was just as glad to see him.")[13]

The regimental ballplayers read no account of their game in the *Stars and Stripes*, however, because the publication spiked its sports page the same week. This was the work of Lt. Grantland Rice of the 115th FA. Granny was unhappy about being yanked from the field to help edit the army paper in Paris. "Lieut. Grantland Rice, hired to be sporting editor, promptly canned the sport page for the duration of the war and went off to report the front."[14] *Stars and Stripes* explained its rationale in a long editorial, later attributed to Rice:

> It was sport that first taught our men to play the game, to play it out, to play it hard. It was sport that brought out the value of team play, of long, hard training and the knack of thinking quickly at a vital point of the contest.
>
> But sport as a spectacle, sport as an entertainment for the sideliners, has passed on and out. Its glamour in a competitive way has faded. Its leading stars are either in the iron harness of war—or forgotten—until Germany is beaten.[15]

The 342nd FA team nonetheless continued playing Sunday games. Alexander later recalled with amusement one game that *didn't* happen during training at Camp de Souge.

There was a team in the south of France which wrote our outfit that they were the champions of the world, or words to that effect, and wanted to play us. Our major was our manager, and he wrote back to that bird that we had a few young fellows who didn't know much about the game, but if they had the money to put up, as they said they had, we'd take a chance.

He said he had a youngster named Noyes—you know he is one of Connie Mack's stars; Ward and Mitchell, two inexperienced kids—they belong to Brooklyn; Lambeth, a Cleveland kid, and a kid pitcher named Alexander. He also added that he had a few college boys who could fill in. Potsy Clark of Illinois, Lewis of Missouri, Lindsey, a University of Kansas star, but that, of course, these college boys weren't regulars. We never heard from that outfit again.[16]

Alexander's squad did play two games that garnered considerable ink in the United States. These contests with navy fliers at Naval Air Station Pauillac received more coverage than the outfit's other games and perhaps more than any game played anywhere in France. The first game was at Pauillac, a large seaplane base in the hamlet of Trompeloup on the Gironde estuary thirty miles north of Bordeaux. The site was meaningful to Yanks because the Marquis de Lafayette had sailed from there to join the American Revolution in 1777. The date of the ball game is uncertain, but it may have been August 4. Alexander took the mound for the soldiers.

"The Base Champs had an unbroken row of victories over the best army teams in France until they went up against Alexander," an amateur ballplayer wrote to the *Chicago Tribune*. "In the first game against Pauillac, Aleck pitched the entire game and won, 3 to 0."[17] Another newspaper picked up the tale: "Word comes from France that Grover Cleveland Alexander, the Cubs' star pitcher, hasn't lost his skill. Alexander recently pitched for his regimental team, the 342d field artillery, against the reputed champions of the American army 'over there,' and scored a 3 to 0 victory. The big right hander was in great form and allowed only one hit, which was made in the ninth inning with two men out. Alexander's strategy won a cup for his regiment in honor of which the Y. M. C. A. gave a banquet after the game."[18]

Writers noted that Alexander had never tossed a no-hitter in any league. At Pauillac he came "within an ace of letting his opponents down without a hit, but with two men out in the ninth inning, a player on the other side cracked one of 'Alex's' offerings for a clean single," a newspaper reported. The no-hit jinx, it added, "appears to have followed him to France."[19]

The artillerymen played at Pauillac again on August 11. The sailors attempted to slow the soldiers with a big meal beforehand. "The navy eats met with great favor among the khaki players. As he negotiated his last yard of steak Alexander was heard to remark, 'I wish I had joined the navy now.'"[20] The game was a fourteen-inning, 5–3 thriller. The box score shows that all six of the army team's professionals played against the sailors, as did Potsy Clark, Ad Lindsey, Poge Lewis, and Lloyd Wait. A young navy pitcher identified only as Miller went the distance against three army hurlers, "pitched great ball against this array and was well supported."[21]

Lambeth tossed the initial six innings and left with the score tied 3–3. Win Noyes followed with five scoreless innings, using "a 'slippery elm' delivery, much to the amusement of the fans." Alexander then moved in from left field to take the mound in the twelfth. "Aleck used the best he had in his heaving wardrobe to stop the threatening Trompeloupers," the *Chicago Tribune*'s amateur correspondent wrote. By the fourteenth inning the navy players were "quite tired out and the show was getting cold. So Chick Ward, being an accommodating chap, lined one to center for a count of two. Then the quartet of frogs in a near by moat croaked 'The End of a Perfect Day.'"[22]

The *Pauillac Pilot* judged the event "the greatest exhibition of the national Yank game yet staged in la belle France."[23] The *Tribune* added, "Sports may not be the most decisive factor in winning the war. . . . But we are unsophisticated enough to believe that an exhibition of the old game like Pauillac and the army here is the greatest little morale booster on the military market."[24]

The 342nd FA team kept playing, beating the 136th FA of the Ohio brigade on August 18 at the Stade Bordelais stadium in Bordeaux. "Noyes and Lambeth held the opposition to one run and five hits," reported a newspaper in Portland, Oregon, where Noyes and Ward had played Pacific Coast League ball in 1915–16. "Ward, playing short for the 342d, was up two times at bat and crashed out a single and a double and scored one run. Lindsey tripled and homered. Noyes fanned eight of the 136th F. A. players and walked two."[25] The paper offered no score. Other sports pages mentioned victories of 7–3 and 8–1; "I worked the last three innings striking out eight men," Lambeth wrote of the latter.[26] One of four additional games versus unnamed opponents involved pitcher Chester Torkelson, Lambeth's Cleveland teammate in 1917, now a private in the Sixty-Second Regiment of the Coast Artillery Corps.

The ballplayers often thought of the campaigns they were missing back home. Alexander even served as an overseas scout for Cubs manager Fred Mitchell. "Grover Alexander writes that he can name six pitchers, none of them having any special reputation before the war, but every one of them a whale, well worth using on any big league team," Mitchell told reporters. "He has also found some corking batsmen and nifty outfielders. Alexander will look after our interests among the boys. He will deliver some of the best to the Chicago club—and the best the Chicago club has won't be too good for these youngsters, who fought like men and will come home to please the public."[27]

The Major League season back home ended a month early on Labor Day, the result of a government order requiring all young men in non-essential occupations (such as baseball) to join the armed forces or find work in a war-related industry. "No doubt you fellows will have the pennant won by the time you get this letter," Alexander wrote to Bill Killefer. "I am sorry I am not with you and I certainly will be pulling for you in the world series. Tell Mitch and the boys I wish them all the luck in the world. I would like to pitch one of the games, but I am over here fighting for a cause and I hope to do my share before I get back."[28]

The Cubs remembered Alexander after losing the World Series in six games to the Boston Red Sox. "They sent me $50 as a world series bonus for the three games I had pitched at the start of the season before I went into the army, which I thought was pretty nice of them," the hurler recalled years later. "It was war time, and naturally the world series didn't draw as under normal conditions."[29] The 342nd FA team ended its season at nearly the same time as the Major Leagues. Even had there been another opportunity, the artillerymen couldn't have played again at the front because their uniforms, shoes, bats, balls, and gloves all were lost during the move forward.

"The team had met all comers while at the Artillery Camp near Bordeaux and had won every series," the Eighty-Ninth Division history boasts.[30] The regimental players figured their two victories over the naval aviators gave them bragging rights in France. "Have not been able to find any club that can beat us," Lambeth wrote home, "so we claim the championship of the A. E. F."[31]

Two days before the regiment left Camp de Souge, Col. Earl Biscoe of the 342nd noticed Alexander, Lambeth, Noyes, and Ward listed on the roster of a suggested army all-star team. "These enlisted men are holding important positions in the regiment and it is earnestly requested that steps be taken to prevent their being detached," he wrote to the brigade commander, Brig. Gen. Edward Donnelly, at headquarters. "Further, the above mentioned enlisted men do not desire to be separated from their organizations." Biscoe added an immodest observation: "In view of the fact that a selected team eliminates competition," he wrote, "it might be stated that the baseball team representing the 342nd Field Artillery can hold its own with either an A.E.F., or the winner of the World's Champion Series Team, should said team visit France."[32]

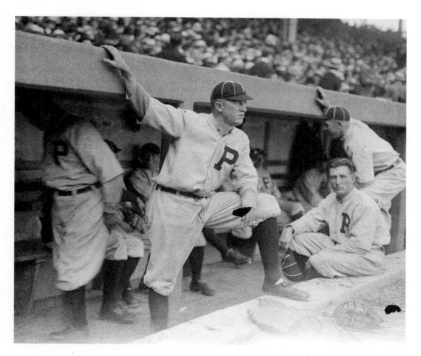

1. Pete Alexander with the Philadelphia Phillies, 1917. Library of Congress.

2. "Alexander the Great" by Robert Ripley, after winning Game One of the 1915 World Series. The Boston Red Sox then swept the final four games from the Phillies to take the championship. Jim Leeke Collection.

3. Gen. Leonard Wood throwing out first ball, Polo Grounds, New York, April 11, 1917. Library of Congress.

4. Camp Funston, Fort Riley, Kansas, October 1917. Library of Congress.

5. First day at Detention Camp No. 2, Camp Funston, 1918. National Archives.

6. Maj. Paul Withington, August 9, 1919. *Boston Globe.*

7. 342nd Field Artillery baseball team, Camp Funston. 1: Eddie Croak, 2: Potsy Clark, 3: F. D. Brown, 4: Poge Lewis, 5: Ad Lindsey, 6: Win Noyes, 7: Major Andruss, 8: Colonel Nugent, 9: Pete Alexander, 10: Clarence Mitchell, 11: Otis Lambeth, 12: Chuck Ward, 13: Lloyd Wait, 14: Dutch Wetzel, 15: Charles Ballingall, 16: Joe Novak. *Spalding's Official Base Ball Guide, 1919.*

8. Pete and Aimee Alexander (right) on their wedding day, with Georgia Merz,
June 1, 1918. Union Pacific Railway Press Bureau.

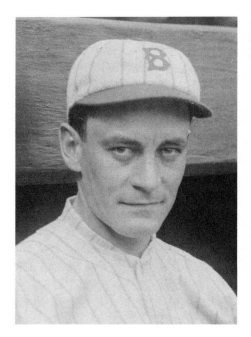

9. Clarence Mitchell with the Brooklyn Dodgers, 1922. Library of Congress.

10. Win Noyes with the Philadelphia Athletics, 1919. Jim Leeke Collection.

11. Adrian Hobart "Ad" Lindsey,
Kansas halfback, 1916. Jim
Leeke Collection.

12. John C. "Jick" Fast, Kansas
halfback, 1916. Jim Leeke
Collection.

13. SS *Justicia* in dazzle paint, ca. 1917. Naval History and Heritage Command.

14. "Lambeth's Strikeout Arm Going Great as He Dodges German Bombs and Shells." Syndicated cartoon, November 1918. Jim Leeke Collection.

15. Doughboys in French boxcars, April 1918. Library of Congress.

16. Camp de Souge, France, April 1918. National Archives.

17. Naval Air Station Pauillac, France, ca. 1918. Naval History and Heritage Command.

18. Loading 155-millimeter howitzers on a French train, March 1918. National Archives.

19. An artillery regiment on the march in France, March 1918. National Archives.

20. A howitzer crew in action in France, October 1918. Library of Congress.

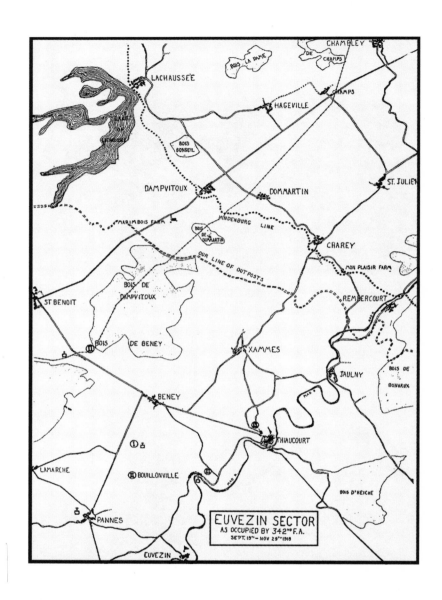

21. Euvezin Sector, September 19–November 29, 1918. Chubb, *Regimental History, 342nd Field Artillery, 89th Division.*

22. Route of march, November 29–December 15, 1918. Chubb, *Regimental History, 342nd Field Artillery, 89th Division.*

23. Euvezin, France, chateau and church, 1918. *Pennsylvania in the World War*.

24. Bouillonville, France, January 1919. National Archives.

25. The Army of Occupation passing through Luxembourg, December 1918. National Archives.

26. Doughboys with artillery horses in Hundsdorf, Germany, 1919. National Archives.

27. "He's Still Over There" by Robert Ripley, *Boston Globe*,
March 6, 1919. Jim Leeke Collection.

28. Cubs cartoon, December 4, 1918. *Boston Post*.

29. American Expeditionary Forces championship football team, 1919. Kneeling: Withington, third from left; Lewis, fifth from left. Standing: Lindsey, far left; Clark, far right. English, *History of the 89th Division, U.S.A.*

30. SS *Rochambeau*, which returned Alexander from overseas, shown here in 1917. Library of Congress.

31. "Sergt. Grover Alexander" by Roy Grove, from a photo taken on board ss *Rochambeau*, 1919. Jim Leeke Collection.

TWELVE

St. Mihiel

I'm just a wee bit throaty and perhaps a trifle hoarse;
My accent isn't soothing and my diction's somewhat coarse;
I've never studied grammar and my style is poorly planned,
But I speak the only language that the Boche can understand.

—LT. GRANTLAND RICE

P ete Alexander and the 342nd Field Artillery (FA) team likely
didn't play a scheduled game on September 15, their final Sunday at Camp de Souge. "We began preparation for the trip to the
front from the 12th to the 16th," the Battery F history states, "all moves
being easily remembered by the fact that numerous strict instructions
always preceded the event."[1]

George Nugent was a new brigadier general and no longer commanded the regiment, which was as ready for the front as possible in
such hectic circumstances. "The training of the past year has seemed
irksome and hard at times," Nugent had written ten days earlier to
Col. Earl Biscoe, the new commanding officer, "but both officers and
men have continued at the task with commendable enthusiasm and
spirit, and now with the training period drawing to a close, the regiment is soon to be put to the supreme test which is the ambition of
every soldier."[2]

The 164th First Artillery Brigade took possession of the guns, equipment, and animals of another brigade training at Camp de Souge, making it as fully equipped as any other outfit rushing forward to join Pershing's First Army. The brigade's headquarters company left for the front on September 8. The three regiments soon followed, again in numerical order. The 340th FA entrained with its 75-millimeter guns on September 12. The 341st FA left two days later, and the 342nd soon began loading its two dozen 155-millimeter howitzers on short notice. The regiment had nearly six hundred draft horses, about a hundred riding horses, and approximately five hundred mules.[3] During this trip the small French boxcars would transport eight horses apiece. The regiment also owned a big Dodge touring car, which no doubt went along as well.

Alexander, Mitchell, Ward, Noyes, Lambeth, Wetzel, and the rest of the 342nd FA departed by rail on Monday, September 16. "The schedule called for eight train sections to leave at six hour intervals from the long loading ramp at Bonneau Station near the Camp," the regimental history states. "Although loading materiel, horses and mules was distinctly a new problem, the difficulties of it did not prevent the trains from pulling out on time."[4] The doughboys rode in relative comfort for once, with fifteen rather than forty men per car and with rolling kitchens supplying hot food. "We left the camp and loaded on the train with all our equipment and rode about three days and nights," a Missouri corporal wrote to his sister. "Sure was some trip. We passed through some beautiful country and got to a big town near the front and unloaded and had to travel about 20 miles by road."[5]

The big town was Toul, 180 miles east of Paris and 25 miles southeast of a town on the Meuse River called St. Mihiel. "Until then we had no idea what sector of the western front we were going to," Chuck Ward wrote. "After unloading our large 6 inch howitzers from the train and finishing our corn willie dinner with hard tack we proceeded on our way to the front, to join in the big game and deal the necessary blow in the pinch."[6]

The Eighty-Ninth Division had gone into action two weeks earlier in the sector north of Toul. Capt. Paul Withington, the division's former athletic officer, was now a medical officer for the First Battalion, 354th Infantry. The Harvard man's actions during a gas attack the night of August 7–8 far surpassed any of his exploits on a playing field. "He worked all night in the gassed area, not only as attending surgeon but even as litter bearer when necessary. His superb physical strength and great determination carried him through the trying period, although he received burns as severe as those for which he evacuated many of the soldiers. He administered treatment to himself during intervals in his treatment of others and escaped with painful but not permanent injuries to his eyes."[7]

Days later the division was heavily engaged in what became known as the St. Mihiel offensive. The French town lay at the western tip of a German salient into allied lines. Occupied early in the war, the area "ever since has stuck like a great thorn into the side of France."[8] Thirty-five miles wide by twenty miles deep, that thorn had become untenable. The Germans were pulling back to a shorter, more easily defended line when a joint French-American offensive jumped off the morning of September 12. The Eighty-Ninth was one of six American divisions fighting on the right flank, with the French on their left.

"In the first days the 89th advanced an astonishing 8 km [five miles] through well-prepared positions," a battlefield guidebook explains. "The German forces had already begun their withdrawal, and the barbed wire, laid down years before, had become brittle and susceptible to the barrage."[9] With its artillery brigade not yet arrived from Camp de Souge, the division had relied on the Thirtieth Division's 55th Field Artillery Brigade and various French units.[10] The allied armies attacked in overwhelming force, the Eighty-Ninth capturing all its early objectives while sustaining 833 casualties. The division consolidated its position on September 13–15, "digging first shallow pits usually called fox holes, then connecting these up so as to form a trench, stringing wire in front and generally preparing the ground for their own comfort and security against harassing fire and attack."[11]

The battle officially ended after four days when it became clear the Germans weren't going to counterattack. "We had restored to France

200 square miles of territory and had placed our army in a favorable situation for further operations," General Pershing wrote. "The new American position in the Woëvre [Plain], almost within reach of Metz, now stood as a threat against the great fortress on the Moselle that defended Germany on that part of the front."[12] World War I historian Mitchell Yockelson adds, "The reduction of the salient was not only an important strategic victory but a morale booster for Pershing's newly minted First Army, which had impressed the Allied commander [French field marshal Ferdinand Foch] in its first operations."[13]

The 342nd FA arrived too late for the big push. The fighting at St. Mihiel had largely ended by the time the laddies from Missouri boarded their train for Toul. "It appeared that the reason for the haste was the scarcity of artillery in the sector following the St. Mihiel drive, and it was more the assurance of artillery support than the necessity for action, that required the haste."[14] The 340th FA, which had left earlier than the Missourians, fired the brigade's first shot at ten o'clock the night of September 16. The 342nd FA unloaded at the Toul station near the city's old fort on the evening of September 19. The end of the offensive didn't mean there was no fighting yet to do.

"We transferred our equipment to wagons, and discarded all unnecessary luggage," Battery F's history states. "We pulled out headed for the front just at dark in a 'nice' gentle French rain, it soon getting so dark it was black. We were hampered to a great extent by slick roads, and the condition of our horses, numerous changes being made to the extent of riding horses being put into the draft."[15] The regimental history adds that a few of the 342nd FA's exhausted animals had died during the train journey from Camp de Souge. The regiment struggled forward for two days through the backwash of the recent fighting. The Eighty-Ninth Division history describes the terrain where Alexander and the others were headed: "North of the heights of Euvezin the ground dropped . . . into a valley down which flowed the little stream called the Rupt de Mad, on the banks of which stood the villages of Bouillonville and Thiaucourt. After rising sharply from this valley the ground stretched away to the north and east in a high, bare plateau on which were situated the villages of Xammes and Beney, with dense forests on the east and west."[16]

The 342nd FA's headquarters company arrived first and established a command post at Pannes, about twenty miles north of Toul. The three battalions marched a couple of miles farther to positions near Beney (Beney-en-Woëvre today) and Bouillonville. "On our way to the front . . . we saw all kinds of dugouts, barb wire entanglements, trenches, ammunition and machinery of war," a private in Alexander's Battery F wrote.[17] The first taste of combat varied from battery to battery. The regiment's opening barrage came the night of September 20 when Battery A opened fire for adjustment on German-held Dampvitoux, several miles to the north. "The other batteries were allowed more time for digging gun pits, arranging camouflage, and getting up ammunition, but all went into action shortly after arrival."[18] Cpl. T. B. Thompson wrote that Battery E reached the front the next day "and we have been 'hitting the ball' ever since."

> It was about 5:30 in the evening of the 21st that we first heard the shells from Fritz' big guns. We were marching through a little village called Essey, about four miles from the front line trenches, when they began dropping shells into the town.
>
> We could hear them screaming when they were [within] a mile of us and I thought every one of them was coming a little nearer. I have never heard them scream so loud as they did that first day and I have had them bursting all around me several times. On two occasions they came so near that a piece of the shell hit the ground within ten feet of me and I picked them up but they were too large to carry home as a souvenir.[19]

Battery F observed the same shelling. "We saw that the first shell had landed in the town," the battery history reports. "A number of shells followed making the bunch have a sort of feeling similar to the game of checkers, everybody wanted to move at once."[20]

Otis Lambeth's Battery D sustained the regiment's first casualties that evening when German 150-millimeter shells hit its position. The explosions killed four men outright and cut down eight others; two of the latter soon died of their wounds, while another succumbed to pneumonia later in an army hospital. Remarkably, despite many subsequent losses to wounds and disease, these seven would be the 342nd FA's only combat deaths. Pvt. Dutch Wetzel, the former Minor Leaguer and future St. Louis Brown, wasn't in Battery D but "nearly lost my own life" in the shelling as well.[21] The barrage also killed fourteen horses. "Whether the Boche had observed the exposed picket-lines from his planes, or whether he was merely picking a likely location for a target is unknown."[22]

An Arizonan in the 340th FA wrote home the following day about adapting to life under fire. "One learns things very fast up here, and believe me, one of the first things you learn to do is to kiss the ground and do it quick," the corporal informed his father. "I have all the skin off my face now from going to the ground so much."[23]

Pete Alexander and Battery F dug in near Bouillonville at a position overlooking the little waterway the doughboys called the River Mad. "The men of the battery were called to the valley and given their initial test of endurance in the form of an entirely new exercise, which they were soon to become nightly subjected to, viz.: That of hauling 'peanuts,' otherwise known as shells, up the steep hillside," the history notes. "Our first lesson over, we repaired ourselves to the valley and spent our first night at the front under wagons and in the mud without mishap, but with more or less discomfort."[24]

The men camouflaged their gun emplacements with large fish nets tied with raffia or dyed burlap. But netting offered little protection from counterfire, especially if enemy spotter planes were up. *Field Artillery Journal* later recalled the simple rules of survival that artillerymen like Alexander quickly learned: "Do not space the guns equally. Pick broken ground for the battery position. Pick a position which can be reached without leaving trails, either by men going to the guns or by ammunition supply. Pick positions which are not subject to enemy fire for other reasons. Keep spoil covered. Get rid of blast marks. Do not erect camouflage which will cast shadows, thereby revealing the fact that there is something important enough to be hidden."[25]

Good camouflage couldn't prevent but only reduce the frequency and accuracy of enemy shelling at the front. Alexander later recalled that he had been sleeping the first time Battery F came under fire. "'It happened at night,' Aleck says. 'We were in our pup tents when the shells started hitting around us. I just rolled over and over all night. Guess I was trying to figure whether I'd rather get it in the back or in the face. Most of the boys did the same thing, too. I thought of baseball for just one minute. If they were going to get me I wanted them to do a good job of it. I didn't want them to cripple my pitching arm and let me live.'"[26]

The pitcher also joked about a shell that had skittered nearby without detonating, on a day now unknown. "I didn't know what to do with this dud," he said. "I suppose I ought to have fielded it, it landed but didn't penetrate the ground and came at me like a regular bounder. I didn't know what it might do on every bounce, so I let it go by me, and believe me, I was glad to see it on its way."[27] The newspaper back home in St. Paul described the incident as the "closest call Grover ever had . . . they all were peeking just inside the pearly gates, as the explosion of that shell meant death and destruction to him and his companions."[28]

The men of Battery F scrambled September 22 on hearing the alarm for a gas attack. Fortunately for anyone who couldn't locate his gas mask amid the scattered equipment and debris of their few days in the field, it was a false alarm. Battery F fired its first shells Tuesday afternoon, September 24. "The fire was for adjustment only, using as our target a tower in the village of Dommartin. Our first shots fell with accuracy in the heart of the village."[29]

The battery's war began in earnest over the following days. The regiment moved September 25 into the Bois de Mort Mare (Dead Sea Wood) south of Euvezin. The old German positions snaking through these woods north of Flirey in the former St. Mihiel salient were muddy and uncomfortable. Conditions were even tougher for the horses. "Originally in poor shape, and pulled down by the railroad trip, some of the animals never recovered from the pull from Toul, and were lost," the 342nd FA history states. "When it later became necessary to evacuate a considerable number with thrush and mange, the regiment was in part immobilized for lack of transportation, and it became a problem to keep the horses in shape for the daily work of hauling rations and ammunition."[30]

An estimated eight million horses died during the Great War. Combat was at least as terrifying for animals as for soldiers. The Missourians would have preferred the promised tractors and vehicles that didn't break down or die shrieking from shrapnel wounds. But the doughboys had little more freedom than their animals.

On the night of September 25 and into the next day, Alexander and Battery F "got their first experience in bombardment and barrage work," the battery history states. "It was the memorable night that marked the beginning of the last lap of the war when the great drive started on the whole from the coast of Belgium to the Swiss border."[31]

THIRTEEN

Euvezin

Come to the centre of the world's red heart,
Amid the graves of those who've done their part,
Where blood-swept France is beckoning to-day
Through those who've given more than life away,
Before the last great valiant chance is gone,
Come on—come on—come on!

—GRANTLAND RICE, 1917

After St. Mihiel much of the First Army pivoted for an immense new offensive in the Meuse-Argonne Sector. Before the Americans could launch their attack, Col. George C. Marshall, General Pershing's chief of operations, first had to move half a million men, two thousand artillery pieces, and nearly a million tons of supplies and ammunition fifty miles northwest—all secretly, under cover of darkness. The monumental task made Marshall's name in the army.

Coordinating with broader allied operations, the First Army was ready to go over the top early on September 26. The forty-seven days of combat that followed would end the war. "To call it a battle may be a misnomer," Pershing later wrote, "yet it was a battle, the greatest, the most prolonged in American history."[1] The Eighty-Ninth Division, however, wasn't involved in the initial assault. The Fighting Farmers instead maintained the positions they had held at the end of the St.

Mihiel fight. The 164th Field Artillery Brigade stayed with the division it had finally rejoined after their long separation.

The area of northeastern France in which Cpl. Pete Alexander and his howitzer crew now found themselves bore various names. To the division it was the Limey-Flirey-Pannes Sector, extending some six miles northwest to southeast, from Lachaussée to outside Rembercourt. The 342nd Field Artillery (FA) called it the Euvezin Sector, for the village south of the front lines where the division had established its headquarters. The Americans here faced a portion of the Hindenburg Line, a strong German defensive position that stretched from the Belgian coast southeastward through France to the Swiss border.

The *New York Times* described the Hindenburg Line for readers: "It consists of an elaborate system of trenches, multiple lines of barbed wire entanglements, concrete positions for artillery, blockhouses for machine guns, and shelters for the infantry."[2] The Eighty-Ninth Division history adds that the formidable defenses "had been prepared by the German engineers in entire deliberation and after prolonged study both of the ground to be occupied by them and the ground to be occupied by us."[3]

Beyond the Hindenburg Line and only twenty-five miles northeast of Euvezin lay the fortified German city of Metz. Situated on the east bank of the Moselle River, Metz was a road and rail hub that had been fought over since the days of the Roman legions. France had relinquished Metz and the rest of the Alsace-Lorraine region in 1871 following the disastrous Franco-Prussian War. The city then became the capital of German Lorraine, where French- and German-speaking residents had lived uneasily together ever since. Metz also was the gateway to the iron ore region of Briey, which the Germans had occupied at the start of the war. In September 1918, writes historian Mitch Yockelson, Metz was "a key to the entire German defenses along the western front."[4]

In front of Metz the 342nd FA received instructions on how to fire barrages. The barrages might precede allied attacks, defend against

German thrusts, or coordinate with artillery activity in neighboring divisions. The batteries also got directions for conducting harassing, reprisal, and interdiction fire (the latter focused on bridges, crossroads, villages, and railways). The regiment fired its first real barrage early on September 26, coinciding with the beginning of the huge offensive farther north. The men unloading shells from the ammunition train spread out so that no single enemy shell could kill or wound a large number of soldiers.

"For the regiment this was the first experience of waiting at the lanyards for the H-hour and the first experience of the flash and roar as a general bombardment broke loose," the regimental history relates. "Although only a small raid was attempted that night on the right of our sector, the firing lasted from midnight till after dawn, expending about 300 rounds per battery."[5] Sgt. Carey Maupin of Battery E described the firing as a "heavy 7-hour barrage upon certain objectives behind the enemy's lines."[6] Pvt. John Ziehl of the same battery recalled it decades later: "Our 155s fired every two minutes so they wouldn't get too hot. Our gun captain would order us to bring certain types of shells up. One of our gunners would install the fuse, and we'd be ready for loading."[7]

Maj. Gen. William Wright, now commanding the Eighty-Ninth Division, inspected the 164th Field Artillery Brigade early on the morning of September 27. The 340th FA was well dug in and "looked very fit," he noted in his diary. "On my way back stopped and inspected a battalion of the 342nd. At Bouillonville we inspected two battalions of the 341st and another battalion of the 342nd. Found everything in good shape."[8]

Despite all the activity, Euvezin was considered a "quiet sector."[9] For a time the 342nd FA was restricted to firing ten rounds per gun per day to conserve ammunition. The army's strategy was to keep the enemy occupied and guessing where the next assault would come. The division's artillery therefore fired bombardments for attacks that never came or that supported only small raids.

Thus the Germans were induced to retain in the vicinity of Metz several reserve divisions that might have been used to stop the real attacks elsewhere. . . . The artillery brigade gradually settled down to a schedule of harassing fire by day and all kinds of fire by night. The men always preferred to fire in the daylight hours, but in the course of time it became a matter of routine for them to wake in the dead of night, calculate the necessary data, and send off shell after shell until the desired number was completed. The church steeples of Charey, Dommartin, Dampvitoux and the other towns in the Hindenburg line came in for a good share of this shelling, because of their convenience as registering points for adjusting fire on the organized strong points of the enemy in the towns and in Marimbois and Monplaisir Farms.[10]

Pete Alexander was promoted again October 3 and sewed a sergeant's three chevrons onto his sleeves. The eight men in a 155-millimeter howitzer crew each had specific duties. Alexander became a gunner. The history of another regiment defined the gunner's responsibilities: "Sets deflection angle of sight and elevation and calls out to Chief of Section the data set-off for each round, lays gun in direction and elevations and refers it, records base deflection on shield, sets angle of elevation on quadrant used and hands it to No. 1, calls 'ready' and raises hand when piece is laid for each shot."[11] After the war sportswriters and biographers would speculate that Alexander had damaged his pitching arm by continually yanking the lanyard that fires a howitzer. That was the duty of the number one crewman, however, not the gunner; it's possible Alexander had served as number one at Camp de Souge before his latest promotion.

Important combat jobs such as gunner wouldn't have been assigned to a soldier simply because of his baseball skills. Alexander was a natural noncom. Ballplayers back home had always admired his level head on the diamond. "You got no nerves at all, kid, have you?" Pittsburgh Pirate great Honus Wagner had once asked.[12] "One thing the army will not need to teach Grover Cleveland Alexander is coolness under fire," the *Omaha Bee* had observed even before he reached Camp Funston.[13] Once overseas, the army later observed, Alexander was "a non-chalant soldier. In war he wore the same air of sang-froid as he carried into the pitcher's box in a tense moment."[14]

The Nebraskan certainly possessed a casual steeliness. Phillies pitcher Charles Bender recalled waking one night in a Pullman car during the 1917 season, in pain from septicemia in his arm. He woke Alexander. The hurler promptly sterilized the blade of Bender's pen-knife with boiling water, applied a tourniquet, and drained the infection in a sort of field surgery. "Next day the doc told me he couldn't have done a better job himself," Bender recalled. "He said old Pete probably saved my life."[15]

As a sergeant Alexander clearly had the confidence of his lieutenants, Potsy Clark and Jick Fast, as well as the trust of the enlisted men in Battery F. One day during a lull in the firing Clark remarked that if he survived the war he would return to the University Illinois and coach the baseball team. "Yes, if we both get out alive I'll help you," Alexander replied.[16] Until then, they kept firing. "I had charge of the fighting of one of the guns of our battery which was sending over shells toward Germany," Alexander later remembered. "In fact I took it all the way through. I did pretty near everything in the battery."[17]

After barely two weeks in the field, however, the brigade was still green and minimally trained. The brigade commander, Brig. Gen. Edward T. Donnelly, was a regular army man and "an artilleryman of long experience."[18] Donnelly was less impressed with his batteries than General Wright had been. Their gunnery inevitably fell short of his standards during the early days at the front—sometimes literally so. The brigade's operations officer soon fired off the kind of memo that no regimental commander wanted to receive. "A number of complaints concerning rounds falling short have been made against units in this brigade," it stated in dry army language. "Most complaints have proved to be groundless but unfortunately some have been shown to have foundation."[19] In other words, shells fired by the brigade had fallen near or among doughboys rather than atop the Germans. The October 5 memo issued specific instructions concerning observation and firing procedures so that no such friendly fire incident would happen again.

Two days later Alexander's new regimental commander, Colonel Biscoe, received a rocket directly from Donnelly himself. The general pointed out that the 342nd FA had taken fifteen minutes to swing into action against a German target near St. Julien. "It is reported that in your fire on a battery target today, your shots fell beyond and short of the target, which stood still during the firing of the series and then proceeded on its way unharmed." Donnelly acidly demanded a report on the measures that Biscoe would take to correct such "poor gun service."[20]

The regiments overcame the deficiencies and the Eighty-Ninth Division soon was satisfied with the brigade's performance. "The high state of discipline and training of our artillery brigade, the fine dash and enthusiasm of its officers, the excellent liaison established with the infantry, all contributed to make this period of trench warfare highly satisfactory, so far as the cooperation of the two arms of the service was concerned," the division history states.[21] Sergeant Alexander and the men of the 342nd FA grew into their roles, as did the doughboys of the two companion regiments. "In the course of time . . . the receipt of orders over the 'phone, the assignment of missions, the rousing of the officers and calculations of data became a commonplace, and usually within fifteen minutes after receipt of an order the men were out, lighting devices set, and the first shell over. 'Rounds complete' became merely a grateful signal for the men to curl up in their blankets and fall asleep, just as though hurling a few tons (more or less) of high explosive across miles of country had been a custom for years in the Ozarks."[22]

General Wright had learned during his tour of the batteries that the Eighty-Ninth Division soon would shift position and join the Meuse-Argonne offensive; "the Forty-second Division would leave the line and we would have to take over their entire sector."[23] Ohio's Thirty-Seventh Division, in turn, would relieve the Eighty-Ninth in the Euvezin Sector.

The Buckeyes had seen hard fighting and were in bad shape. "The long range guns from Metz barked a welcome as the relief proceeded far into the night," the Thirty-Seventh Division history states.[24] The repositioning was supposed to be done by ten o'clock on the night of October 7, but the division wasn't finally in place until the night of October 8. General Wright had little sympathy for tardiness. "This division, the Thirty-seventh, apparently does not function," he wrote in his diary. "I think the staff is poor, the organization is an unsatisfactory one."[25] The Buckeyes had no high opinion of the Fighting Farmers either. "The entire sector was in a very disorderly and unhealthy condition," the Thirty-Seventh Division history coldly states. "When the Eighty-Ninth Division had advanced to this position, they were tired troops and naturally little had been done to clean up. There were dead horses, food wastes, debris, unsalvaged equipment and the general rack and ruin of battle everywhere."[26]

The 164th Field Artillery Brigade was again separated from the Eighty-Ninth Division, staying behind to support the arriving Thirty-Seventh, which likewise had been shorn of its artillery.[27] It wasn't unusual in France for guns to remain in place rather than to move with the parent division. General Pershing later recalled that lack of horses had made American artillery "almost immobile."[28] A modern historian adds that as battle plans evolved, "the AEF [American Expeditionary Forces] became ever more accustomed to assigning divisional artillery to whatever portion of the line was convenient to avoid needless movement of artillery pieces."[29]

"It was with deep regret that we parted with the artillery brigade when the division was relieved, and many an effort was made thereafter by General Wright to secure its return to us for use in the great coming battle," the Eighty-Ninth Division history reports.[30] Wright later stated that he had "made repeated requests for the return of this Artillery Brigade with the view of establishing closer liaison between the Infantry and Artillery. Unfortunately, the Army was unable to comply with this request."[31]

The brigade worked with the Ohioans only a short time. "Nine days later the 37th Division was relieved by the 28th Division, and since the 28th also was without artillery the 164th Brigade, much to its disappointment, was forced to remain in the sector."[32] Increasingly ill from the miserable weather, the Buckeyes weren't sorry to move up into Belgium after days under German shellfire. "The entire tour of duty in the sector was a dismal, trying experience; there were no tears when, on 15th October, the 'warning order' to prepare for relief and movement to another area came."[33]

The arriving Twenty-Eighth Division was mainly Pennsylvania national guardsmen. Traveling by foot and trucks in a "miserable, drizzling rain," the Keystone Division relieved the Thirty-Seventh on October 16.[34] The Pennsylvanians gave the area yet another name, the Thiaucourt Sector. Now supporting its third division in ten days, the 342nd FA began "a period of especial interest and activity for the artillery."[35]

The regiment used steeples and crumpled buildings in the villages and small towns along the Hindenburg Line as aiming points. The devastated terrain made accurate observation difficult. "The Hindenburg Line opposite us had been built about two years before," the regimental history records, "and was characterized by the usual reverse slope positions, extensive use of concrete in dugouts and emplacements and double lines of wire. . . . It was accordingly rarely possible for us to observe directly the results of our fire, even when weather conditions were favorable."[36]

The weather generally was miserable. "We are now located in what you might call a mud hole, having plenty of rain, cloudy weather and very little sunshine," wrote a private in Battery A. "I don't know where they get that stuff 'Sunny France,' as the sun is very seldom seen over here."[37] As the artillery kept firing, Sergeant Alexander and Battery F surely recognized what French soldier-poet Albert-Paul Granier had called the War Song:

Dame Death is glad, and very drunk—
for there's blood in full flow out there,
a heavy red brookful in every ravine.

Accompanying her weird dancing
is the tom-tom of guns in the distance:
"Tom-tom-tom! tom-tom-tom! Come then, White Lady,
come dance to the sound of the drums!"[38]

Battery F fired 119 rounds at a camouflaged enemy position near Monplaisir Farm on October 23. "That night a patrol from the infantry lines found a wrecked concrete mixer at the place, with the bodies of fifteen Germans, lying in a partially constructed concrete dugout, mute evidences of the accuracy of Battery 'F.'"[39] The tom-tom beat grew louder for Alexander and the doughboys manning the howitzers. "Time passed fast during the time that we were on the firing line, and we did not know half of the time what day of the week it was," Chuck Ward of Battery C later wrote. "Furthermore, we did not care much, as all we had in mind was to get it over as soon as possible."[40]

Ward and the regiment knew that the tide had turned in their direction. Otis Lambeth of Battery D wrote an upbeat letter to a friend in Cleveland after German ally Bulgaria had signed a separate armistice on September 29. "This has been a very nice day and Fritz rested all morning," the pitcher wrote. "Perhaps he got some of our gas in his cheese. But he is now making up for it by a lot of activity. But all the good it will do him is to make more trouble for himself, for we are replying with a few high hard ones. And we don't miss very often either."[41]

An American raid on German positions at the Bois de Dommartin on October 27–28 illustrated the variety of the brigade's targets. All three regiments and the trench mortar battery were engaged during the night. The 342nd FA alone fired on multiple positions: a place called Maimbois Farm; a matériel depot; a small warehouse; a machine-gun emplacement; wire, railway tracks, and roads; and an important crossroads. At the height of the bombardment the 155-millimeter howitzer crews each fired five rounds a minute.[42]

Sports editors and columnists back home kept track of Alexander, Ward, and the others as best they could. Many noted that Lambeth had been born in tiny Berlin, Kansas, and wanted to see the German capital. "I don't want to die until I reach Berlin," Lambeth wrote to a friend. "I just want to see if they resemble each other in something else besides the name."[43] The Indians hurler noted in another letter that Americans were singing a new song at the front: "Hell, Heaven or Hoboken by Christmas."[44]

Many sports pages published a brief report that Lambeth had been awarded a medal "for bravery in action, according to word that has reached his friends in Cleveland."[45] The *Iola Register* in Kansas declared, "Otis is our famous ball player and his gallantry on the battlefield being given such special note, while the cause of local pride, comes as no surprise as we expect nothing less than the highest honors for all our boys in action."[46] But the report was a case of mistaken identity. The hero was a Lambeth relative, a physician who had received the Military Medal while serving under fire with the British Army. The mix-up also led a sports columnist to write mistakenly later that the pitcher had risen to the rank of major. The little *Register* may have been the only newspaper in the country to run a correction, while also noting that Lambeth had two brothers and two more cousins serving in the U.S. Army.

> Nobody who knows Otis Lambeth will doubt that he is a good soldier and will do his duty gallantly. But in order that the record may be kept straight the statement ought to be made that it is not he who has been decorated for gallantry as a number of newspapers have erroneously reported, but his cousin, Dr. George Lambeth. . . . [Otis] would be the first if he knew it to protest against being accredited with a decoration which had been won by another. So far as the Lambeth family is concerned, in the language of Admiral Schley, "there is glory enough to go round."[47]

Sergeant Lambeth would have disputed the glory. "Fritz has tried to shell me, to gas me, to bomb me, and I presume he is lying awake nights thinking of other means to obliterate me from this earth of ours," he wrote to a Cleveland sportswriter. "So far I have been spared and he has wasted a lot of powder trying to get me. And all the time we have been sending him a little better than he has handed us."[48]

Despite the fluid situation at the front and the optimism expressed in American newspapers, Lambeth, Alexander, Ward, and the other ballplayers knew the fighting was far from finished. Their batteries were in action every day. "Once when on the line I went seven days with only carrots to eat," Sgt. Chuck Ward recalled. "Finally I sneaked away, found the Salvation Army and stuffed myself with doughnuts before I came back with my courage restored."[49] Death, disability, disfigurement, or lung-searing gas might rain down at any moment, as it could upon the German troops the batteries shelled in return. Soldiers made light of the danger in letters home by comparing themselves to groundhogs when under fire.

"I had a pretty narrow escape the other morning as I was down getting my breakfast," a corporal in Battery F wrote on October 11. "I heard a shell coming so I ducked down and a slab of iron went over my head and went right through a post about 5 inches in diameter, but I was too quick for Fritz that time altho' I sure believe it was meant for me. Ha! Ha!"[50]

Even the doughboys' own ammunition could be deadly to them, as the brigade learned again on October 28. "Last night while firing a barrage on the German lines we had the misfortune of having a gun explode," a first lieutenant wrote to the mother of Pvt. Arthur A. Wight Jr. of Battery D, 340th FA. "Your son was helping serve the gun, and when the explosion occurred a piece of steel struck him on the head. I personally rendered first aid as rapidly as possible and rushed him to the infirmary, from which he was rapidly taken to a hospital three miles back where he soon succumbed. . . . I will place a small but substantial remembrance at the head of his burial place so that the place may be easily recognized as such."[51]

The batteries continually shifted positions during the brigade's first weeks at the front. The men often lived in shelters abandoned by the enemy, for German dugouts were more comfortable than those occupied by Britishers and Yanks. American infantrymen had discovered lavish German officers' quarters complete with a wine cellar in a chateau at Euvezin, the only sizable building aside from the church in the village. "There were two tiers of rooms with broad balconies in front and all lighted by electricity," an Associated Press correspondent wrote. "In the lower floor was an elaborate sitting room, containing richly upholstered furniture, a piano, oil paintings, inlaid tables and beveled mirrors. This apparently was the headquarters of a high officer, for in it were found many maps, plans and a telephone switchboard. Outside was a bowling alley and a small swimming pool."[52]

German enlisted men likewise lived in dugouts that generally were better constructed and more livable than those within the British or American lines. The arriving artillerymen scavenged abandoned stoves and furniture and scooped up enemy equipment to send home as souvenirs. "I have several helmets, rifles, and other German things, which I have found close by," wrote the 340th FA soldier who had earlier learned to kiss the ground, "but they are so common up here that it don't pay to save them."[53] A sergeant in the regiment described his frontline home to folks in Arizona: "I wish you could see this dugout. It was a sort of artillery emplacement just back of the trenches, and talk about the comforts of a home, the Hun surely had them here. These dugouts are built of concrete, with hot and cold baths. There were pianos and upholstered furniture, in fact everything for a neat and cozy home. We all were dazed with the splendor of the scene."[54]

Alexander's regiment, too, was "far from being a sad-eyed, gloomy bunch," a Missourian wrote home, noting that "there is enough Americans here now to whip the whole German army and then some if they would turn us loose."[55] A sergeant major added that the Germans "are on the move and like a pig going down hill on ice, couldn't stop if they wanted to."[56] Alexander wrote Aimee on November 7 that Battery F was busy supporting the front-line infantrymen. "Aleck incidentally voiced the opinion that the Germans were cracking and that he thought he would be through fighting in plenty of time to report to the Cubs for Spring practice."[57]

American troops called the enemy the Hun, the Boche, or (inaccurately) the Dutchmen. The artillerymen all hated the airplanes that strafed them, spotted their positions, and helped to adjust German fire. The 342nd FA one day saw two men parachute from a flaming observation balloon shot down by a German plane. "I am more afraid of them than any thing on the front," a Missourian in the 341st FA confided in a letter to his mother. "They can drop bombs on you or turn their machine gun on you, but the thing to do when they are around is to hide and get where they won't see you."[58]

Another soldier in the regiment had an encounter with an enemy aviator his first day at the front. "I was riding one horse and leading one down a road and a Dutchman in an aeroplane turned a machine gun on me and the way I went wasn't slow. I think about it and laugh. But he missed me by a little."[59] Americans weren't entirely defenseless on the ground. A sergeant in the 342nd FA medical detachment wrote to an uncle, "Our Anti-Aircraft guns play us a tune and fill the skies full of smoke whenever a Boche plane comes over. Mr. Boche goes home then as he does not like the music."[60] Sometimes allied airmen appeared overhead to chase away the Germans. "American pursuit planes drove enemy machine down back of hostile lines, while diving to make escape the observer fell from enemy plane—body found behind our lines," the 342nd FA war diary recorded in early November.[61]

The weather grew colder as Alexander and Battery F pressured the Hindenburg Line. "Perhaps the most tangible evidence we had that our firing was effective," the regimental history states, "was the fact that we kept on excellent terms with the infantry of the various divisions which we supported. We had occasional visits from the infantry officers who led the raids, and their comment was uniformly favorable as to our accompanying fire."[62]

Farther north the Fighting Farmers of the Eighty-Ninth Division were among the nearly 1.25 million doughboys hotly engaged in the Meuse-Argonne offensive. The First Army had driven forty-three German divisions about thirty miles since September 26, "over some of the most difficult terrain and most heavily fortified positions on the Western Front," an army history states. "It had inflicted over 120,000 casualties on the Germans and captured 468 guns."[63] Doughboys had suffered over 115,000 casualties in breaking the enemy lines.

Capt. Paul Withington again distinguished himself while accompanying a patrol that pushed ahead of the division's main lines near Barricourt. The patrol entered the town of Nouart, "occupied it on the night of November 2 and 3, and was in possession when troops of the 178th Brigade entered it on the following day."[64] During the second day, Withington tended a wounded soldier in the open under heavy shelling. The former Harvard footballer was later cited for "distinguished and exceptional gallantry."[65]

In the Euvezin Sector, meanwhile, "information was received indicating a withdrawal by the enemy along the entire front."[66] The 164th Field Artillery Brigade learned of armistice talks from an enemy leaflet that bore the headline "The German People Offers [sic] Peace."[67] "One nice, windy afternoon the Germans came over with a couple of planes filled with propaganda and dumped it out. It looked like a big snowstorm was coming," a private from the 340th FA wrote home.[68]

The 342nd FA now anticipated an actual sustained assault on Metz, not more small-scale raids and reconnaissance parties. The Twenty-Eighth Division was among seven American and nineteen French divisions set to launch an offensive beginning November 14. The Pennsylvanians meanwhile received orders November 10 to make a smaller attack the next day. The artillery brigade got word to prepare to move forward too. Sgt. Chuck Ward wrote that "it was rumored in the ranks that they wouldn't stop until they had occupied Berlin."[69]

FOURTEEN

Armistice

How quiet now the lost trench seems,
How still across the fold
Where lately through our broken dreams
The nightly thunder rolled. . . .

—LT. GRANTLAND RICE

T he American Expeditionary Forces' commanding general took a hard line on peace with Germany. "Pershing, like most of the Allied generals and political leaders, wanted abject surrender," a historian wrote a half-century later. "The armistice must attest to the victory which the Allies had won on the battlefield, and it must leave Germany so weak militarily that the Allies could impose peace terms."[1] But the allied heads of states and governments agreed on an armistice rather than a surrender; the fighting would stop under harsh terms for the Germans, with a peace conference to follow.

German officers agreed to the armistice before dawn on November 11, with all firing to stop late that morning. One of the 342nd Field Artillery's (FA's) lieutenants later wrote to his parents in Missouri about America's strength in the field as the end neared. "Had not the Germans signed the armistice terms when they did 'hell would have broken loose on that front in a short time,'" a Sedalia newspaper reported, quoting from the lieutenant's letter, "as 140 batteries of 6-inch guns and fifteen regiments of '75s' were being transported to the Toul sector in addition to the great quantity of cannon of all sizes already there and prepared for action."[2]

Soldiers on both sides meanwhile kept fighting. The 342nd FA's last position was about two miles north of Euvezin at Bouillionville, "sometimes known as 'Soup Town,' (for several reasons, but mostly because of the muck)," a young second lieutenant recalled years later.[3] The 342nd FA fired nearly 2,500 shells the night of November 10–11, so many that Sgt. Pete Alexander later joked that he had kept his arm in trim "partly by pitching shells at the Boche."[4] The regiment received the long-awaited news at five thirty that morning, and the adjutant recorded it in the war diary: "3rd Battalion Radio picked up message that armistice effective 11:00 a.m. had been signed."[5] The diary didn't say what the artillerymen thought of waiting for the symmetry of the eleventh hour of the eleventh day of the eleventh month before they ceased firing.

Some American commanders weren't inclined to risk their troops' lives during the last hours of combat, but Maj. Gen. William Wright drove the Eighty-Ninth Division hard. His reasoning has been debated and criticized for a century. Wright later reported to Pershing:

> Since the Division had been in the line a considerable period without proper bathing facilities, and since it was realized that if the enemy were permitted to remain in Stenay, our troops would be deprived of the billets and of the probable bathing facilities there, instructions were sent to the Infantry Commander at Laneville, to push forward directly and take Stenay, not waiting for any assistance or support of the 90th Division.... The German High Command made an official complaint that the American troops on the Stenay-Beaumont front had not ceased attacking at 11:00 hours but continued their advance.
>
> Orders once fully understood were, however, loyally obeyed, although there was no regret that the Division had up to the last hour continued to carry out its offensive instructions to the fullest possible extent.[6]

The Fighting Farmers sustained nearly four thousand casualties during a month's fighting in the Meuse-Argonne offensive, including more than three hundred on November 10–11.[7] Wright later told a congressional hearing that his 354th Infantry had lost "three men killed and about twenty-odd wounded" to shellfire at ten thirty in the morning.[8] The general ultimately received no official reprimand for what a modern historian terms "placing cleanliness above survival" during the war's final minutes.[9]

In the Euvezin Sector sixty miles to the southeast, Alexander likely didn't know that the former National League pitcher whose records he coveted had reached the Twenty-Eighth Division. Christy Mathewson, once the New York Giants' star hurler, was now a captain in the army's Chemical Warfare Service. Maj. Branch Rickey and several other Major League executives and players were "Gas and Flame" officers as well.

Mathewson had reached France after the baseball season and been hospitalized with influenza soon afterward. Later he and Capt. Ty Cobb of the Detroit Tigers had been exposed to poison gas during a training accident. Cobb suffered no lasting damage, but effects from the accident and exposure to gas in the field possibly contributed to Mathewson's early death from tuberculosis in 1925. Like most of the men in the Twenty-Eighth Division, Matty was a Pennsylvanian.

"Captain Mathewson although in France for several months did not get into any real fighting, but saw considerable of the battlefields," a Bucknell University alumni magazine reported. "Three days before the armistice was signed he was ordered to join the 28th, 'The Iron Division,' and he reached them as they were in the front line trenches on the day that the war was over." Mathewson believed he had seen more of the war than most officers because he had roamed between sectors as a gas officer. "Most of the gas was used by the artillery and the shells containing it were thrown from artillery guns," he said later. Gas was especially effective against concealed enemy artillery, he added, because "it would burn thru houses, fences or brush coverings of the guns."[10]

Alexander knew something about gas, too, having received special training back at Camp de Souge. The orders as the armistice approached were for concentrated fire on German positions. The 342nd FA had opened fire the day before to support the long-awaited push toward Metz. "On the afternoon of the 10th the artillery brigade covered the advance of the infantry to the wire of the Hindenburg line," the division history reports.[11] The main assault was set to begin on the eleventh, but suddenly the war was nearly over. "We were on the Hindenburg line and staring Metz right in the face and if the war had lasted a week longer we would have been in Metz," a corporal in Battery C wrote.[12]

Battery F and Alexander were "up and about early, eager to give the Huns the final blow" the morning of the eleventh.[13] They fired gas shells into German lines until 10:54 a.m. Altogether, between five thirty and eleven o'clock that morning, the 342nd FA fired 641 shells at the enemy. Orders throughout the regiment changed at 10:50 a.m., ten minutes before the armistice. "After firing every day at targets unknown to them, the gunners were allowed to pick targets of their own, and the last rounds of the regiment were in most cases fired by the Chiefs of Section."[14] Officer's wristwatches ticked off the final hours, minutes, and seconds. A colonel in the Twenty-Eighth Division had never seen such terrible shelling in both directions as during the final three hours. "I estimate in the area occupied by the 112th Infantry about 3,000 shells fell, and most remarkable to state, not a casualty from one of them. This seems almost impossible, yet it is a fact. The last gun that I heard fired from our side was just three seconds to eleven o'clock. The last shell that I heard coming from the enemy was a six inch one that fell within seventy-five yards of my P. C. [post of command], but fortunately it was a dud."[15]

The final shells of the war detonated miles away from the camouflaged positions from which they had been fired. At the top of the hour grimy hands cautiously released howitzer lanyards. Then . . . nothing. Soldiers stood awed in the silence.

"It was like a great thunder storm, the artillery rearing, the machine guns puttering and the aeroplanes buzzing, then it all ceased just as though they had all run out of ammunition," wrote Cpl. T. B. Thompson of Battery E. "We heard the dough boys give a yell in the front line trenches over the hill and it was picked up by the artillery and carried on from one battery to another till it was almost as loud as the firing. We all felt sure that the long looked for victory had come."[16] Pvt. Ralph H. Hull of the regiment's medical detachment wrote home later that day, "This stillness here seems queer, not a gun firing. I have become so used to their noise that it seems lonesome without them."[17] At Xammes the men of Battery F, 340th Field FA, covered the muzzles of their 75-millimeter guns for the last time, then held a mock burial for one of the final German shells fired at them—a dud that hadn't exploded.

Every artilleryman in France and Belgium likely believed that his gun had fired the last shell of the war. Many had a reasonable claim. "I will never forget it, although our battery was off in a woods miles from any civilization," Chuck Ward of Battery C wrote to Charles Ebbets Jr. "Our gun, of which I had been made sergeant two weeks before the end, fired its last shot at 10:59, the eleventh day and the eleventh month of the year."[18] The planned push on Metz was forgotten; *Stars and Stripes* called it "the great unfought battle of the war."[19]

That night Alexander and Battery F watched an astonishing spectacle as "the hillsides and villages where, up to this time, not even the faintest gleam of light showed at night, were flaring with hundreds of campfires, and thousands of red, white, blue and green rockets shot skyward from every direction in celebration."[20] Chuck Ward was struck by the peaceful splendor afterward. "I just stepped outside of our dugout before I started to write this letter, for a few moments, and what a beautiful Fall night it is, with a full moon shining brightly and not a cloud in the sky," he wrote to a friend in Portland during the wee hours. "This is a very unusual thing to witness over here, after the many rainy days that we have experienced. It just seemed as though the Almighty sent peace on us by giving us a bright moonlight on the very night of the armistice, which would make any fellow in the trenches feel happy."[21]

Pvt. George Rigney of Battery D walked out between the lines the following day in what would had been a suicidal act twenty-four hours earlier. "Tuesday morning, four of us went out in no man's land," he wrote to his mother in Long Island City, Queens. "We saw about 200 or 300 Germans there, waiting to be sent back. They were talking to us. Some of the fellows were trading coins with them, but I did not have any U. S. money, only lots of French money. They only wanted U. S. money."[22] The 342nd FA war diary briefly noted the scene as well: "Armistice in effect. Considerable fraternizing in no man's land. German soldiers tearing off buttons and insignia to give Americans as souvenirs."[23]

The 342nd FA ended the war with a good reputation. Despite his sharp criticism when the regiments had first taken the field, Brigadier General Donnelly now held a high opinion of the 164th Field Artillery Brigade. "You can't find any better artillery men in France," he told journalists later back in the United States. "The boys are wonders. They would just as soon keep shooting for two or three days as not. Sleep means nothing to them, and neither does rain nor mud nor cold. If they have work to do they go right ahead and do it regardless of what is going on, and they never stop to question why. They are wonderful boys, every one of them, and I'm proud of them."[24]

Maj. Gen. William H. Hay, the Twenty-Eighth Division commander, felt much the same way about the Missourians. Hay shared with his doughboys a letter commending the division's performance during the days leading up to the armistice; he also made a point of noting that the 164th Field Artillery Brigade had "done much towards the success of these operations."[25] Donnelly received a personal memo from the general's chief of staff:

> The Division Commander desires me to express to the officers and enlisted men of your command his appreciation of the excellent work which they have done during the time that the 28th Division has been in this sector.
>
> Our infantry states that the barrage work of your brigade is uniformly good, and the proof that your artillery work is good is that it has the confidence of the infantry of the 28th Division.[26]

The brigade had been fortunate in the Euvezin Sector. The Eighty-Ninth Division history shows only two brigade officers and twenty-three men killed and four officers and 185 men wounded or gassed during nearly two months at the front. The 342nd FA had seven men killed, twenty-five gassed, and twenty-eight severely wounded. These were very light casualties compared to those in the infantry units that the 342nd supported. "By way of recapitulation it is to be noted that the brigade had seen fifty-six days of continuous service in support of three different divisions. It had fired about 200,000 rounds of ammunition. Though it had been frequently shelled, good luck and good management kept the casualties down."[27]

One of the 342nd FA's few casualties was Sgt. Carey J. Maupin, the Missourian in Battery E who had overcome his father's attempt to have him exempted from service. Maupin was wounded by shellfire in October. The preacher's son minimized the severity of his wound in a letter he wrote four days later from a base hospital in Limoges, which his parents wouldn't receive until late November. "I would not have left the battery only it was necessary to have my arm dressed, and when they got me started they just kept me moving," he wrote. "I suppose this will be a sort of vacation, but I fear it will be hard for me to get back to the front after my stay here."[28] He was somewhat more forthright in a subsequent letter. "The enemy continued to make each day and night exciting. On the night of the 22nd [of October] he tried to bomb us. In return we gave him a barrage and on the 23rd he began a bombardment of our positions. He winged me and now my only regret is that I could not return in time to celebrate the ceasing of hostilities, or to help fire the last shot or to accompany the boys in their march to the Rhine."[29]

Former Major Leaguers who had preceded Alexander to France had experienced a hard war too. Lt. Harry McCormick had returned to the United States suffering from shell shock. His former Giants teammate Capt. Eddie Grant had died in action October 5, killed while leading his battalion in the Argonne Forest. Capt. Ed Lafitte had served in France and England with the army's first plastic and oral surgery unit, patching soldiers' ruined faces. Marine Hugh Miller had earned the Distinguished Service Cross for his actions during the vicious fighting at Belleau Wood; wounded twice later and hobbled for life, he was Organized Baseball's most decorated warrior. Alexander and the other ballplayers in the 342nd FA, in comparison, had been fortunate. Chuck Ward wrote a letter home November 12 that *The Sporting News* later paraphrased: "Ward writes on to say that often he, Alexander and the others, as they lay in the mud, talked about the good old times in first class hotels, the lower Pullmans and wondered if they ever would be on such velvet again. They were full of hope, since none of them had been hurt much, in spite of several narrow escapes from dropping shells."[30]

But none could have been unaffected by the sights, smells, and sounds of war—the awkward sprawl of dead animals, the terrifying whiff of gas, the deafening tom-tom-tom of the howitzers. We know a bit of what Alexander did and saw. Former National League star second baseman Johnny Evers gave an account of him upon his return from France, where Evers had served as a Knights of Columbus athletic director. Evers had toured the front several times, often encountering Major and Minor League players.

"Grover Alexander, Clarence Mitchell, Otis Lambeth, Chuck Ward, Win Noyes and others who were members of the baseball battery did heroic work," Evers said. "When last I saw them they were up in the front lines . . . and their guns were spreading havoc among the Huns. There had been a report that Alexander was injured, but he was as sound as a dollar when I met him and enjoying every minute of the big scrap."[31]

"None of our men was gassed and none was wounded, though we went through some heavy shelling at times," Alexander told an interviewer that winter. "But I guess it wasn't heavy compared with what some of the others got. The time went faster than I thought it would at a time when the end might be near for any one of us. I stood it better than this waiting—that is what is tiresome."[32] He apparently was speaking only of his own crew, but all of Battery F was remarkably lucky as well; it had only two men gassed and none killed or severely wounded. For the rest of his life the laconic Nebraskan shrugged off the dangers of combat in France and didn't discuss what his service there might have cost him. "I've never been afraid," he said nearly a quarter-century later. "I wasn't afraid when I was a gunner with the 342d F. A. in the front lines in 1918 . . . and I wasn't afraid of the best hitter I ever faced—[Rogers] Hornsby."[33]

Sgt. Otis Lambeth summarized the effects of combat in brief holiday greetings that he, Alexander, and several other ballplayers wired to a Boston newspaper for an article printed on Christmas Day 1918: "There's one thing about this war. It takes all a fellow's nervousness away. I don't care how the Red Sox and Tigers try to ride me any more. And I won't be a bit afraid of getting beaned in the future. Maybe [manager] Lee Fohl and the bunch in Cleveland will be glad to hear this."[34]

Sgt. Chuck Ward also shared war memories in his armistice letter to Portland. "This bunch surely know how to fire these big shells, and every one was made to hit the right spot when these gunners fired them," he wrote. "Night after night, while on the firing line, Alexander and myself thought of the many happy days we had while playing baseball and living in the best of hotels and wondering if we would ever come back to the States alive. After dodging machine gun bullets and big shells a fellow cannot but be happy that he came through without receiving a scratch." The infielder added a thought about the homefolks: "I can imagine how many hearts have been made happy in the States when they received the news of the armistice, while we know that there are many sad hearts among the mothers and wives who have been informed that their sons and husbands have died fighting their way to victory. Although it is hard to realize that their bodies are buried somewhere on the battlefields of France, they should be very proud of them to know that they paid the supreme price to make the world a better place to live in."[35]

Ward summed up his war experience in his letter to Charles Ebbets Jr. "Baseball never did and never will have the thrills the big game had," he wrote. "A fellow going to sleep at night, if anything like sleep could be had, would remark in the morning, 'Well, boys, I am still in the game.' Charles, I could write more than one book on my experiences and close calls, but here I am, still in the ring. I wouldn't want to go through it again for millions, but wouldn't have missed it for thousands."[36]

FIFTEEN

The March

Slogging through the mud of France,
    Camping in the rain;
Hiking in a frozen trance
    Down some German plain;
"Fall in!"—hear the Sergeant yell,
    Far from home and clover;
Tell me, who the bally hell
    Said the war "was over"?

—LT. GRANTLAND RICE

The Euvezin Sector was lightly held following the armistice. The doughboys accepted prisoners, stayed within their own lines, and received maps and information from the Germans according to the terms of the armistice. Many troops who weren't needed began training in rear areas.

"The artillery remained for a week or so in the dugouts of the positions and then gradually moved to the slightly more comfortable quarters afforded by the ruined towns," the 342nd Field Artillery (FA) history states. Batteries A and B occupied German barracks at Hattonville, Batteries C and D moved into Beney, and Batteries E and F "made the best of quarters in Bouillionville."[1] Safe and more comfortable than they had been for weeks, the doughboys' thoughts drifted toward home. "After the armistice was signed we were under the impression (of course like all soldiers) that we should be among the first 500,000 to get back," Pvt. Dutch Wetzel wrote. "Everybody was figuring how many days it would be before we would embark."[2]

The good news from home was that Major League baseball—in limbo since the conclusion of the early World Series in September—would restart in 1919. "The positive assurance that major league baseball would be resumed next Spring was made in Chicago yesterday by President Ban Johnson of the American League after he had received a letter from General March, Chief of Staff," the *New York Times* reported December 5. "The representative of the War Department informed Johnson that there was no reason why the game should not be resumed in accordance with the regular schedules. . . . It is believed that all the players who are now in the service will be discharged from the army before it is time for the Spring training trips."[3]

Such optimism was misplaced. Four days after the armistice General Pershing formed the Third Army of Occupation under Maj. Gen. Joseph Dickman. It included troops from the regular army (First Division through Fourth Division), the National Guard (Thirty-Second Division and Forty-Second Division), and the National Army (Eighty-Ninth Division and Ninetieth Division). Joined by soldiers from Belgium, France, and Great Britain, the total allied occupation force was about 1.25 million. Rather than again taking small French trains, the Eighty-Ninth Division began a 175-mile march into Germany as winter set in.

The Fighting Farmers soon learned what their artillerymen already knew about army horses in France. "Shaggy, wild-eyed, tired horses, some of them straight from the farms back home and that understood English, began to come in," the division history relates. "Animals also came in that did not speak or understand English—captured German horses, and horses that the Germans had captured from the Russians and that we, in turn, had captured from the Germans, and Spanish mules and French horses."[4] Once they had enough animals, the doughboys set about cleaning and repairing their harnesses and wagons. For once the 342nd FA was ahead of the game, but Pete Alexander, Clarence Mitchell, and the others were forced to set aside their dreams of heading home in time for Christmas . . . or Easter, and perhaps Memorial Day, or even the Fourth of July.

Alexander showed no bitterness over the delay in going home. One soldier who knew him then was 2nd Lt. Francis X. Fitzpatrick. The shavetail had reported to the regiment only ten days before the armistice and had little reason to expect kindness from Battery F. Yet he would always remember Sergeant Alexander lumbering up to him on a snowy morning when the men were grooming the horses on the picket line. Alexander stood a head taller than the diminutive officer. "Lieutenant," he said, "you put on these gloves, as you look kind of cold." Fitzpatrick tried to decline, but Alexander "just wouldn't have it. I mention this merely to show his heart."[5]

The occupation army set off in waves to Germany. The first wave passed the Eighty-Ninth Division headquarters at Stenay on November 17. The Fighting Farmers stepped off a week later. The 342nd FA had orders to follow eventually and rejoin the division, but they spent Thanksgiving Day still in quarters. Battery F started the November 28 holiday with a five-mile hike before returning to a dugout on a hill at Bouillionville, where they dined on regular army chow rather than turkey. "Extra horses had been drawn and on the morning of November 29th the regiment took the road for Germany."[6]

Battery F rose at four o'clock with orders to march at eight thirty. "At that hour we left our position, which had come to seem like home to us, and headed for the Rhine," the battery history states. "We were somewhat elated at seeing the country of our enemy."[7] The lead elements of the Third Army were very far ahead, tramping toward the enemy's fatherland a day behind the rear guard of the retreating Germany army. A staff officer briefed newspaper reporters later on the remarkable journey. His description applies as well to the Eighty-Ninth Division and the 164th Field Artillery Brigade as to other units in the huge American force: "You will readily see the necessity of marching a division on at least two roads when I tell you that a complete division, in route column, without distances, occupies 31.8 miles of road space. Remember now that the support divisions were two days' march, or say twenty miles, in rear of the advance divisions, and each division on two roads occupies fifteen miles of depth, so you see that the depth of the two leading corps was at least thirty-five miles, and was more generally nearly forty miles deep."[8]

Twenty-seven-year-old 1st Lt. Harold Jacobus led the way for the 342nd FA. He was the former insurance man bemused by the Ozark men back at Camp Funston. More recently Jacobus had been a battery reconnaissance officer in charge of preparing maps; during the long trek to Germany he was a regimental billeting officer. He roved ahead of the column, speaking French and later German, arranging shelter for the doughboys trudging along behind him. His captain wrote that Jacobus "had a great deal to do and moreover he went ahead each day in a machine and so did not walk or ride horseback as some of us did."[9]

The regiment made slow progress over shattered roads. "For three days we marched through French occupied territory," a doughboy in the headquarters company wrote. "Here we came in close contact with inhabitants that were oppressed and it was very evident that they were happy over being liberated by the Americans. At first many were terrified by the sight of the Americans and many of them did not know who we really were until the news spread."[10] Alexander and Battery F reached the village of Woël the first day out and Allamont the second, tired men and horses taking shelter in ruined houses. "We found pioneers and engineers still engaged in blowing up the mines in the vicinity," the regimental history records. "On the next day's march it was something of a relief to leave the ruins of the war zone."[11]

"Can you imagine Alexander, Noyes, Lambeth, Lieutenant Wait and myself traveling for miles on horseback," Sgt. Chuck Ward asked in a letter, "pulling big batteries behind us and going into big shell holes large enough to bury a whole detachment?" Ward had "a little hard luck with [the] mount when his back became sore from the saddle," so he walked the rest of the way into Germany.[12]

The artillerymen reached pretty Xivry-Circourt in fair weather on December 1. They halted the next day at Villers-le-Montagne, where the people seemed exhausted, "partly by previous celebrations and partly by a forlorn depression over their ruined fortunes, for the Germans had stripped the country of all its live-stock, food and other valuables."[13] Battery F crossed into Belgium on December 3. The Chicago Cubs learned the same day that Alexander and the 342nd FA were rejoining the Eighty-Ninth Division and heading for Germany. "This information was received by Manager Fred Mitchell today and dissipates hope that the manager had entertained, he said, that the pitcher would be available for duty next season."[14] Sportswriters began to suspect that Alexander and the others might be playing ball in Berlin come summer. "In spite of Gen. March's assurance regarding early release of ball players in the army, the Chicago Cubs and other clubs that have players in the 342d field artillery are disturbed. The regiment includes a notable lot of ball players, including Grover Alexander, Chuck Ward, Otis Lambeth and others. Reports indicate it is with the army of occupation in Germany, where it is likely to stay awhile, and the only hope for the ball players to get out is through preferential discharges."[15]

Battery F marched through the Belgian border town of Aubange and continued north to Messancy, which was decorated with evergreens that reminded the men of Christmas trees. "At either entrance of the town was hung an imitation of the Kaiser, representing him with his hand grip [suitcase] and shabby uniform retreating before the approach of the visitors." Able to buy alcohol for the first time since Toul, "the boys went very heavily on this light beer, but were unable to hold enough to produce a 'jag,' as they soon found it was useless to overload themselves."[16] The next day the artillery column left Belgium near Arlon and turned eastward.

The men marched through rain into a hilly, forested part of Luxembourg, neutral but occupied by Germany during the war. This was "a place that had not been touched by shell-fire," Ward wrote, "and here we saw some wonderful scenery while hiking along the foothills overlooking a beautiful valley with its winding rivers. We were treated like kings while traveling through Luxemburg."[17] The artillerymen stopped the first night at Saeul. Turning northeastward the second day, Battery F reached the city of Ettlebruck, where citizens held a parade for several hours.

"We were able to buy eats, rent rooms with cozy beds, buy beer, wine, 'snops' and best of all we were able to get candies, but at high prices."[18] The doughboys would have liked to linger there but were ordered back onto the road the next day. "The eighth day out brought us through the most interesting country of the trip and into the most ancient of the towns. We passed through the City of Diekirch and thence through Tandel and Fouhren, over the hills and suddenly down into the valley of the Sauer River, where Vianden was located."[19] The doughboys of Battery F enjoyed the latter town nearly as much as they had Ettlebruck.

All of the Major Leaguers in the regiment except Clarence Mitchell managed to gather together at some point, perhaps for the first time since Camp de Souge. "Alexander, Noyes and Lambeth and myself sat down in one of the towns of Luxemburg for over two hours," Ward wrote, "relating some of the great times we had while playing ball and wishing that we were again in the real country, the good old U. S. A., getting ready for the spring training trip to the southern climate instead of trying to make these people understand us. We can hardly wait for the time to come when we will again board a ship that will take us across the Atlantic to our dear old home, the land of the Stars and Stripes."[20]

The 342nd FA reached Germany on December 7, two days behind the advance elements of the Eighty-Ninth Division. The border was only a fifteen-minute march from friendly Vianden. The doughboys paused, unfurled their colors, and heard the regimental band play "The Star-Spangled Banner." The division's history captures the soldiers' mood on marching into the enemy's country: "Should we mention our feelings on seeing green fields well kept—roofs and chimneys whole on the houses—fat cattle and well fed people in unharmed

Germany—all after devastated France? Other emotions were sometimes excited. It is related that a disgusted K. P., engaged in digging a kitchen sink, was overheard to make the following complaint, 'This is a h—l of a country; not even a shell hole to throw things in!'"[21]

General Pershing's headquarters had issued strict orders to troops entering Germany: "So long as a state of war continues, Germany remains enemy territory, and there must be no intimate personal association with its inhabitants. A dignified and reserved attitude will be maintained on your part at all times." The orders warned of the "severest penalties known to our military law" for any doughboy who embarrassed the army by looting or acting violently toward residents.[22] Battery F saw by "the expressions on the faces of the inhabitants that we were among the conquered." Alexander and the men marched past the Germans without hatred or roughness, "but always keeping aloof and strictly to business."[23]

Ward had expected the doughboys' reception from Germans "would be altogether different from what we had experienced in the allied country, and above all, we would not receive any more good eats. But to the contrary, we feasted fine."[24] The regimental history records that food was plentiful; "the absence of the men had not prevented the cultivation of the land, due to the fact that the women were well accustomed to manual labor in the fields."[25]

The regiment marched through rain along more bad roads before stopping in the village of Burg. After resting a day, the artillerymen moved on again and spent the next two nights in Boden. On December 11 they reached Bitburg, where both the Third Army and the Eighty-Ninth Division had established headquarters. "There the natives turned out to see the guns that made Fritz change his mind and learn that other people live besides the Huns," Dutch Wetzel wrote to a friend.[26] Battery F marched through the city and then another twenty-one miles to reach Pickliessem. Here Alexander and Battery F rested, cleaned equipment, and cared for the horses. The regiment's other batteries scattered through nearby towns, which like Pickliessem the doughboys found "dirty and inconvenient."[27]

The doughboys had hoped to see the city of Coblenz, where the Moselle meets the Rhine. Battery F instead marched back through Bitburg on December 15 to the village of Alsdorf, where the battalion established its headquarters. The men set up a washroom and bath-house, "and the cootie [lice] population soon diminished consider-ably, and our clothing began to show the effects of soap, water and elbow grease."[28]

The trek into Germany had been long and arduous after weeks in combat. Still, it could have been worse; the 342nd FA had always slept under shelter rather than canvas during the wet weather. Horses and mules had been kept under cover most nights as well, and only four animals had died along the way. Battery F began a light drill sched-ule in Alsdorf, letting exhausted men rest at last. The doughboys also began planning for the holidays.

Back in Chicago manager Fred Mitchell was fretting. No one had heard from Alexander since his November 7 letter to Aimee, who was living in Newport, Kentucky, until his return. "Officials of the Chi-cago Cubs are anxiously awaiting some word from Grover Alexander to show that he was not injured during the last four days of the war."[29] Mail from France took weeks to reach the United States under good conditions and was delayed even more when a regiment was march-ing. News that the Cubs' craggy right-hander was unharmed finally arrived like a gift from Santa.

"A merry Christmas to all the good fans in the States," Alexan-der wired to the *Boston Post*, the paper that had solicited greetings from Major Leaguers serving in the American Expeditionary Forces. "Only wish I were home to eat my turkey in God's country. Hope to be back with the boys next spring. Expect to be on the firing line in Chicago in June."[30]

Having survived the war, the doughboys now faced the same deadly threat as families and loved ones back home: the Spanish influenza. The pandemic killed millions around the world. "I had the flu and my fever was 103," a private in Battery E wrote home. "The flu is something bad and I see in the papers that people sure have been dying in the states."[31] A corporal in the 340th FA wrote of his worry over the spread of the virus in his Arizona hometown. "Sorry to hear that the flu was in Clifton, but not many sections of the country escaped. I was in the hospital about two weeks with it and I promise you it gets a fellow."[32]

Lieutenant Jacobus had helped to arrange shelter for the regiment during the long march but now fell ill as Christmas neared. By roaming ahead of the column by automobile, his captain wrote, he "did not get the hardening that the rest of us did and consequently was not in shape to combat the cold which he took the day we arrived in this place [Alsdorf]." Jacobus was ill three days before doctors sent him to a hospital at the nearby city of Trier. He died Christmas Eve of pneumonia, which often followed the flu. "I realize the futility of words at a time like this but I do wish to express our great admiration and love for Harold and to extend our heartfelt sympathy to his parents," the captain wrote.

The regiment buried the lieutenant beneath a headstone that bore a simple inscription: "Gentleman—Soldier—Patriot."[33] Jacobus had been lucky in war but unlucky in peace. Despite crowded conditions in the batteries' German billets, "the regiment came through the season without any serious epidemics."[34]

SIXTEEN

Occupied Germany

When the doughboy hits the dirt
With Rhine mud on his shirt—
    And a year ago this morning they were winning;
Now they stand by in a daze
As we pull off double plays
    In a land that never knew a "seventh inning."

—GRANTLAND RICE, 1919

T he 342nd Field Artillery (FA) occupied billets in three small towns closely situated along a river road south of Bitburg. The Third Battalion (including Battery F) was at Alsdorf, the Second at Niederweis, and the First at Irrel. A corporal in the headquarters company wrote home from Irrel that the Germans were "just a little afraid of so many soldiers but they try to treat us fine." Residents endured rather than liked the doughboys, he added, "but really if you could see how accommodating and nice some of them try to be you would be more than ever convinced that we were fighting their government more than their people."[1]

The regimental history later damned the Germans with faint praise as "law-abiding to the point of servility."[2] A private from the 341st FA wrote home to Missouri from another small town, "The Dutch [sic] sure try to make it happy for us all. They treat us so much better than the French do."[3]

The 342nd FA remained at Alsdorf during the holidays. "No trouble was experienced with the inhabitants, and the Christmas and New Year celebrations were none the less merry for being spent in hostile territory."[4] The doughboys were in "very pretty country through here for we are in the mountainous region," Dutch Wetzel wrote from Irrel. "They are having a wet season here now and it rains every day. It hasn't been real cold yet but we expect it every day."[5]

A light snow fell before dawn on Christmas Day. The Third Battalion gathered at ten thirty that morning for an athletic program. "Our regimental band being present, we were soon in the proper spirit to enjoy a program of horse riding, mule racing, mounted wrestling, centipede races and other forms of entertainment," the Battery F history relates. "We returned to our billets, each one to prepare himself for the big feed, which came at 3:00 p.m."[6] Captain O'Fallon had put Sergeant Alexander in charge of the battery's Christmas party, which included two hogs barbecued Missouri-style and plentiful trimmings. The men were already seated when Alexander appeared. Lt. Francis Fitzpatrick knew the big Nebraskan had been "frolicking" as soon as he came through the door. Alexander saluted his captain and beat a hasty retreat. He said later he had "only been rushing the holiday celebration a bit."[7]

John Barleycorn had begun tightening his grip on the pitcher. Years later Alexander recalled that although he had drunk beer all his life, he had first turned to hard liquor in France. "Overseas, everybody knew he was going into battle continually and no one knew whether he would be alive tomorrow or not," he wrote. "So a lot of men who had never drunk before drank over there. But fortunately for them, it didn't get a hold of them like it did of me."[8]

The dinner and entertainment Alexander had planned were nonetheless a success. The festivities went on for hours, boosting morale in Battery F when spirits were low in other outfits. The battery enjoyed a leisurely holiday through the rest of December. Many men enjoyed passes to Trier. "New Year's day was spent without any formation whatever, and, with the exception of the boys drawing a little mail and Christmas boxes, was without incident."[9] Chuck Ward wrote a long New Year's Day letter to Charles Ebbets Jr. back in Brooklyn: "This war has taught us many a good lesson, and I know my interest in baseball would be greater than ever. Sunday is a real day of rest and consequently we have that day to ourselves—that is, after the horses and mules are fed. So my intentions are to saddle up a steed and take a ride to the next village, Niederweis, where Mitchell is located, to talk over the coming year's baseball season."[10]

Alexander, Mitchell, and the other professional ballplayers in the regiment surely welcomed the news printed in the *Stars and Stripes* two days later. "The American and National Leagues will resume baseball on a 140-game basis, instead of playing 154 games as heretofore," the army newspaper reported, "and the American Baseball Association managers have announced that they will start banging the old horsehide in that circuit on April 29."[11]

The announcement offered no insight into when Alexander and the others might expect to head home, however. Players in the armed forces serving stateside were already being discharged, simply because it was quick and economical for the War Department to discharge them. Tris Speaker of the Indians and Wally Pipp of the Yankees had begun training as naval aviators following the season, and both had been discharged by the end of November. Alexander's pal Bill Killefer was now a sergeant at Camp Custer, Michigan, mustering out doughboys returning from France. "It is not at all impossible that Killefer will have a hand in the mustering out of Aleck after the latter returns," the *Chicago Tribune* had reported.[12] Reindeer Bill said of Ol' Pete, "I've heard from him from time to time and know how badly he wants to get back here."[13]

No one knew when the 342nd FA might start for home. Alexander indicated in a letter to Cubs infielder Fred Merkle that the regiment's Major Leaguers were ready to rejoin the sport. "He writes that all the ball players in the battery are in good health and that all came through the war with nothing more serious than scratches and powder burns from their own guns."[14]

Other ballplayers overseas were caught in the same wait-and-see situation as the artillerymen. Color Sergeant Hank Gowdy of the Boston Braves, the first active Major Leaguer to enlist, also was part of the occupation army, at Rolandseck. About three dozen other active Major Leaguers were in the army in France; they included Sherrod "Sherry" Smith of the Dodgers, Mike Menosky of the Senators, and Hal Carlson of the Pirates. Roughly fifteen former players were in France, too, as were Yankees co-owner Lt. Col. T. L. "Cap" Huston and several other front-office men. A handful of active players in the navy served aboard warships or in overseas shore billets as well. Most of these servicemen could count on going home ahead of the poor fellows in Germany, despite long waits for transports. Capt. Ty Cobb had somehow scooted home ahead of everyone a week before Christmas, but Capt. Christy Mathewson's managerial job in Cincinnati would be gone before he returned in February. The U.S. Army had two million men overseas at the armistice. It would take many months to get them all home again.

Alexander meanwhile continued serving as an unofficial Cubs scout while in Germany. One of his lieutenants—Potsy Clark, the former Illini quarterback—topped his list of prospects. "Clark played on the same army team with Alex and aside from the pitcher was said to be the star, being a speedy outfielder, a smart base runner and an unusually heavy hitter," a newspaper had reported at Christmas. "Clark has all the requirements to play on a major league club and there was no doubt in his mind he could make good. . . . Whether Clark will desire to follow baseball as a profession is not known, but it is the disposition of the officials of the Cub team to give him the chance to earn a berth on Alexander's recommendation."[15]

Battery F moved to roomier billets in Meckel, east of Alsdorf, on January 10. The men finally got rid of their cooties, no small relief, while the army kept everyone busy with inspections, hikes, and collecting German war matériel. The regiment also stood guard along the Sauer River, each battalion stationing a detail at Echternach, Luxembourg, and other towns along the border for two weeks at a time. The men directed traffic, prevented smuggling, and kept order. "It is not to be concluded that the winter was by any means comfortable," the regimental history declares. "The man with a bed was fortunate and the man who could keep clean was enterprising."[16]

The battery shifted again in early February, to Holsthum, west of Alsdorf. "We reached this place about 10:00 a.m. and found that our Billeting Sergeant, Grover C. Alexander, had everything arranged in advance."[17] Despite the generally law-abiding nature of the Germans, the regiment had occasional problems during the occupation. Not surprisingly, one involved alcohol. "Some of the backcountry peasants were severely fined for selling home-made 'Schnapps' and before the arrival of Spring this latter form of law-breaking was responsible for an incident in which two Germans were accidentally shot. Otherwise, the occupation of our area was peaceable."[18]

The regiment also prepared to surrender its horses and mules. Doughboys didn't treat the animals that had hauled their batteries through France and into Germany like pets. As a Battery F private wrote in December, "If a mule don't kick me I think I will have a good chance to come back home."[19] And like the entire American Expeditionary Forces (AEF), the 342nd FA was bedeviled by a serious shortage of hay. "Our troubles in this direction were, however, finally relieved by the long-delayed arrival of tractors and motor vehicles toward the middle of March," the regiment's history states. "The men and officers undertook the transformation with zest and it was only a week or so before the regiment was on the road with its full equipment. That a body of men only superficially and partially trained to handle this equipment was so successful and rapid in learning the operation and maintenance of the tremendous quantity of machinery was not at the time considered astonishing, but to those who were familiar with the nature of the problem it will remain a source of satisfaction, if not of wonder."[20]

Battery F alone received ten five-ton tractors, eleven trucks, a large staff car, a detail car, and a rolling kitchen. Few men grew wistful during their long-overdue and now largely useless mechanization. "Our horses were turned in in small bunches and everyone was glad to see the last one leave," the battery history states.[21] The animals didn't remain long in Germany, even though local farmers were using oxen and cows to pull their plows because they had no horses left. "The price of a horse is from five thousand dollars and up," a Battery E man wrote in late March. "I think this battery will turn in the rest of the horses this week. Two-thirds of them have been sent back and are sold to the French. I hope they will go this time, as we have tractors for the guns, instead of horses."[22]

The ballplayers grew anxious for the voyage home. "What a grand and glorious feeling that will be for the gang; we all have said it will be the happiest days of our lives," Chuck Ward had written in January.[23] Clarence Mitchell had penned a letter about the same time to Dodgers owner Charles Ebbets. "We were told for our Christmas that we would be homeward bound in another month, so expect to be in time to start spring training the same as ever."[24]

Any quick return was unlikely, however, and Ward was impatient. "One night I had an impromptu sparring match with Lambeth, greatly to the edification of the natives, in the middle of the street in the village of Irrel," he said. "Maybe I won't kid him when I get him on the diamond again. . . . But what is the chance of getting home instead of staying here and playing for the expedition championship?"[25]

Managers and magnates at home also worried about their players' mental and physical condition once the troops returned from wartime service. "The $50,000 idol of the Chicago fans, Grover Alexander, may find that carrying a rifle and a pack in France has destroyed his usefulness as a pitcher," a wire report speculated. "Jack Barry, star second baseman of the Red Sox, may discover that life as a gob has unfitted him for the diamond."[26] New York Giants manager John McGraw was sympathetic but typically candid in speaking about Alexander and others who had fought in France.

I am afraid that Aleck and the other boys who have seen active service on the battle front will find it impossible to play the old game like they did before they went through that experience. The life which they have led for the past few months has been sterner than anything they ever had known before, and while they have gained the glory which is the due of all our fighting men, they have lost something, I believe, which they can never get back. That which they have lost is the physical condition and the mental poise so necessary to the major league ball player.[27]

Stars and Stripes asked whether exposure to poison gas might affect ballplayers who had fought in France. "The report has been widely circulated here [in America] that the prevalence of gas along the old battle front has affected the stamina and breathing apparati [*sic*] of many ball players and that their work may be considerably affected for this reason," the army paper reported. "This may be true of an individual case or so but the general effect will be small. A few rounds of old-fashioned steak and few whiffs of United States air will very likely have the desired results, so far as conditioning is concerned."[28]

The German weather was lousy for baseball, but Alexander and Battery F could cheer other army sports. The Eighty-Ninth Division had organized football, basketball, indoor baseball, and soccer teams soon after arriving. Capt. Paul Withington assembled a crack gridiron team for a unique late-winter AEF championship series. Nearly sixty divisional football teams participated, many filling out their rosters with former collegiate stars.

The Eighty-Ninth Division team practiced on a small field a few hundred yards outside Kyllburg, where the division now had its headquarters. The starting eleven included three familiar faces from the 342nd FA: lieutenants Potsy Clark, left halfback; Ad Lindsey, right halfback; and Poge Lewis, center. Withington played left guard. "Although equipment had not arrived, the men began practice in their O. D. trousers and hob-nailed shoes by the 25th of January, in the snow and slush. The division's old battle cry—*Wright Wood Winn*—was readily seized upon as a fetish, and, in huge letters of black on a field of red (for Harvard and Coach-Captain Withington), led the 89th loyal rooters in many hilarious snake-dances on fields from Coblenz to Paris."[29]

The team's first game was February 14 versus the Ninetieth Division at nearby Wittlich. After losing Clark to a separated shoulder on the first play, the Eighty-Ninth eked out a 6–0 win with a third-quarter touchdown. The team was "in striking distance of the goal again and again, but the tightening of the defense and the slippery field saved the losers from a larger score."[30] *Spalding's Official Foot Ball Guide* later reckoned that both teams had been "handicapped by little practice."[31]

Withington's squad easily dispatched the Third Army headquarters team, 30–0, a week later at Coblenz. It next faced the Fourth Division on February 27, again at Coblenz, with the victors moving on as Third Army champions. "It was Harvard against Harvard," the division history records, "the captains of the teams being two of the greatest players who ever wore the Crimson—Paul Withington for us and Hamilton Fish for the 4th."[32] Correspondents reported that doughboys slapped down bets totaling around half a million francs (about $100,000). *Spalding's* offered a breathless account:

> In the final game, when army sport writers in Coblenz ran dry of superlatives, before a crowd that smashed all records in a contest that beggared description, the 89th defeated the 4th, 14–0. This game was played on an island in the middle of the Rhine, with a castle, once the home of William Hohenzollern, glowering in the distance. Curious Germans looked on silent, phlegmatic. Not a tree branch that would support the lightest Doughboy, not a roof top, not a telephone post, not an eminence of any sort near the field of play, was untenanted. "S.R.O."—there wasn't anything else but standing room.[33]

The Eighty-Ninth Division squad defeated the Eighty-Eighth Division, 13–9, in a March 5 practice game at Trier before traveling to Paris for the AEF championship series. The first game was March 14 versus the Service of Supply team from St. Nazaire. The site was the Auteuil

Vélodrome, a racetrack almost in the shadow of the Eiffel Tower. Eddie Hart of Princeton University coached the St. Nazaire team, which included Eddie Mahan, one of Harvard's greatest kickers. The first half was scoreless. Ad Lindsey then scored a touchdown in the third quarter but missed the point after. The highlight of the game came later in the same quarter as Withington's men stood with their backs to the goal on their 1-yard line. "Four straight, desperate, Herculean plays were thwarted. Lindsey punted out of danger. The game was over, then and there."[34] Potsy Clark wriggled across to score in the fourth quarter to make the final score 13–0.

The Service of Supply Intermediate Section from Tours was next, on March 22 at the Vélodrome. The first half ended with Service of Supply leading 3–0. Withington's team came back with two touchdowns by Clark and a Lindsey field goal for a 17–3 victory. "The game was a typical 89th Division victory, finishing with a victorious punch after coming from behind."[35] In the lead-up to the AEF championship game March 29 versus the Thirty-Sixth Division, *Stars and Stripes* hailed the Fighting Farmers' eleven as "one of the greatest fighting football teams ever developed."[36]

Special trains delivered thousands of troops from France, Belgium, and Germany for the championship. General Pershing joined fifteen thousand fans packing the Vélodrome. The Eighty-Ninth Division team wore special "Withington shoes" for the contest. "The shoe is just like the ordinary football footgear, but instead of leather cleats it has rubber fibre cleats."[37] Excitement ran high in Paris. "The whole atmosphere was reminiscent of a game at Yale, Harvard or Princeton, or the annual Army and Navy game, with the exception of the colors in the stands. The spectators presented a solid mass of olive drab, relieved here and there by the blue of the uniforms of the women army workers."[38]

The Thirty-Sixth struck first, scoring during the opening quarter on a recovered fumble in the end zone. General Winn, again commanding the Eighty-Ninth, visited the locker room with the division trailing 6–0 at halftime. Potsy Clark remembered every word of the pep talk years afterward. Winn declared that the division had never failed to obey an order, whether from him, General Wood, or General Wright. "You have taken every objective," he barked. "You know those written orders that have been sent out from our headquarters. Right now I haven't time to write one out, but I am giving you an oral order. *I order you to take this game.*"[39]

Clark obeyed, becoming a "mud-covered streak of maroon" in the second half.[40] He scored in the third quarter on "a triple pass with Gerhardt and Lindsey."[41] He scored again during the final quarter on a 65-yard run. "Clark darted through a hole opened by his linesmen, and slipping away from the first defencemen, bore down like a French taxi driver on the last man in his path. The latter was unable to move in the mud, and Clark was past him like a streak."[42] The final score was 14–6. *Spalding's* later applauded the Eighty-Ninth's team for "one of the most interesting seasons in the history of the game."[43]

General Pershing walked onto the field moments after the final whistle. Exhausted players and jubilant doughboys at first didn't notice the AEF commander. Black Jack waved for silence and spoke to the khaki-clad throng. "I am glad of this opportunity to thank you for the splendid game you have played today and for the wonderful spirit you have shown. You have carried out the letter and the spirit of the plans adopted to promote clean sports in the American Expeditionary Forces. You have gone at this athletic program and this game today with the same dash and spirit you showed on the fronts, and that is the spirit that makes America and Americans great."[44]

Alexander wasn't there to cheer at the championship game or enjoy the celebrations, banquets, and trophy presentations later in Germany. Only Major League baseball mattered to him now. "A man can't play baseball all his life and I wish I could get back in the game while I have the stuff in me," he had confided to correspondent Junius Wood in late February.

No, a man can't play ball all his life. He must make hay while the hay [*sic*] shines. The pitchers especially must do so. If the government is going to muster out the United States Army this summer I hope it will do so within the next few days so that I can go home and get time to get into shape this season. Our team starts training on March 16. All the other players here are in the same fix as I am. I talked with our colonel yesterday and he said that the rules were against applying for a discharge at this end. This ties our hands and any work to get us back must come from the other end. Possibly I can get home some time in May and then I will need a month's training before I can get into shape to go on the diamond. That means tough sledding, for nobody has time to bother much with late comers.[45]

New York World sportswriter Hugh Fullerton had commented two days before Christmas on what he called the Cubs' "unwise move . . . in sending a representative of the club to Washington to try to use a little persuasion and perhaps pull to get Grover Cleveland Alexander released from service." The army sought to avoid any appearance of favoritism, Fullerton had added, "and a howl might go up if Alex was allowed to return and other less favored privates retained."[46] The Cubs had then quickly denied they would seek special treatment for anyone in the armed forces, even Alexander. "The club let it be known that not only had it made no move to get Alexander out," one newspaper had reported the day after Christmas, "but that it disapproved of any such propaganda on the ground that the major leagues already had suffered too much criticism in matters relating to the army, and that it could ill afford to take any chances now."[47]

Speculation about Alexander's return had grown as the weather warmed. A *Chicago Tribune* correspondent reported March 5 from Kyllburg that the right-hander would leave Germany within twenty-four hours. "That's the best news I've heard all winter," Fred Mitchell exclaimed. "I'll admit I was getting worried for I hadn't heard anything from him for a long time and then only indirectly through Mrs. Alexander. . . . Everything looks fine for the Cubs now."[48] Chicago held its collective breath when no other news followed.

Sportswriter Grantland Rice was back in mufti after his own artillery service. "Alexander can be counted upon in normal times for thirty victories. But to-day he is still gazing moodily across the Rhine, toying with a caisson or rubbing down a wheel," Rice wrote in the *New York Tribune*. "Now Alexander may get back by May. Then again he may not return before June or July."[49] Fred Lieb of the *New York Sun* was more optimistic: "Perhaps the Giants would just as soon have seen 'Aleck' drinking Rhine water all summer, but the great Grover will be back in America long before May 15."[50] That was the date by which Major League clubs had to pare down their rosters to twenty-one players.

Unknown to the scribes, Alexander already had started for home. The 342nd FA received a telegram via the brigade from AEF General Headquarters at Chaumont, France, in late February, "stating that request for discharge of G. C. Alexander has been received. Asking if he desires discharge and can be spared from service."[51] He did and he could. Colonel Biscoe replied to the brigade February 28, recommending the sergeant's discharge.

The news took time to reach Chicago. It arrived on March 18 in a brief cablegram from General Pershing to manager Mitchell: "Alexander has left station en route to United States."[52] Sportswriter I. E. Sanborn wrote in the *Chicago Tribune* that when the message arrived, "All gloom disappeared from Cub headquarters. . . . Cub officials were delighted, because at worst it is believed Alexander will be here in time to join the Cubs during the spring training trip."[53] It didn't matter that Pershing offered no specifics about Alexander's arrival. "He may have departed from the main depot of the H. H. and C.—Ham, Hocks and Cabbage—at Coblenz, or it might be he has sailed from Brest," an Iowa newspaper happily noted. "It is enough to know that Alex is on the way with his freckled smile, his war medals and his fast one to thrill the inmates on one-day stands along the spring exhibition circuit."[54]

Alexander headed for home before any other Major Leaguer in the Army of Occupation. Even Color Sergeant Hank Gowdy, Organized Baseball's most popular war hero, wouldn't reach America until nearly two weeks after the Nebraskan. Despite the Cubs' earlier denial, Alexander later wrote that he had no doubt his release was due to "Mr. Wrigley's influence."[55] Announcement of his departure by Pershing himself confirms that strings had been pulled at the highest levels of the U.S. Army.

"Hereabouts we are all hoping he will have the opportunity of stopping off for a short visit," the *St. Paul Phonograph* told Alexander's neighbors in Nebraska, "as he wends his way westward, to Pasadena California, where his team mates are already hard at work fitting themselves for the big work that is before them."[56]

SEVENTEEN

Safe at Home

It's sweet enough to dream and hear the lonely night wind calling.
With ghosts of voices blown across the weary miles between;
To hear them whisper back to you, as soft as rose leaves falling,
Of life where summer days were long and summer fields were green.

—LT. GRANTLAND RICE

Sgt. Pete Alexander faced a long trip home to Nebraska. Along the way he probably heard and perhaps sang a haunting, bittersweet song popular among British and American troops. "There's a long, long trail a-winding / Into the land of my dreams, / Where the nightingales are singing / And a white moon beams."[1]

Traveling as a casual slowed his progress, but Alexander had lots of companions. He reached the First Replacement Depot at St. Aignan, France, about the same time that news of his return reached Chicago. At the depot he turned in his jerkin, pistol, and holster and reported to Casual Company 2950. Another casual in the company was much-decorated Sgt. Sam Dreben, a Jewish immigrant and well-known soldier of fortune from Ukraine. General Pershing called Dreben "the finest soldier and one of the bravest men I ever knew."[2]

Alexander played a little ball at St. Aignan for the first time since Camp de Souge. "The $15,000 pitching star toed the slab for five innings for the team from the Prisoners of War Enclosure against the Medical Labor Corps' nine and struck out seven and allowed but two hits, his team winning 4 to 1," *Stars and Stripes* reported. "Ten thousand soldier fans saw the game."[3] The box score indicates that Sgt. Mike Menosky, a Washington Senators outfielder, played first base and hit a triple. Alexander recalled the game years later while chatting with another veteran. "Alex talked of some games played . . . between a prison camp and a casualty camp and he pitched three or four innings for the prison camp—not that he was an 'active' member of the latter outfit."[4]

The next stop for the eighty-six doughboys in the casual company was a camp in Le Havre on the English Channel. The army issued the returnees special clothing for the voyage home. "In the Embarkation Instructions they are described as 'suits of blue denim clothing,' and to even the unknowing this is just a nice way of saying overalls. . . . The idea is to protect soldiers' uniforms during the voyage, so that when they land they will not look as if they had just come out of a delousing shop," *Stars and Stripes* reported.[5] On Friday, April 4, Alexander, Menosky, and other casuals boarded the second-class French liner s s *Rochambeau*, newly back from a week in drydock.

Lt. Joe Jenkins, a backup catcher for the White Sox, went on board too. Jenkins had earned a field commission while fighting with the Thirty-Third Division. Menoksy had served at American Expeditionary Forces General Headquarters at Chaumont; he acknowledged that manager Clark Griffith had pulled strings to send him on his way home. "Griff cabled me to hurry up and get my release, as I was needed in the line-up," he said. "With that cablegram in my hand it was comparatively easy to get my orders to leave for Havre." The three ballplayers got together once aboard the ship. "Needless to say, they spent considerable time together after that."[6]

Around 1,300 passengers crowded on board *Rochambeau*. They included civilians, war workers, doughboys, French and Belgian soldiers headed for a Victory Loan tour in the United States, and ten Belgian war dogs famous for hauling machine guns across battlefields.[7] Alexander may have felt he was in a seagoing kennel himself once the ship left port. "Aleck the Great came back as a casual bunking down in the stuffy hold with his bunkies of the A. E. F., and his presence was unknown to most of the civilians on board," the *Chicago Tribune* reported. The liner crossed the Atlantic in ten days, reaching Hoboken on Monday, April 14. "Grover Cleveland Alexander, premier pitcher for the Chicago Cubs, arrived here tonight . . . looking fit to pitch the Cubs through anything," the *Tribune* added. No longer wearing denim, he stepped onto the deck looking sharp in his olive-drab sergeant's uniform, overcoat, and overseas cap. Hundreds of doughboys who recognized the right-hander sent up a whoop. "There goes the National league pennant for the Cubs," a private yelled.[8] Reporters clustered around for questions and photographs.

"There was no opportunity abroad to get up a game, for the weather was bad, mostly rain all the time, and so I have had but little practice, except games of catch," Alexander said somewhat inaccurately. "I feel in fine shape, and, after I see my mother, there is a contract awaiting me to sign in Chicago with the Cubs."[9]

The pitcher sounded optimistic about the coming season. "My object now is to win thirty games for the Cubs and get Chicago into the next world's series," he said. "I do not think my absence from the game will hurt my pitching, for I kept myself in good shape by light work abroad."[10] Alexander knew he wouldn't be ready in time for the Cubs' opening day. "Give me seven more days, however, and I'll be in shape," he promised. "I'll be pitching real ball by May 1."[11] Someone asked whether his arm had been endangered during the war. "Not in the least, although the command I was with was on the St. Mihiel front for seven weeks at a stretch," he said.[12] Photographers snapped photos to rush onto the news wires for newspapers across the country.

The liner had arrived too late for the army to process Alexander's discharge paperwork that day. A colonel gave him a twenty-four-hour pass instead. That was fine with the hurler. "It won't make me mad at all," he said.[13] Leaving the ship, he called out to the doughboys: "So long, boys, I'll see you in Chicago."[14] Charles Wrigley stood on the pier waiting to greet his returning star. Aimee had planned to be there too but had been delayed traveling from Kentucky. "Wrigley was at one of his warehouses, half a mile from where we landed," Alexander explained. "He was watching with a field glass trying to spot me on the boat. With all those thousands wearing the same uniform he didn't have a chance, of course. But one of the hands there asked Wrigley if he could see me. 'Sure; there he is,' Wrigley answered. Then he dashed over to the wharf and took care of us after that."[15]

The following day was hectic. Sgt. G. C. Alexander, serial number 2845730, turned in his canteen, haversack, eating utensils, shelter half, and other equipment and clothing. He had a physical exam, received dental treatment, and filled out army forms. His character was officially adjudged excellent, as it had been when he'd entered the army at Camp Funston. The sergeant was entitled to wear a war service chevron on his lower left sleeve; he had suffered no overt injury, so he wore no wound chevron on the opposite sleeve. It probably was late in the afternoon before Alexander received his honorable discharge. He left New York by train the next day with Aimee and Wrigley.

"It is expected that all Grover will have to do on his arrival at the Cub office is to sign his contract, unless he has already signed. Mr. Wrigley is supposed to have taken the paper with him," the *Tribune* reported. "The Cub official wired to Vice President William Veeck that Alexander is in fine shape. After a short stay here Alexander will go to St. Paul, Neb., to visit his mother, and then return here to join the team."[16]

Alexander, Aimee, and Wrigley reached the Windy City at 9:40 a.m. on Thursday. "It looked as if Chicago were preparing to entertain a new president when the Twentieth Century Limited rolled into the La Salle street station," sportswriter John Alcock wrote. "There was a big battery of camera men—movie and still variety. There was a great gathering of reporters. And there were commoners galore too many to count. . . . Aleck's head was not turned by this demonstration. It was only a repetition of what they gave him in New York."[17]

Three hundred fans greeted the train. Speaking with waiting journalists, Alexander again gave himself a bit of time to get ready for baseball. "I am in good shape right now; in fact, never was better at this time of the season," he said, "and I think I can be ready for regular work within ten days from the start of the season."[18] He and Aimee then left to check into the Sherman Hotel. Columnist Ring Lardner recorded his supposed reply to Alcock after the couple's arrival: "'Do you know Alexander the Great?' So I said 'Yes I did know him before he died.' So he said 'Oh, no, this bird is not dead because Mr. Wrigley just brought him back from N. Y. city.'"[19]

Alexander and Aimee set out by rail again that night. They traveled six hundred miles to reach St. Paul on Friday. "Grover and his bride received the congratulations of their many friends upon their happy marriage . . . and he departed for France about three weeks later, so they are spending their honeymoon now," the *Phonograph* reported. The newspaper was strangely formal, calling the town's favorite son Dode only three times in a long article. Aside from mentioning the German shell that hadn't exploded, Alexander shared little about his seven weeks in combat. "He says conditions were all right, as good as could be expected, and here is one man who did not expect the government to perform the impossible. . . . After the war was over the work became irksome, and much dissatisfaction resulted, as all the boys wanted to come home. . . . He tells us the Germans treated the American soldiers better than did the French, and between the Germans and the English he would take the Germans every time."[20]

Dode wasn't the relaxed discharged soldier he appeared to be. His drinking would increase. Although he said he had never been sick in the army, he had been treated for a stomach condition at Camp Funston and in France. His epilepsy would continue, hidden from public view. And effects of combat jangled his nerves and his psyche, as they did for many ex-soldiers.

Many biographers and historians have written that Alexander suffered from shell shock, which today is known as post-traumatic stress disorder, or PTSD. He didn't say so himself, but it helps to explain his later self-medication and hard drinking. British doctors had coined the term in 1915, believing the symptoms resulted from the concussive force of exploding shells. "But by 1916," *Smithsonian* explains, "military and medical authorities were convinced that many soldiers exhibiting the characteristic symptoms—trembling 'rather like a jelly shaking'; headache; tinnitus, or ringing in the ear; dizziness; poor concentration; confusion; loss of memory; and disorders of sleep—had been nowhere near exploding shells."[21] Rather, shell shock resulted from psyche-rending sights and sounds experienced on a battlefield.

The condition during Alexander's era often was wrongly associated with cowardice or moral failing. Sportswriter Hugh Fullerton wrote about the "yellowness" of a former Major Leaguer who had been sent home from France suffering with shell shock.[22] Such attitudes added to the mental weight borne by returning soldiers. A junior officer from the 342nd Field Artillery would die in 1921, perhaps by his own hand, as "the result of a nervous breakdown, due to severe shell shock during the war which had since greatly impaired his health."[23] It's difficult to say definitely today that Alexander also suffered from shell shock, but clearly he had emerged from the army a troubled and damaged man.

He and Aimee stayed only the weekend in St. Paul before returning to the brighter lights of Chicago. They arrived on a Tuesday afternoon. "A little bit of the Argonne forest was transferred right to the loop in Chicago last night at dinner, when Lieut. Joe Jenkins happened to be seated at the next table to Sergeant Grover Cleveland Alexander," the *Tribune* reported the next day. "Both had chased the boche through that historic wood in France."[24] Jenkins left that same night for St. Louis and the White Sox's opener versus the Browns.

The Cubs' home opener was scheduled for Wednesday afternoon, April 23, versus the Pittsburgh Pirates. Alexander expected to throw out the first ball to Bill Killefer, now also out of the army; the game's postponement due to rain surely didn't surprise a veteran of France. "Alexander was at the north side for the morning skull practice," *Tribune* sportswriter Jim Crusinberry wrote. "If it had been a bright, warm morning he intended to put on a ball suit and take his first workout. As it was, he joined a game of pinochle with Fred Merkle, Dode Paskert, and Pete Kilduff. Pinochle was a favorite game with the soldiers, and Aleck has some new stuff to spring on his baseball mates."[25]

The next day was clear but so frigid that "expectations for a huge crowd to greet the National league champs and the Pirates went glimmering."[26] Alexander and Cubs pitcher James "Hippo" Vaughn each signed a 1919 contract before the game. Vaughn was starting the season for Chicago versus fellow left-hander Wilbur Cooper for Pittsburgh. The club cut back on the opening ceremonies because of the unusual cold, but Cubs players who had served in the armed forces carried Old Glory out to the flagpole. Crusinberry described the scene that followed: "The flag was raised and the procession marched back to the diamond. Grover Cleveland Alexander immediately went to the rubber and warmed up, then pitched the first ball without half the crowd knowing who it was. Those who did see him hurl that first ball thought he did it in such stylish form that he will be on the rubber for a regular battle in a few days. Aleck himself says he thinks he can pitch a game in two weeks. Maybe he can if the weather will warm up." Bundled in coats and blankets, Cubs fans cheered as Chicago put on "such a hot rally in the second inning that they knocked the Pittsburgh Pirates flat, 5 to 1, and made everybody forget the Christmas breeze off the lake."[27]

More than two weeks passed before Alexander was ready to take the mound in a game. Fans in Cincinnati meanwhile saw him coaching at third base on May 4, while manager Mitchell "sat on the bench in a close study of the enemy."[28] While preparing for his debut, Alexander rubbed shoulders with Abraham Lincoln "Sweetbread" Bailey, a rangy Cubs rookie from Joliet. Bailey, too, had served in France with an artillery regiment, but he hadn't seen combat. According to articles published earlier in Chicago, he twice had defeated Alexander in army games overseas. Alex the Great set the record straight. "My team never lost a game," he said. "I didn't see Bailey over there. I know we weren't beaten. . . . I might have met Bailey over there and not known it."[29]

Alexander finally stepped onto the mound May 9 at home versus the Reds. He lost a 1–0 heartbreaker to right-hander Ray Fisher, back from stateside army service. "Alex was right, all right, but Fisher was righter," one account stated.[30] "The big fellow wasn't quite up to his old time standard, but seemed to lack nothing except control," Crusinberry agreed. "He walked five batsmen, and it was one of those walks that was turned into the lone tally. He seemed to have the old curve ball working, and about 90 per cent of his old time speed. Another week of training and the great slab star should be right back in his form of ball and preceding years."[31] A United Press sportswriter added, "The Cub fans are not disappointed. Alex remains Alex the Great."[32]

The loss began a winless streak for Alexander. "When he came down the gangplank in the Spring of 1919, he was thinner, weary, looking about the same. But he wasn't the same," sportswriter Jack Sher wrote decades later.[33] To make matters worse, a thief relieved Aimee of rings and jewelry worth $8,000 during a road trip to Pittsburgh. "That's a swell reception for a returned hero," Philadelphia sports editor Robert Maxwell grumbled.[34] Grantland Rice observed the pitcher's slow start from New York. "When Grover Cleveland Alexander reached the middle of May without having turned in a victory, his chance of reaching the thirty-victory [mark] this abbreviated record season had practically vanished," Rice wrote. "Thus explodeth another record unless the ex-cannoneer has more ammunition at hand than he has ever had before."[35]

The Phillies showered Alexander with gifts on his return to Philadelphia, then walloped the Cubs, 7–2. "The big boy had speed and his control was so perfect that his pitches cut the heart of the platter," Maxwell wrote. "These were ideal for clouting purposes and the home-town boys surely soaked the pill."[36] By the end of the month Alexander was 0–4 in five starts, with a four-out save in relief against the Dodgers. The drought ended June 2 in Chicago. "After five unsuccessful attempts," I. E. Sanborn wrote in the *Tribune*, "Sergt. Alexander went over the top into the 'won' column yesterday by licking the Pirates, 7 to 0, in the first game of a double header. . . . For the first time this season Alex had perfect control and did not issue a pass, usually having the batsman in the hole."[37]

Alexander struggled to sixteen victories and eleven losses in 1919. While acceptable for most Major League pitchers, the record was substandard for Alexander the Great, who nonetheless posted the league-leading ERA (1.72). Ol' Pete's explanation for his poor season applied as well to many other ex-serviceman pitchers.

"Army life did a lot for me physically. I never felt better in my life. But it undoubtedly held me back in pitching," he said. "One has got to keep his hand in all the time to retain his form, and I had mighty little opportunity to do much real pitching in the army." Brooklyn southpaw Sherry Smith had been in France, too, and agreed with Alexander. "You're right, Aleck," he said. "If you are going to play good baseball you have got to play baseball all the time. I came out of the army feeling like a two-year-old, but it took me half the summer to make the old ball behave rightly."[38]

EIGHTEEN

Postwar

You've sent along your orders through the shadow and the rain,
And the guns have barked their message to the Hun across the plain,
But the echo's hardly settled to a breath of a refrain
Till you wonder how they are back home.

—LT. GRANTLAND RICE

N o ballplayer who had served with the 342nd Field Artillery overseas had an outstanding 1919 season. The veterans needed time to settle into peacetime routines, if they managed it at all. The Dodgers began the year awaiting the return of Clarence Mitchell, although they weren't much interested in having him pitch. The club had traded Jake Daubert over the winter and needed Mitchell at first base.

"Mitchell is a natural first baseman," shortstop Ivan "Ivy" Olson gushed. "He plays the bag as if he were born there. If he hadn't got that fool notion in his head that he was a great pitcher he would be known as one of the greatest first sackers of the game."[1]

The spitballing sergeant sailed from Marseilles on April 22 in a casual company on the Italian liner ss *Caserta*. He reached New York on May 8, received his discharge at Camp Mills, and reported to manager Wilbert Robinson a week after landing. Mitchell upset Olson's prognostication, not appearing once as a Dodgers infielder. "He was on the Brooklyn payroll as utility first baseman and pinch hitter when a shortage caused him to be used as an emergency pitcher," Tom Rice of the *Brooklyn Eagle* explained. "He technically won two games in which he went to the rescue."[2]

Mitchell finished the shortened season with a 7-5 record. While mediocre, the former artilleryman was better overall than the Dodgers, who ended at 69-71 in fifth place in the National League. He was good at the plate, pinch hitting eleven times while posting a .367 batting average. After the season the Major Leagues banned his specialty pitch, the spitball, but Mitchell and other practitioners were allowed to continue tossing the wet one until they retired.

Brooklyn captured the pennant the next year and met Cleveland in the 1920 World Series. During Game Five Mitchell hit a liner to Bill Wambsganss, who made an unassisted triple play. Later in his career the hurler played with Alexander on the St. Louis Cardinals in 1928–29, and he pitched in the Major Leagues into 1932. Mitchell returned to the Minor Leagues (1934–37) and ran for sheriff of Franklin County, Nebraska, in 1934 while pitching for the Mission Reds in the Pacific Coast League. He campaigned by postcard—"No scores for crime with MITCHELL in the sheriff's box"—and finished fifth in a six-person race.[3]

The southpaw retired after a final Minor League appearance in 1942, during World War II, having pitched in over 1,300 games. The reason for his longevity seemed simple: "You never heard of a spitballer with a sore arm," Mitchell said.[4] He later operated a tavern in Aurora, Nebraska.

Chuck Ward had hoped to return to America with Mitchell. The Dodgers were eager to have him back. Ward had written in late February 1918 that the Major Leaguers in the 342nd Field Artillery expected to be on their way within a month and to be discharged by May 1. "It was the report among the ball players that all of them who could show employment awaited them would get special action on their requests for discharge."[5] Ward and Lambeth had requested permission to leave

Germany ahead of their division. They didn't get it. Nor were Noyes or Wetzel permitted to leave early for home. All four remained with the regiment along with their football-champion comrades.

The 342nd Field Artillery sailed from Brest on May 18 on the former German liner ss *Prinz Friedrich Wilhelm*. The ship reached Hoboken on May 27. After processing at Camp Upton, the artillerymen entrained for the Midwest, paraded in St. Louis, and stepped down June 8 back at Camp Funston. "The detachments were then discharged one by one and by the evening of June 11, 1919, all members of the 342nd Field Artillery had been discharged and were homeward bound."[6]

Ward returned to the Dodgers in July. "It is Manager Robinson's intention to inject Chuck at third base at once, for that seems the weakest point in the Dodgers' defense," *The Sporting News* reported.[7] Ward played in forty-five games at third base, posting a .233 batting average and a .920 fielding percentage.

He continued with Brooklyn into 1922, followed by two seasons in the Minor Leagues. Rutgers University appointed him head baseball coach in 1938. Ward served for twelve seasons and later scouted for Philadelphia and Cincinnati. He secured future Hall of Fame pitcher Robin Roberts for the Phillies by buying him two steaks for dinner.

Otis Lambeth returned to the Indians in 1919 only to be sent down to the Columbus Senators in the American Association. "It may be that Lambeth, because of his war experience, has sustained an injury of some sort, or perhaps the Indians could not wait for him to get into condition," a wire service speculated.[8] The *Iola Register* offered a bitter interpretation: "He has been 'bumped' out of the big league, given way to some shipyard working ball player or exempted man who played ball while he took part in several engagements in France."[9] But a paper in Topeka, where Lambeth had been a popular Minor Leaguer, probably had the right explanation: "Lambeth's late arrival from France found Cleveland well supplied with pitchers and the club is forced by the player limit to reduce to twenty-five men."[10]

Lambeth never again pitched in the Major Leagues.[11] He spent two losing seasons in the Minors before leaving baseball altogether.

Later he worked as an undersheriff, postmaster, and rural mail carrier in Kansas, "known to virtually every person who has lived in Allen county for any length of time."[12]

Win Noyes returned to a dreadful Athletics team. A headline in Philadelphia proclaimed: "Looks As If the Only Win Connie Mack Can Get in the American League Is Win Noyes."[13] He first pitched August 8 in the second game of a doubleheader at home, in relief during a 6–2 loss to the league-leading White Sox. Philadelphia fans were glad to see him. "Only redeeming feature of the afterpiece was the return of Winnie Noyes to A. L. box scores."[14]

The pitcher's scoreless debut was the highlight of his season. The 1919 Mackmen finished in last place in the American League with a 41-99 record. Noyes was 1-5 when Chicago picked him up off waivers in late September. He pitched one game for the White Sox without a result and wasn't eligible for the tainted 1919 World Series. Chicago marked the last stop in his professional baseball career. As with Lambeth, the war had robbed Noyes of at least one season and perhaps more. He became a druggist, pitched for semipro and independent teams, and later operated a drugstore for many years in Washington state.

Dutch Wetzel played what remained of the 1919 season with the Flint Halligans in the Class B Michigan-Ontario League. He reached the Major Leagues the following year and played sixty-eight games for the St. Louis Browns in 1920–21. He then returned to his long career in the Minors as a player, player-manager, and owner. Dutch later worked as an electrician for a Hollywood movie studio with several other former Major Leaguers.

None of the 342nd Field Artillery football stars attempted a return to their sport. All ended their playing days with the American Expeditionary Forces championship in Paris; indeed, army service had extended their time on the gridiron beyond the usual university years. Degrees and commissions were advantageous in peacetime. The former officers resumed their postwar careers more easily and successfully than the ballplayers they had once commanded.

Potsy Clark went back to coaching as an assistant under Bob Zup-pke at Illinois. In late January 1920 Alexander kept his battlefield prom-ise to help his old lieutenant whip the university baseball team into shape if they both survived the war. "Little more was thought of the matter until one day about three weeks ago, when Clark and Alexander met in the lobby of a local [Chicago] hotel," a wire service reported. "Clark reminded Alex of his promise and the big pitcher said he would make good."[15] The Cubs' star duly arrived at the Urbana campus and began working with the Illini pitchers, "showing his pupils just how he does it."[16] He stayed more than a week before heading to his own spring training in California.

Clark later was head football coach at Kansas (1921–25). He jumped to the National Football League in 1931 to coach the Portsmouth Spartans, who in 1934 moved north and became the Detroit Lions. In 1937–39 Clark coached the National Football League's Brooklyn Dodgers before returning to the Lions for a season. He then coached at the University of Grand Rapids in 1941 with future president Ger-ald Ford as his line coach. Clark returned to the armed forces during World War II and coached a navy team at Pensacola, Florida. "Lieut. Comdr. George Clark is one of the most popular officers on the post," columnist John Kieran wrote. "Well, why not? He's the fellow who invites them out to play games, isn't he?"[17] After the war Potsy was athletic director for the University of Nebraska, and he later became a stockbroker in California.

Ad Lindsey likewise returned to coaching. His University of Kan-sas baseball team won the Missouri Valley Conference title in 1920. The following year Lindsey was the freshman football coach under Clark. The old army comrades hosted a reunion of the Eighty-Ninth Division championship team at a Kansas game that autumn. Lindsey became head football coach at the University of Oklahoma (1927–31), and he returned to Kansas as head coach (1932–38).

Lindsey had retained his reserve commission following the war. He, too, returned to active duty during World War II, serving with the Ninety-Sixth Division during hard fighting in the Philippines. "It's just like football," Lieutenant Colonel Lindsey said of his job as chief of intelligence. "You have to figure what the opposition is capable of doing. If you guess or deduce right you're a hero. If you're wrong, you better start looking for another job."[18] He saw Japan as a full colonel following the surrender. After the war Lindsey managed a family lumber business in Kansas. Fittingly, when he retired from the army, he commanded the Eighty-Ninth Reserve Division from Colorado, Kansas, and Nebraska.

Paul Withington, the division athletic director and football coach, rose to major and briefly remained in Europe following the armistice. During the summer of 1919 he switched sports to coach and compete in rowing. "He himself stroked the American four and sculled in Inter-Allied and Henley races, also in the Marlow regatta in France."[19] Withington was assistant football coach at Columbia University in 1923 under Percy Haughton, then became head coach following Haughton's death the next year.

Withington later returned to Hawaii to practice medicine in Honolulu. Like Clark and Lindsey, he returned to active duty during World War II. He switched to the navy medical corps and rose to captain, the naval equivalent of colonel. Withington flew over two hundred thousand miles around the Pacific during sixty-one months' service.

Unlike his former teammates, Jick Fast didn't pursue a sports career. Soon after his discharge he returned briefly to Lawrence, scene of his University of Kansas football exploits. "Fast lacked seventeen hours of being able to graduate from the School of Engineering at the University at the time he enlisted and is here to see if he can get his degree for war work."[20] In May 1920 he entered a Kansas City hospital; a newspaper in his hometown of Hutchinson later reported that he was "recovering from his injuries received while overseas in France."[21]

Fast isn't listed in the various histories as having been wounded, but his registration card for older men during World War II noted a spine bone graft. Fast was able to work, however, and rose to the position of chief draftsman for a Kansas City steel company.

Pete Alexander had the toughest reentry to civilian life. The introduction of Prohibition in January 1920 didn't slow his heavy drinking; a famous ballplayer always got served in big-city speakeasys. "After he came back he would get a bottle and drink it up, afraid that somebody else would get to it first," Aimee said later. "He never used to drink that way."[22]

America was only beginning to understand how many of its veterans were struggling to cope. The armed forces had treated seventy-six thousand troops for shell shock. By the end of the year more than 12,000 discharged soldiers, sailors, and marines still would be receiving treatment, nearly 5,600 in hospitals run by the U.S. Public Health Service, a forerunner to the Veterans Administration.[23] An army lieutenant colonel suffering from shell shock would write that although he was back in his own country, among friends and scenes he loved, he felt he was "not back at all." He would decry what he saw as "the quick abandonment of interest in our overseas men by Americans in general. . . . This fact burns in the minds of the thousands of men who at this very moment are living their broken lives in almshouses, jails, insane asylums, and hospitals, or wandering, hopeless, about the streets."[24]

Alexander's performance on the baseball diamond, however, was remarkably good in 1920. He led the National League with twenty-seven wins while posting the best ERA in the Major Leagues, 1.91. But Alexander never again posted thirty wins in a single year, and he remained tied with Christy Mathewson with three consecutive thirty-win seasons. "The Great War put an end to my day dreaming of various records," he said.[25]

Former star second baseman Johnny Evers took over as Cubs manager in 1921. The club fired Evers that August, when the team dropped fourteen games below .500, and named Bill Killefer player-manager. Alexander's pal steered the Cubs until July 1925, when he, too, was fired. Alexander remained with the club only into the following summer. Joe McCarthy, named manager in 1926, soon got fed up with the pitcher's drinking and rule breaking. The Cubs put Alexander on waivers in June after eight-plus years in Chicago. Folks in his hometown got the bad news on the front page of the newspaper.

"Time and drink has taken its toll of the Great Grover Alexander of Nebraska, and today he is nearing the end of his baseball career," the *St. Paul Photograph* reported, in an article picked up from an Omaha paper. The weekly added a postscript: "The idol of the St. Paul fans, the great man of the county, it is indeed too bad that such a condition should arise, when his friends hereabouts were looking forward this year to a good baseball season for the veteran."[26]

Killefer had meanwhile landed in St. Louis as a Cardinals coach and player-manager Rogers Hornsby's right-hand man. Reindeer Bill spoke up now for his old pal: "They say Pete is through. He's not, Rog. As long as he can stand on his feet, he's still the pitcher I'd want out there if we were in a rough spot."[27] Hornsby listened and claimed Alexander off waivers. Shrugging off his early-season 3-3 record with Chicago, the pitcher went 9-7 for St. Louis and helped the Cardinals into the postseason. Having arrived in disgrace, Alexander found brief redemption during the season's final innings.

"The 1926 World Series, pitting the Cardinals against a powerful Yankee team featuring veteran bombers Babe Ruth and Bob Meusel and young guns Lou Gehrig and Tony Lazzeri, cast the Alexander legend in stone," writes baseball historian Jan Finkel.[28] Alexander won Games Two and Six and was sitting in the bullpen at Yankee Stadium for Game Seven, believing his season over. The Cardinals led 3–2 in the seventh inning as the Yankees loaded the bases with two men out and New York's sensational rookie second baseman Lazzeri coming to the plate. Like Alexander, Lazzeri suffered from epilepsy, which he kept secret during his playing days.

With starter Jesse Haines faltering, Hornsby called for a reliever to face "Poosh 'Em Up." Alexander was nearly forty years old and had thrown a complete game a day earlier. "There was a breathless pause, and then around the corner of the stand came a tall figure in a Cardinal sweater," the *New York Times* reported. "His cap rode rakishly on the corner of his head. He walked like a man who was going nowhere in particular and was in no hurry to get there."[29]

"They say I stopped to pick daisies on my way in," Alexander said over two decades later. "I didn't but what the hell did they want me to do—run in? I'd a been all out of breath." He saw Lazzeri anxiously knock dirt from his spikes. "So I thought to myself I'll give him plenty of time to worry."[30] With the count at 1-1, the rookie smacked the third pitch down the left-field line. The ball landed well beyond the fence but barely foul. Lazzeri then swung and missed at Alexander's fourth offering to strike out and end the threat. The aging gunner pitched two more scoreless innings to deliver the championship to St. Louis. Writers and fans could hardly fathom what they had witnessed.

"There you see the man who gave us today the greatest pitching feat baseball has furnished since Christy Mathewson shut out the Athletics three times in a row" in 1905, said Giants manager John McGraw.[31] "That is one they will reconstruct and retell down the ages in the spirit of the ancient Roman epic of Horatius at the Bridge," sports editor Harry Grayson wrote seventeen years later.[32] Hollywood even used Lazzeri's strikeout as the climactic scene of *The Winning Team*, a 1952 movie starring Ronald Reagan as Alexander and Doris Day as Aimee.

A narrative soon developed that the Nebraskan had been either drunk or badly hung over when called into the game. Participants in the game both affirmed and dismissed the notion over the following decades. Alexander himself always insisted he had been sober; Aimee continued declaring it decades after his death. "Alexander was expected to be effective, but no one had any reason to expect such remarkable pitching from this 39-year-old veteran. . . . But all glory to Aleck the Great," sportswriter Fred Lieb wrote after the game. "He pitched with heart and head, and the National League does well to venerate him."[33]

The *St. Paul Phonograph* welcomed the prodigal son home after the series and especially praised Aimee, "that good woman who has been with the big boy all the time cheering him on by her presence and words of love and encouragement . . . who worked so heroically behind the scenes to have our old friend and associate of many years accomplish that which no man believed him capable."[34]

Twenty thousand people—twelve times St. Paul's population—converged on the town on October 27 for a celebration and ballgame in which Alexander pitched a few innings. Some people drove two or three hundred miles to be there. The *Phonograph* reported suspiciously little of what Alexander did or said, but published a letter from a Howard County pioneer recalling the pitcher's late father. The *Phonograph* obliquely reported the occasion more accurately more than a quarter-century later: "Alex returned to St. Paul after the series and a tremendous welcome was arranged for him; however, he didn't quite measure up to the occasion."[35]

Alexander kept pitching for the Cardinals during the postwar years while fighting his private battles. A British expert had spoken of one effect of shell shock only days before the war's end: "There was an infantry captain with a brave record in the trenches who came to London to recover from shellshock and would never ride in the subway because the sound of the train with its trailing vacuum reminded him of the sound of big shells coming through the air."[36] Pitcher Bill Hallahan, a St. Louis teammate, saw a similar incident with Alexander.

During one spring training game kids began setting off fireworks in the grandstand, Hallahan said, causing ballplayers on the bench to jump. Alexander never budged. "He just sat there stiff as a board, teeth clenched, fist doubled over so tight his knuckles were white, staring off into space like he was hypnotized," Hallahan recalled. "When finally somebody came and chased the kids off and the noise stopped, he turned and looked at me with a sad little smile."[37]

Ol' Pete was still with the Cardinals in 1929, but Aimee was no longer around. Weary of his drinking and the ups and downs of their marriage, she had filed for a divorce, which became final that October. "Few women probably ever loved a man or loathed his situation more than Aimee Arrants," St. Louis sports editor Bob Broeg wrote nearly fifty years later. Alexander kept pitching, often in relief. Broeg saw him as a boy while a member of the Knothole Gang at Sportsman's Park. As an adult he still vividly recalled watching the revered "old man" hurry down to the left-field corner, "unsmiling and with a too-small cap perched like a peanut shell atop his head. He would warm up hurriedly, throwing with a short, semi-side-armed delivery across his chest."[38]

Alexander tied the late Christy Mathewson's record for most National League victories at 372 in St. Louis that summer. "The veteran pitched a typical Alexander game, his greatest asset, control, being in evidence from start to finish," the New York Times reported. "No bases on balls, no wild pitches or hit batters marred his performance."[39] The beautiful August 1 game was a final gift from baseball's gods to an aging, alcoholic pitcher. Alexander broke Mathewson's record nine days later, in relief at Philadelphia. "It was Old Pete's 373d triumph as a Philly, a Cub and a Cardinal," the Times reported. "Alex entered the game in the eighth with the Phillies in the lead, but the Cards tied the score in the ninth and won with a two-run attack in the eleventh."[40]

Ten days later Alexander was again in deep trouble, "sent home from New York . . . by Bill McKechnie, Red Bird manager, after Alex disregarded the manager's warning that his next escapade would be his last."[41] St. Louis traded him away to Philadelphia that winter. Alexander never won another Major League game, going 0-3 in nine outings before the Phillies released him in June 1930. He was again front-page news back in St. Paul. "It is too bad to see 'Old Pete' turned loose after all these years in the front rank doing his bit for the team he was with," the Phonograph's editor wrote.[42] The Sporting News declared that not only had Alexander repeatedly disappointed fans, "he has disappointed his friends, and those who have tried to render him that kind of assistance which is good to a man who needs it, as Alexander does."[43]

The hurler took his release quietly. "I'm just going to sit tight here for a few days and see what turns up," he said. "I haven't a thing in view just at present; that is, no connections."[44] Wade Killefer, Bill's brother, said he'd like to have Ol' Pete on the San Francisco Missions team he managed. The Omaha police department thought it might have a place for him, too, and not in the drunk tank. "To secure Alex the police team would have him tendered a job pounding a beat so that their opponents could pound the air against Alexander's slants."[45] The pitcher instead signed with the Dallas Steers in the Texas League.

The experiment ended badly. Playing in five games before he got suspended for breaking training, Alexander was 1-2 with an ERA above 8.00. A deal to play for manager Casey Stengel's Toledo Mud Hens fell through because Alexander was too sick to take the field. He never played for another team in Organized Baseball. "I've got a bad reputation, and they're mighty hard to live down," Alexander admitted. If he should die on a floor from double pneumonia with eight doctors and nurses as witnesses, he said, everyone still would believe he had passed out from bad hooch. "But I'll tell you one thing," he added. "If I had my whole baseball life to live again I'd never drink a drop, that is, outside of a glass or two of good beer."[46]

A dozen years later his one-game edge over Christy Mathewson vanished. A researcher uncovered a mistake in the 1902 records, a loss that should have been credited as a win for Matty. League statistics were corrected to show Ol' Pete and Matty tied with 373 National League victories apiece. "The two righthanders, both victims of the war, would be forever linked in the record books," writes historian Finkel.[47]

NINETEEN

The Long, Long Trail

But I wonder if ever you miss the thrill
(Where memories hold their tryst)
Where a church spire looms from a distant hill
Or a field through the morning mist,
The thrill again of the swinging beat
As marching men go by,
The swinging beat of a million feet
Under a far June sky?

—GRANTLAND RICE, 1919

Pete Alexander began touring with the popular House of David team in 1931. The bearded ballplayers represented a Michigan religious sect and resembled Old Testament prophets in their baseball flannels. Alexander settled into a stable if nomadic life as they barnstormed around the country. He even reunited with Aimee, remarrying her that June. "They are 'very happy' he said and are enjoying life together," the Associated Press reported. "Alex said he had not taken a drink of liquor for a long time. He admitted he tried to quit several times before but it would not 'stick.'"[1]

Sobriety and stability didn't last. "And now in far-off places, / Beyond those phantom cheers, / Strange whiskers on strange faces, / A whiskered ghost appears," columnist John Kieran wrote in 1932.[2]

Alexander stayed with House of David teams for several years, then tumbled through a series of odd jobs, illnesses, hospitalizations, and occasional encounters with the police. "Maybe you passed him on a street in Pittsburgh one night," sportswriter Jack Sher later wrote. "Maybe you sat next to him in a bar in Denver, Springfield, or Cleveland."[3] For a while the Major Leagues put Alexander on a sort of stipend, under the care of a farmer in Nebraska.[4]

The *St. Paul Phonograph* reported in January 1936 that Alexander had left for a radio job in Louisville. "He is in good shape and ready to go to work at anything he may be asked to do. This is a good job and his many friends hope it will be a permanent position."[5] It wasn't. Late that summer Howard County residents read that the former pitcher had been hospitalized in Evansville, Indiana, after being found lying unconscious in a gutter. "Physicians said he suffered a severe brain concussion. Police have been unable to determine whether he fell or was slugged after an evening visiting local taverns."[6]

Plans were then under way to build the National Baseball Hall of Fame in Cooperstown, New York. Christy Mathewson and Walter Johnson were among the first inductees in 1936, with Cy Young chosen the following year. Alexander was elected to the third class in January 1938. By then Alexander was working as a greeter at a hotel in Springfield, Illinois. "It's swell. I certainly appreciate the honor," he said on hearing the news. "I want to thank the writers for selecting me and tell them all 'hello.' . . . Yes, I still yearn to pitch a few innings, but the old soupbone isn't what it used to be."[7]

Alexander said he would like to attend the Hall of Fame's dedication and baseball centennial in June 1939. He meanwhile left Illinois to work in a penny arcade and flea circus on West Forty-Second Street in New York City. There he spoke to customers who paid a dime admission about the Lazzeri strikeout and his seasons with the Phillies, Cubs, and Cardinals.

An anonymous benefactor probably helped Alexander get upstate to Cooperstown in time for the celebration. He stood between Honus Wagner and Tris Speaker for photos of ten of the eleven living members of the hall (Ty Cobb arrived too late to participate). The *New York Sun* labeled the group "baseball immortals."[8] During public introductions retired slugger Babe Ruth "received far and away the greatest ovation with Johnson and Old Pete Alexander running neck and neck for second honors."[9] The *New York Post* found the troubled Nebraskan standing "slim and erect" despite his recent stint at the flea circus. "Old Pete said life had kicked him around a bit, but that he had no regrets. A non-conformist, a rebel who took his fun where he found it, Pete is not one to whimper at the vicissitudes of fate."[10]

Cooperstown was Alexander's last meaningful interaction with Major League baseball for eleven years; the broken-down pitcher resumed his rocky path to nowhere. "They gave me a tablet up at the Cooperstown Hall of Fame, but I can't eat any tablet," he said later.[11] In November 1940 he sought treatment at a Veterans Administration hospital in the Bronx. A claim form listed five complaints: "Nervousness; ear condition; skin condition; stomach condition and rheumatism."[12] The first item might well indicate shell shock.

Current research sheds light on Alexander's struggles. The symptoms of a traumatic brain injury (TBI) overlap those of shell shock (PTSD). Studies suggest that both are risk factors for epilepsy and psychogenic nonepileptic seizures among veterans. Epilepsy is associated with abnormal electrical activity in the brain, while psychogenic nonepileptic seizures are caused by mental or emotional distress; it's possible to have both. "It has been hypothesized that seizures in the veteran population are linked to veterans' history of combat exposure and resulting increased frequencies of TBI and PTSD," a 2015 study states.[13]

These medical issues are relevant to Alexander's long downward spiral. The TBI in 1909; the epilepsy that began in France or earlier; the jumble of combat-related conditions and symptoms that aren't entirely understood even today; the unknown and unknowable details of his combat life in Battery F; hearing problems that worsened with age (not uncommon among artillerymen); and a growing dependence on alcohol—together they constitute a worrying and dangerous combination for anyone, let alone an athlete once at the top of his profession. The surprise wasn't that Alexander had declined, but that he had performed so well after the war.

The hospital in the Bronx readmitted him the following spring, nine months before America entered the century's second world war. "Now, broke, his health gone, his appeals to organized baseball for a coaching spot unanswered, Old Pete has hit bottom," a reporter wrote. "Pete served with the 342d Field Artillery in France during the war and was shell-shocked. Today he figured that the shell shock was more valuable than the fame which attended his best performances in baseball. Fame got him nothing. Shell shock got him a bed in a hospital ward and food."[14]

Doctors removed cancerous skin from Alexander's right earlobe, leaving a hole that led people mistakenly to believe that he had been wounded by shrapnel in 1918. "Never could hear much out of it, anyway, since those days when I was a gunner in France," he said with a laugh. "They used to tell you to stand on your tiptoes and hold your ears, but, hell, you haven't got time for that when you're up at the front."[15] Doctors would remove the ear entirely in 1947.

Alexander found work at a Cincinnati aircraft factory after America entered World War II. "At that time he wanted it known that his physical condition was such that he would welcome a new job in baseball, as a pitching coach or in some other capacity," the *New York Times* recalled.[16] No job offer arrived, nor did he keep the factory job long. In 1944 police in East St. Louis, Illinois, found Alexander wandering the streets in pajamas at two o'clock in the morning. The police took the old pitcher into protective custody until he could be "sent to a veterans' hospital to recuperate from a mental and physical breakdown."[17]

The awful cycle continued after the war. In May 1949 Alexander fell down the stairs of an Albuquerque hotel, fracturing a vertebra in his neck. He signed himself out of the hospital despite a doctor's warning that "another fall or slip could sever the spinal cord."[18] Christmas found him hospitalized again, at County General Hospital in Los Angeles, suffering from skin cancer that may have resulted from his long years pitching under summer suns.

"I'd like to get the chance to work with youngsters and help them get along in the game," Alexander said when released. "A kid has to start young and most of it depends on natural ability. But the right guidance helps. I think I could tell them in a hurry how to add to their ability."[19]

Alexander got that opportunity in the new year at home in Nebraska, working with an American Legion junior baseball program. He returned to live in St. Paul, which hosted a day in his honor. The May 24 event featured a parade, a baseball game between Boys Town and the St. Paul legion team, a banquet, and his commissioning as an admiral in the Nebraska Navy. "The day afforded an opportunity for the baseball hero to enjoy a reunion with two other buddies in World War I of the 89th division, Potsy Clark and Clarence Mitchell," the *Howard County Herald* reported.[20] Aimee was there too. They somehow had found their way back into friendship after their second divorce in 1941, although they never married a third time. "I feel more like a mother to him, with him a small boy," Aimee once said. "He listens to me more than to anyone else."[21]

Except for the company of his army buddies and the love of his life, the day proved disappointing. Few locals turned out. "Wednesday was Grover Cleveland Alexander Day in St. Paul, and everyone loved him but the people of his 'old home town,'" the *St. Paul Phonograph* acknowledged. "Remembering perhaps how he deserted them 14 [sic] years ago on a similar celebration, the people of St. Paul stayed away in droves."[22] Aimee later wrote bitterly to the editor about "fair weather friends." She added that Alexander was "a very sick man and it must have been a bitter pill to take and why he stayed there or went there in the first place to stay, is more than I can figure out."[23]

The American Legion job was a disappointment too. With Aimee living in Omaha, Alexander grew restless and unhappy in St. Paul. Then the Phillies captured the 1950 National League pennant for the first time in thirty-five years—since Alexander himself had pitched their only victory in the 1915 World Series. A Chicago radio program paid for the old right-hander and a young companion to fly to New

York City to watch the Whiz Kids play the Yankees for the championship. The pair stood unnoticed through two innings of Game Three before a Yankees executive spotted them. He took Alexander up to join the writers covering the series.

"One of baseball's immortals, Grover Cleveland Alexander, sat in an obscure corner of the Yankee Stadium press box Friday and watched his first World Series game in nearly 20 years," Will Grimsley of the Associated Press wrote. Alexander was in poor shape. "The aging mound master, once a robust 185 pounds, looked thin and drawn. A patch covered his right ear where a delicate operation was performed last winter."[24] The Phillies lost the game but Alexander considered it "the happiest day of my life."[25] He said he had never seen a game on television and was amazed by the size of the crowds. "Baseball may have forgotten Grover Cleveland Alexander but he has not forgotten baseball," the *New York Times* noted.[26] A *Brooklyn Eagle* reporter caught up with him afterward. "Now sitting in an East Side New York hotel, Alexander is just another good argument for the ball players' pension system. . . . 'It just shows what a difference 30 years makes,' Alexander said. 'I used to speak to everyone I knew. Now most people don't know me.'"[27]

Ol' Pete returned to Yankee Stadium the next day and saw the Yankees complete a sweep of the Phillies. At a victory party that night at the Biltmore Hotel, someone called him to the rostrum for a speech. Although looking ill, he delivered a "sharp and witty talk," the Associated Press reported. "Then he went back home. His young fellow townsman, Quentin Lynch, who arranged the trip, said later: 'This is the greatest thing that has ever happened to Pete. Back home he is just another fellow. Here they have made him a hero. He really is eating it up.'"[28]

Alexander went back to St. Paul to rest. "After the trip, fan letters and requests for pictures and autographs poured in to him here," the Associated Press reported. Lynch said the hurler had "started to live again."[29] But happiness was fleeting. Alexander lost his older brother Nick when the retired well driller died unexpectedly on October 14 while recuperating from pneumonia at a Grand Island rest home. Unlike childless Dode and Aimee, Nicholas Alexander, age seventy-six, left behind a son, three daughters, thirteen grandchildren, and seven great grandchildren. Dode was a pallbearer at his funeral.

The former pitcher wrote unhappy letters to Aimee. He thought himself a fool for returning to St. Paul, where he felt ignored and unappreciated. Getting a drink was difficult because bartenders often wouldn't serve him. "If there is another Hell in this world I don't want to ever get there. St. Paul is enough," he wrote with rare self-pity.[30]

Alexander made plans to leave, despite premonitions that he had little time to live. He delayed a planned visit to Aimee to wait for the arrival of a suit and overcoat he was expecting from an anonymous benefactor. He wrote to her on Saturday, November 4, shuffled downtown to mail the letter at the post office, then returned to his rented room in a private home. His landlady's son found Dode lying on the floor beside the bed in a pool of blood a little after noon. A doctor pronounced him dead of a heart attack.

"Death had been some hours earlier," the *Howard County Herald* reported. "It is presumed Alexander had attempted to arise from bed and fell when stricken. Some writing material was also found near his body, indicating he was preparing to write."[31] The United Press attributed his passing to his recent journey: "The strain of the trip by plane and the excitement of the final game which he watched from the press box at Yankee Stadium in New York, were too much for the gallant old campaigner."[32] Aimee believed he had fallen during a seizure, as he had numerous times before. She speculated later that Alexander had suffocated in his own blood from facial injuries.

News of Ol' Pete's death rocketed around the country. Writers again placed him among baseball's immortals. One paper recalled an "Alexander for President" banner in a St. Louis parade following the 1926 World Series.[33] Others recalled his past glories and mused lightly but forthrightly about his many recent problems.

"Grover Cleveland Alexander died the other day after a tragic life," *New York Times* columnist Arthur Daley wrote. "John Barleycorn,

invincible one, robbed him of health, wealth, happiness and everything else. . . . And now Alexander the Great is gone, a tragic figure
off the field but one of the true titans of the game on it."[34] Six months
later Aimee shared many of his final letters with *The Sporting News*.
"Grover Cleveland Alexander died a bitter man—bitter at St. Paul,"
the *Phonograph* later acknowledged. "This theory is hammered home
in no uncertain words."[35]

Aimee, Potsy Clark, and Clarence Mitchell returned to the small
town for the November 6 funeral. The Cardinals paid for the steel cas-
ket and commissioned a local florist to create a floral piece shaped
like a baseball diamond with a gold ribbon that said *Pete*. The family sent a smaller arrangement fashioned into the shape of a baseball. The club also paid for the service and sent a representative from
their Omaha farm team to attend to the arrangements. Despite Alexander's estrangement from many locals, St. Paul businesses closed
for the funeral hour.

The ceremony began at 1:30 p.m. on Monday at the McIntyre Funeral
Home. Two hundred fifty fans, friends, and family attended. Quentin Lynch served as a pallbearer. Churchwomen sang "Lead Kindly
Light," "Beautiful Isle of Somewhere," and "Going Home." The retired
Methodist minister who officiated "made only slight references to
Alexander's brilliant diamond career which lasted two decades and
placed him in baseball's Hall of Fame. The religious theme of the services pointed out that three weeks ago he attended the funeral of his
brother, Nick, that one never knows when death will come."[36]

The chimes of a nearby Presbyterian church tolled as the entourage
headed to Elmwood Cemetery. Dode's friends and relations buried
him in the family plot beside his parents. The American Legion post
where he had been a member fired a rifle salute and sounded taps for
the veteran of France. "The body of Grover Cleveland Alexander lay
today in a quiet cemetery in the hills not far away from this Central
Nebraska town where he was born," the Associated Press reported.[37]
Either reporters didn't ask his old army comrades for a comment or
Clark and Mitchell chose not to speak of him to outsiders.

Rogers Hornsby announced plans to erect a memorial to the pitcher in St. Paul. "I consider Alexander the greatest, cleverest, gamest pitcher of all times," he told the *Phonograph* early in the new year. "The memorial will be a marble monument of imposing nature."[38] The paper started a fund but the campaign soon sputtered, perhaps affected by Aimee's blunt comments and the letters she had shared with *The Sporting News*. A monument was never erected in the pitcher's hometown. In February 1952, fifteen months after his death, no marker even indicated his burial site. By June he had two—a modest headstone matching those for his parents but bearing the wrong date of death and a veteran's white government marker ordered by the American Legion.

The Winning Team, the movie starring Ronald Reagan and Doris Day, opened later that month. The *Phonograph* didn't know what to make of the fact-bending film on which Aimee had worked as an advisor. "What puzzled local moviegoers is how Hollywood could produce a full-length 'true life story' of Alexander and NOT ONCE mention St. Paul, his acknowledged home town, where he returned each season, where he died, where he was buried," the editor wrote. "This important fact was entirely rubbed out of the movie script."[39] A baseball historian notes that the movie "is not the definitive word on its subject."[40]

Any hard feelings that tainted St. Paul's feelings for Dode and Aimee faded with the decades. The town now hosts an annual festival named in the pitcher's honor. What began as Grover Cleveland Alexander Day during Nebraska's quasquicentennial in 1992 has grown into a three-day summer celebration featuring a parade, athletic competitions, dances, music, bake sales, and a car show. An area sportswriter notes that the community "not only named its town celebration after the Hall of Fame baseball player, but has references of the sport painted throughout town on buildings, their water tower, and even has a motto that says, 'St. Paul Batting 1.000.'"[41]

Aimee tirelessly guarded Alexander's reputation for nearly thirty years after his death. Jim Murray of the *Los Angeles Times* was among many sportswriters who heard from her whenever she thought Alexander had been neglected in an article or column. Most patiently took her calls. Readers remembered Alexander, not because he had died alone and alcoholic, but because he had accomplished so much for so long, despite his ghosts and dark shadows. "No one came back from Flanders and World War I shell-shocked and deaf in one ear and went on to win 183 more big league games," Murray wrote after visiting Aimee in 1974. "No one made the Baseball Hall of Fame with epilepsy."[42]

Alexander's former wife died in a retirement home at age eighty-six, three days before Christmas in 1979. Aimee had no family; Los Angeles County saw to her funeral. She had guarded Dode's memory to the end. "Alex loved baseball and he loved to play," she had recalled. "His hat never got too small and he was always especially nice to me. He was a very fine gentleman."[43]

ACKNOWLEDGMENTS

Many people assisted in the writing of this book. My thanks first to Dr. Lindsay John Bell for his research help in Cooperstown, New York. Thank you as well to Mitch Yockelson for his advice on accessing the U.S. National Archives at College Park, Maryland, and to several knowledgeable archivists there for their assistance. Alexander biographer Jan Finkel offered advice and encouragement, much appreciated. Editor Sandy Crump ushered wayward sentences back into line.

Obinna I. Moneme, MD, of Columbus, Ohio, was tremendously helpful in sharing a neurologist's view of epilepsy, traumatic brain injury, and PTSD. Thomas Litzinger, MD, generously shared information on sports injury and ophthalmology. Nurse-turned-lawyer Judith Berman likewise provided valuable guidance and advice.

Finally, thanks to author Steve Steinberg for generously sharing his research on Pete Alexander, especially concerning his relationship with the people of St. Paul. Steve also is due an explanation. Soon after deciding to introduce each chapter with a few lines from Grantland Rice, I realized that Steve had used this technique in his biography of pitcher Urban Shocker. Fortunately, Granny wrote enough war poetry for us both. Many of his pieces first appeared in daily editions of the *New York Tribune*, viewable now on the Library of Congress website (www.loc.gov).

APPENDIX A

Selected Athletes of the 342nd Field Artillery

Soldier	Hometown	Rank	Battery	Team/School
Grover "Pete" Alexander (1887–1950)	St. Paul NE	Sergeant	F	Cubs
George "Potsy" Clark (1894–1972)	Carthage IL	1st Lieutenant	F	University of Illinois
John "Jick" Fast (1894–1959)	Hutchinson KS	1st Lieutenant	F	University of Kansas
Otis Lambeth (1890–1976)	Moran KS	Sergeant	D	Indians
Monroe "Poge" Lewis (1894–1971)	St. Louis MO	1st Lieutenant	HQ	Washington University
Adrian "Ad" Lindsey (1895–1980)	Kingfisher OK	2nd Lieutenant	HQ	University of Kansas
Clarence "Mitch" Mitchell (1891–1963)	Franklin NE	Sergeant	E	Dodgers
Winfield "Win" Noyes (1889–1969)	Ravenna NE	Sergeant Major	HQ	Athletics
Lloyd Wait (1893–1956)	St. Louis MO	1st Lieutenant	E	Pirates (prospect)

Charles "Chuck" Ward (1894–1969)	St. Louis MO	Sergeant	C	Dodgers
Frank "Dutch" Wetzel (1893–1942)	Washington MO	Private	A	Browns (postwar)
Paul Withington (1888–1966)	Honolulu HI	Major	89th Division	Harvard University

APPENDIX B

Composition of the 164th Field Artillery Brigade

Unit	Weapon	Largest contingent (state)
340th Field Artillery	75 mm	Arizona
341st Field Artillery	75 mm	Colorado
342nd Field Artillery	155 mm	Missouri
314th Trench Mortar Battery	6-inch	Iowa
134th Field Artillery (temporary)	75 mm	Ohio
314th Ammunition Train	—	Nebraska

NOTES

Typographical errors, misspellings, and missing punctuation have been corrected. Variations of players' names, common in 1917–19, have been updated to currently accepted spellings, *Killifer* to *Killefer* being the prime example.

Abbreviations

KHS-49   World War I Collection #49, Kansas Soldiers, Kansas Historical Society, http://www.kansasmemory.org

NARA-164   Records of the American Expeditionary Forces (World War I), 1918–1919, 89th Division, 164th Field Artillery Brigade, Records Group 120, National Archives, College Park, Maryland

NARA-342   Records of U.S. Regular Army Mobile Units, 342nd Field Artillery Regiment Headquarters, Correspondence, Records Group 391, National Archives, College Park, Maryland

NARA-GCA   Official Military Personal File for Grover C. Alexander, Records of the Army Staff, 1903–2009, Records Group 319, National Archives, St. Louis, Missouri; Persons of Exceptional Prominence, https://www.archives.gov/st-louis/st-louis/pep

NARA-WD   Records of the American Expeditionary Forces (World War I), A.E.F. General Headquarters, War Diaries (89th Division), 342nd Field Artillery, Records Group 120, National Archives, College Park, Maryland

Prologue

Epigraph: Grantland Rice, "At Dusk in Camp," The Sportlight, *New York Tribune*, February 7, 1918.

1. Arthur Daley, Sports of the Times, *New York Times*, November 7, 1950.

2. Skipper, *Wicked Curve*, 8.

3. Louis Effrat, "Old Pete Standee; Sic Transit Gloria," *New York Times*, October 7, 1950.

1. Alexander the Great

Epigraph: Grantland Rice, "The Story of the Drums," The Sportlight, *New York Tribune*, April 10, 1917.

1. Tuchman, *Guns of August*, 146.

2. "America in Armageddon," *New York Tribune*, April 7, 1917.

3. "Moran Refuses to Let Phillies Play," *Washington Herald*, April 7, 1917.

4. Denman Thompson, "Good Weather at Norfolk for Senators-Phillies Game," *Washington Star*, April 6, 1917.

5. "Early Pioneer of Howard County at Rest," *St. Paul Phonograph*, December 14, 1916.

6. Louis A. Dougher, "Alec the Great on Mound Today," *Washington Times*, April 7, 1917.

7. Denman Thompson, "Mighty Alexander Is Rudely Handled," *Washington Star*, April 8, 1917.

8. "President Backs Subscription Plan," *Washington Star*, June 8, 1917.

9. "Base Ball Assured," *Washington Star*, April 8, 1917.

10. "Baseball to Lose Men through Call of War," *Philadelphia Ledger*, April 7, 1917.

11. "Phils' Game with Senators Is Off," *Philadelphia Ledger*, April 9, 1917.

12. Thomas Rice, "Superbas' Chances in Opener Spoiled by Cravath," *Brooklyn Eagle*, April 12, 1917.

13. "Winfield Noyes," *Philadelphia Ledger*, April 12, 1917.

14. "The President's Proclamation," *Washington Star*, May 19, 1917.

15. "Patriotic Landslide Sweeps as Its Sons Rush to Register for Service," *Philadelphia Ledger*, June 5, 1917.

16. "More than 900,000 in the First Draft," *Washington Evening Star*, June 4, 1917.

17. Grover Cleveland Alexander, Registration Card, May 25, 1917, U.S. National Archives, via https://www.ancestry.com.

18. "Registrars' Cares in Slackers' Hands," *Washington Times*, June 7, 1917.

19. "Keep Registration Cards Clean and Handy," *Washington Star*, June 6, 1917.

20. "Eleven Men of the Phils Register for the Draft," *Philadelphia Ledger*, May 26, 1917.

21. "956 in Howard County," *St. Paul Phonograph*, June 7, 1917.

22. "Quota for First Draft Army Picked; Drawing Ended at 2.18 This Morning," *New York Tribune*, July 21, 1917.

23. "Draft Numbers Showing How Men Are to Be Called," *New York Tribune*, July 21, 1917.

24. "Quota for First Draft Army Picked."

25. Capozzola, *Uncle Sam Wants You*, 37.

26. "If You Registered June 5, Here Is What to Do Now," *Richmond Palladium*, July 10, 1917.

27. Sport Chatter, *Bismarck Tribune*, August 6, 1917.

28. "Draft Hits Athletic Line Up," *Oswego Palladium*, August 9, 1917.

29. "Crooked Finger Bar to Player; Heine Groh Out," *Harrisburg Telegraph*, August 8, 1917.

30. Paul Purman, "War Begins Making Inroads on Baseball Stars Abandoned Game to Save Nation," *Bismarck Daily Tribune*, August 9, 1917.

31. J. B. Sheridan, "Players Fear Army Draft," *Ogden Standard*, August 11, 1917.

32. "Alexander Is Against Seeking an Exemption," *Washington Times*, December 9, 1917.

33. Thomas Rice, "No Trouble for Alexander to Clean Up Doubleheader," *Brooklyn Eagle*, September 4, 1917.

34. "Alex Registered Second Double Triumph in His Big League Career When He Humbled the Dodgers," *Philadelphia Ledger*, September 4, 1917.

35. Rice, "No Trouble for Alexander."

2. Laddies from Missouri

Epigraph: Grantland Rice, "The Great Adventure," The Sportlight, *New York Tribune*, November 1, 1917.

1. Chubb, *Regimental History, 342nd Field Artillery, 89th Division*, 3.

2. "Regimental Song," *Topeka State Journal*, June 1, 1918.

3. "Camp Funston," *Monett Times*, October 26, 1917.

4. "Stationed at Camp Funston," *Greenfield Recorder*, October 17, 1917. Although a native of the Northeast, Jacobus had been working for an insurance company in Kansas City when America entered the war, which explains his presence at Camp Funston.

5. Rice, *The Tumult and the Shouting*, 92.

6. "340 Field Artillery Is Real Arizona Regiment," *St. Johns Herald*, April 10, 1919.

7. "George Dryer Gives News of Boys in Camp," *Arizona Republican*, September 30, 1917.

8. Andruss, "Baseball Champions," 267.

9. "Beat This Army Nine If You Can." *Geneva Times*, June 19, 1918.

10. Andruss, "Baseball Champions," 267.

11. "Book Reviews in Tabloid," *Atlanta Constitution*, September 27, 1914.

12. Joe Farrington, "Joe Farrington Writes that There Is More Football than Ever Before," *Honolulu Star-Bulletin*, December 6, 1917.

13. "Paul Withington Chosen Sport Coach for Ft. Riley Cantonment," *Honolulu Star-Bulletin*, October 16, 1918.

14. Ellis B. Usher, "Politics Was Main Activity All Week," *Oshkosh Northwestern*, September 23, 1916.

15. "Cooks, Baths and Great Big New Laundry Features at Fort Riley," *Omaha Bee*, September 10, 1917.

16. "Who's Who with the Pirates," *Pittsburgh Press*, March 23, 1914.

17. No doubt further confounding fans, Gerald Wetzel played for Keokuk in 1915 after Frank had left the club. In another curious coincidence, a different Forest B. Wetzel, likewise nicknamed Dutch, played football in 1915 at Washington University, St. Louis, with one of Frank Wetzel's future Camp Funston teammates, Lt. Monroe Lewis.

18. "Locals and Personals," *Owensville Casconade County Republican*, September 21, 1917.

19. "From the Boys in Camp," *Owensville Casconade County Republican*, October 12, 1917.

3. Gridiron

Epigraph: Grantland Rice, "1918—The Soldier," *New York Tribune*, January 1, 1918.

1. "Want Game with K. U.," *Topeka State Journal*, October 16, 1917.

2. "Illinois Sends Many Athletes to Colors," *Wisconsin State Journal* (Madison), August 6, 1917.

3. "Daily Drift," *Lincoln Nebraska State Journal*, November 20, 1916.

4. John L. Griffith, "Griffith Lists Seven Coe Men on Honor Roll of Iowa Athletes," *Cedar Rapids Gazette*, March 24, 1917.

5. "Football Stars in 'Army, Navy' Game," *Santa Ana Register*, November 24, 1917.

6. "Formidable Tiger Backfieldmen," *Lincoln State Journal*, April 11, 1919.

7. "Up to the Minute Sporting News from Everywhere, by 'Clug,'" *Topeka State Journal*, November 1, 1917.

8. "Army-Navy Game Today," *Lawrence Journal-World*, November 24, 1917.

9. "Some of Camp Funston Gridders Who Clash with Camp Dodge in Omaha Next Saturday," *Omaha Bee*, November 25, 1917.

10. "Army Game at K. C.," *Topeka State Journal*, November 19, 1917.

11. "35 Players in Funston Squad," *Topeka State Journal*, November 22, 1917.

12. "Potsy Clark Gives Funston Touchdown Which Beats Navy," *Omaha Bee*, November 26, 1917.

13. "Funston Beats Great Lakes, 7–0, in Great Scrap," *Chicago Tribune*, November 25, 1917. The *Tribune* reported Clark's run as thirty-two yards.

14. "Zuppke's Eleven to Fight Old Hero," *Rock Island Argus*, November 27, 1917.

15. "Illinois Plays Soldiers Today," *Daily Illini*, November 29, 1917.

16. "Camp Funston Is Defeated, 28 to 0," *Rock Island Argus*, November 30, 1917.

17. "Army Grid Game in Omaha Tomorrow Is Real Treat of 1917 Foot Ball Season," *Omaha Bee*, November 30, 1917.

18. "Field Goal Wins for Camp Dodge in Final Minute," *Chicago Tribune*, December 2, 1917.

19. Fred S. Hunter, "Camp Dodgers Triumph Over Funston Eleven in Gridiron Clash at Creighton Field," *Omaha Bee*, December 2, 1917.

20. Serb, *War Football*, 135.

21. "Heard along the Sideline at the Army Grid Clash," *Omaha Bee*, December 2, 1917.

22. "Last Game of Year," *Topeka State Journal*, December 13, 1917.

23. "Funston Lost to MacArthur," *Kansas City Times*, December 18, 1917.

24. "Funston Eleven Loses to Camp MacArthur," *Salt Lake City Deseret News*, December 18, 1917.

4. Chicago

Epigraph: Grantland Rice, "What of It," The Sportlight, *New York Tribune*, August 1, 1917.

1. "Phillies Startle the Baseball World by Selling Alexander and Killefer to the Chicago Cubs," *Philadelphia Inquirer*, December 12, 1917.

2. "With Alex and Bill Gone, In Order to Draw Crowd, the Phils Will Need a Lead Pencil," *Philadelphia Public Ledger*, December 12, 1917.

3. Alexander, "King Baseball."

4. "Dust Gave Alexander Nickname of Pete," *Brooklyn Eagle*, March 28, 1930.

5. "Alexander-Killefer Deal Has Phil Ball Fans Hanging on the Ropes and Gasping for Air," *Philadelphia Public Ledger*, December 12, 1917.

6. H. O. Hamilton, "Spitball Is Fast Losing Favor," *Salem Capital Journal*, January 22, 1918.

7. H. C. Hamilton, "Alexander Has Shot His Bolt Declares Baker," *Lockport Union-Sun and Journal*, January 3, 1918.

8. "Dooin against Deal," *El Paso Journal*, January 5, 1918.

9. Finkel, "Pete Alexander."

10. "Alexander, 'Wouldn't Touch a Drop,' If Starting Now," *Brooklyn Standard Union*, August 8, 1930.

11. Billy Sunday, "Temperance Notes: Winners Don't Use It," *Maurice Times*, May 16, 1918.

12. "Alexander Called to Army," *St. Paul Republican*, January 17, 1918.

13. "Alexander Is in Class One Draft," *Ogden Standard*, January 16, 1918.

14. "Great Ball Player Puts Country First and Welcomes Draft," *Salem Capital Journal*, January 16, 1918.

15. "Alexander Injured," *St. Paul Phonograph-Press*, quoting the *Galesburg Republican-Register*, August 6, 1909.

16. J. O. Taylor Spink, "'No Regrets—I Got My Memories,' Says Old Alex, Leaving Hospital and Hoping for Cooperstown Job," *The Sporting News*, April 3, 1941.

17. Item, *St. Paul Republican*, August 5, 1909.

18. "Alex Holds Levee," *St. Paul Phonograph-Press*, quoting the *Galesburg Republican-Register*, August 20, 1909.

19. "Alex Is 'Covered Up,'" *St. Paul Phonograph-Press*, quoting the *Galesburg Republican-Register*, August 27, 1909.

20. Ritter, *The Glory of Their Times*, 194.

21. Kavanagh, *Ol' Pete*, 71.

22. Meany, *Baseball's Greatest Pitchers*, 9.

23. Report of Physical Examination, Provost Marshal General's Office Form 1010, January 25, 1918, NARA-GCA.

24. "Loss of One Eye or Finger No Bar to Army Service," *Philadelphia Public Ledger*, June 18, 1918.

25. "Weeghman Says Alexander Will Get Big Bonus," *New York Tribune*, February 7, 1918.

26. Sportettes, *Keokuk Gate City*, February 12, 1918.

27. "Alexander Gets in Line," *Washington Herald*, March 9, 1918.

28. "Will Satisfy Alexander," *New York Sun*, February 8, 1918.

29. Item, *St. Paul Phonograph*, March 14, 1918.

30. "'Alec' Left with the Cubs," *Kansas City Star*, March 13, 1918. Although unsigned, the piece has since been attributed to Ernest Hemingway.

31. Editorial item, *Arizona Republican*, March 15, 1918.

32. James Crusinberry, "Cub Recruits Learn 'Art of Baseball' at Pasadena Camp," *Chicago Tribune*, March 21, 1918.

33. "George F. Alexander," *St. Paul Phonograph*, March 28, 1918.

34. Crusinberry, "Cub Recruits Learn 'Art of Baseball.'"

35. James Crusinberry, "'Subs' Torpedo Cub Ship, 10–6, in Coast Fight," *Chicago Tribune*, March 22, 1918.

36. Matt Foley, "Cubs Are Nosed Out in Tenth," *Chicago Examiner*, April 6, 1918.

37. "Come Right In!," *Chicago Tribune*, April 8, 1918.

38. James Crusinberry, "Army of 8,000 Soldier Boys Sees Cubs Win," *Chicago Tribune*, April 7, 1918.

39. James Crusinberry, For the Fan, *Eagle Magazine*, June 1918.

40. James Crusinberry, "Cubs Get Taste of Discipline at Army Camp," *Chicago Tribune*, April 8, 1918.

41. Matt Foley, "Cubs Give Soldier 9 Thumping," *Chicago Examiner*, April 8, 1918.

42. "Cubs Win Two Shutouts," *Deming Graphic*, April 12, 1918.

43. Foley, "Cubs Give."

44. L. B. Blanchard, "Army Umpire Supreme, Say Cubs Players," *Lockport Union-Sun and Journal*, May 13, 1918.

45. Crusinberry, "Cubs Get Taste."

46. Crusinberry, "Cubs Get Taste."

47. "Cubs Win Two."

48. "Grover Alexander Drafted; Great Pitcher Soon in Camp," *Brooklyn Eagle*, April 12, 1918.

49. "Alexander, Called to Army, Will Pitch Opening Game," *New York Tribune*, April 13, 1918.

50. Jack Keene, Dishing Up the Sport Dope, *Richmond Palladium and Sun-Telegram*, April 20, 1918.

51. James Crusinberry, "Gloom in Cubs Ranks," *Chicago Tribune*, April 13, 1918.

52. "Weeghman Out $50,000 If Alexander Is Called," *Chicago Examiner*, April 13, 1918.

53. Crusinberry, "Gloom in Cubs Ranks."

54. "No Chance to Call Me a Slacker," *Philadelphia Inquirer*, April 13, 1918.

55. "Alexander Not Called in Draft," *Ogden Standard*, April 13, 1918.

56. John Alcock, "Aleck Probably Lost to the Cubs by Draft," *Chicago Tribune*, April 13, 1918.

57. "Alexander Call in Doubt," *Chicago Examiner*, April 13, 1918.

58. Larry Woltz, "Alex Sees Cub Heads; Goes Back," *Chicago Examiner*, April 16, 1918.

59. George E. Phair, Breakfast Food, *Chicago Examiner*, April 15, 1918.

60. John Alcock, "Alexander Here for Conference Before Opener in St. Louis," *Chicago Tribune*, April 16, 1918.

61. "Aleck's Board Calls More Men," *Chicago Tribune*, April 16, 1918.

62. "Alexander to Be Given No Favors in Naval Service," *Great Lakes Bulletin*, April 18, 1918.

63. Woltz, "Alex Sees Cub Heads."

64. "Alex Must Serve in Army, Says Board," *Philadelphia Public Ledger*, April 17, 1918.

65. James Crusinberry, "New Cub Machine Slips Cog and Loses, 4 to 2," *Chicago Tribune*, April 17, 1918.

66. James Crusinberry, "Cubs Pass Idle Day; Face Loss of 4 Men, Possibly 6 to Army," *Chicago Tribune*, April 18, 1918.

67. Matt Foley, "Four Star Cubs, in Draft Class 1, Think Seriously of Joining Uncle Sam's Navy," *Chicago Examiner*, April 18, 1918.

68. Ring W. Lardner, In the Wake of the News, *Chicago Tribune*, April 18, 1918.

69. "What about Alexander?," *Stars and Stripes*, April 19, 1918.

70. "Aleck Called!," *Chicago Tribune*, April 19, 1918.

71. "Great Alex Asks Permit to Join Forces of Navy," *Omaha Bee*, April 17, 1918.

5. Fast Nine

Epigraph: "The Old Game and the New," *Stars and Stripes*, August 9, 1918 (unsigned, attribution by author).

1. "Maj. Gen. Wood Wounded in France," *Washington Herald*, January 28, 1918.

2. English, *History of the 89th Division, U.S.A.*, 37.

3. "Details of How Gen. Wood Was Wounded in a Trench," *Washington Star*, March 19, 1918.

4. "Camp Funston Has Crack Squad for Basketball," *Albuquerque Journal*, December 16, 1917.

5. "Camp Comment," *Topeka State Journal*, March 30, 1918.

6. "Athletics," *Alumni Quarterly*, June 1, 1916, 376.

7. Andruss, "Baseball Champions."

8. "Strong in Field," *Topeka State Journal*, Trench and Camp edition, March 16, 1918.

9. Andruss, "Baseball Champions."

10. "Funston Liberty Loan Record Good," *Omaha Bee*, May 20, 1918.

11. "Chuck Ward Off to the Army and Robbie Sore Beset," *Brooklyn Eagle*, March 29, 1918.

12. "Boots and Bingles," *New York Tribune*, August 19, 1916.

13. Paul, "The Life and Times of Clarence Mitchell."

14. Thomas Rice, "Southpaw Clarence Mitchell Enters Superba Ranks," *Brooklyn Eagle*, March 7, 1918.

15. Andruss, "Baseball Champions."

16. "Big Game for Army Team," *Kansas City Times*, March 28, 1918.

17. Andruss, "A Corner in Horsehide."

18. H. E. Fisher, "Ball Season On," *Topeka State Journal*, Trench and Camp edition, April 6, 1918.

19. "342 F.A. Well Represented," *Topeka State Journal*, Trench and Camp edition, April 6, 1918.

20. "Brooklyn Infielder Now Camp Funston Sergeant," *New York Tribune*, April 7, 1918.

21. Andruss, "A Corner in Horsehide."

22. "White Sox Notes," *Chicago Tribune*, April 11, 1918.

23. "Champion Sox Win Slug-Fest Easily in Listless Tilt," *Rock Island Argus*, April 13, 1918.

24. I. E. Sanborn, "10,000 Funston Boys Watch Sox Bombard Camp's Team, 13 to 1," *Chicago Tribune*, April 13, 1918.

25. "Funston Wins," *Topeka State Journal*, April 13, 1918.

26. "If Funston Soldiers Fight Like They Play Ball—Oh, Boy, Oh, Joy!," *Topeka State Journal*, April 15, 1918.

27. "Turned Back Army Drive," *Kansas City Times*, April 29, 1918.

6. Through a Door

Epigraph: Grantland Rice, "The Champions," The Sportlight, *New York Tribune*, January 8, 1918.

1. "Alex in Army by Farm Shortage," *Chicago Tribune*, April 21, 1918.

2. Editorial item, *Omaha Bee*, April 22, 1918.

3. Jack Veiock, "Call for Mr. Aleck," *Schenectady Gazette*, April 23, 1918.

4. James Crusinberry, "Aleck Tames Redleg Crew in 9-1 Clash," *Chicago Tribune*, April 22, 1918.

5. "Aleck Hurls Today, Then Goes to Army; Drive on for Bonds," *Chicago Tribune*, April 26, 1918.

6. "Alexander Will Hurl Last Game for Cubs Today," *Salt Lake City Deseret News*, April 26, 1918.

7. "Alex Puts Money into Loan Bonds," *Bridgeport Times*, April 27, 1918.

8. Matt Foley, "Alexander Closes Pitching Career with Two-Hit Triumph over Cardinals, 3–2," *Chicago Examiner*, April 27, 1918.

9. James Crusinberry, "Veni, Vidi, Vici; Aleck Subdues Cardinals, 3 to 2," *Chicago Tribune*, April 27, 1918.

10. James Clarkson, "Star Gets Ovation from Fans," *Chicago Examiner*, April 27, 1918.

11. W. J. Macbeth, "Young Scintillates Again in Ebbets Field Debacle," *New York Tribune*, April 27, 1918.

12. "Following the Ball," *Lincoln State Journal*, April 27, 1918.

13. See, for example, "Cleveland Loses Lambeth," *New York Sun*, April 22, 1918.

14. "Local News," *St. Paul Phonograph*, also quoting the *Ord Weekly Journal*, May 9, 1918.

15. "Twelve Men Go to Funston Tuesday," *St. Paul Republican*, April 25, 1918.

16. "What St. Louisans Saw on a Visit to Camp Funston," *St. Louis Post-Dispatch*, April 23, 1918.

17. Crowell and Wilson, *The Road to France*, 71.

18. "Alexander at Funston; Most Popular Rookie," *Oklahoma City Times*, May 2, 1918.

19. "Men Shoot the Chutes," *Lincoln State Journal*, May 19, 1918.

20. Bowen, *The Medical Department of the U.S. Army in the World War*, 69.

21. "Camp Funston 'Chutes' Official to St. Louis," *Hutchinson News*, May 15, 1918.

22. "Alexander, Star Twirler in Service at Funston," *Guthrie Leader*, May 3, 1918.

23. "Men Shoot the Chutes."

24. Physical Examination at Place of Mobilization, Camp Funston, May 2, 1918, NARA-GCA.

25. J. O. Taylor Spink, "'No Regrets—I Got My Memories,' Says Old Alex, Leaving Hospital and Hoping for Cooperstown Job," *The Sporting News*, April 3, 1941.

26. "Grover Alexander Taken into Army," *Los Angeles Herald*, May 3, 1918.

27. "Men Approve of Army Life," *Lincoln State Journal*, May 19, 1918.

28. "Aleck in Artillery at Camp Funston; Will Play Baseball," *Chicago Tribune*, May 2, 1918.

29. "No Fourth Officers School at Funston," *Arizona Republican*, May 7, 1918.

30. "Wallops Alex Team," *Topeka State Journal*, May 25, 1918.

31. "Men Approve of Army Life."

32. "A.B.C. of Army Slang," *Yuma Arizona Sentinel*, March 7, 1918.

33. "Bugle Calls Set to Words by Men at Army Camps," *Washington Times*, January 28, 1918.

34. "Alex. Good Soldier," *Topeka State Journal*, May 22, 1918.

35. Document no. 267, Box 1797, NARA-342.

36. "Grover and His Bride," *Topeka State Journal*, June 8, 1918.

37. Andruss, "Baseball Champions."

38. "The Palms," advertisement, *Columbia Missourian*, May 16, 1918.

39. "Alexander May Pitch Sunday Ball," *New York Tribune*, May 19, 1918.

40. "Cubs' Star in Khaki, Grover Alexander, May Hurl Game Here," *Chicago Tribune*, May 19, 1918.

7. Camp Funston

Epigraph: Grantland Rice, "Revenge," The Sportlight, *New York Tribune*, January 19, 1918.

1. "A Letter from Camp Funston," *Monett Times*, September 28, 1917.

2. Showalter, "America's New Soldier Cities."

3. "Letter from Alton Boy at Camp Funston," *Alton Telegram*, November 21, 1917.

4. W. S. Travis, "The Kansas Wind," *Topeka State Journal*, Trench and Camp edition, October 12, 1918.

5. "Stationed at Camp Funston," *Greenfield Recorder*, October 17, 1917.

6. "Efficiency and Cleanliness Is Slogan of Arizona Boys Training at Camp Funston," *Arizona Republican*, December 12, 1917.

7. "Funston Zone," *Topeka State Journal*, March 30, 1918.

8. "Come to the Zone," *Topeka State Journal*, Trench and Camp edition, March 2, 1918.

9. "Hard Work and Fun Well Mixed," *Jasper News*, April 11, 1918.

10. *History of Battery "A,"* 3–4.

11. "Letters from Our Soldier Boys," *Troy Free Press*, May 3, 1918.

12. "Letters from Our Soldier Boys," *Troy Free Press*, May 3, 1918.

13. Jones, *History and Roster of the 355th Infantry*, 27.

14. "Funston Boys About to Start to Battle Front," *Omaha Bee*, May 22, 1918.

15. "General Wood Barred from Duty at Front," *New York Tribune*, May 28, 1918.

16. *New York World*, quoted in "General Wood's Internment," *New York Tribune*, May 29, 1918.

17. "Gen. Wood Reviews Men He Trained and Says Farewell," *New York Tribune*, June 3, 1918.

18. "Base Ball Benefit Play a Success," *St. Paul Phonograph*, July 1, 1915.

19. Item, *St. Paul Phonograph*, August 5, 1915.

20. "Alexander the Great Unmarried," *St. Paul Phonograph*, December 2, 1915.

21. "Famous Pitcher, G. Alexander, to Wed Omaha Girl," *Omaha Bee*, May 29, 1918.

22. "Baseball Star Married," *Topeka State Journal*, June 8, 1918.

23. "Aleck Marries His Sweetheart of Boyhood Days," *Chicago Tribune*, June 2, 1918.

24. *Omaha World-Herald*, May 29, 1918, reprinted in "Grover Alexander to Wed Saturday," *St. Paul Phonograph*, May 30, 1918.

8. Camp Mills

Epigraph: Grantland Rice, "Base Camp No. 1 Speaks (St. Nazaire)," The Sportlight, *New York Tribune*, March 16, 1919.

1. "Letters from Soldier Boys," *Hayti Herald*, December 13, 1917.

2. "From a Taney Boy 'Going Over,'" *Taney County Republican*, June 13, 1918.

3. "In Camp and Field," *Emporia Weekly Gazette*, June 22, 1918.

4. "Leave Taking of Camp Funston Boys," *Monett Times*, June 14, 1918.

5. Rayburn, *History of Battery F, 342nd F.A., 89th Division*, 7.

6. "Baseball By-Plays," *The Sporting News*, July 18, 1918.

7. Crowell and Wilson, *The Road to France*, 91.

8. "Alex Passes Through," *St. Louis Star*, June 5, 1918.

9. "Parade at Kewanee," *Galva News*, June 6, 1918.

10. "Alex on Way to Berlin," *Pittsburgh Press*, June 5, 1918.

11. "Letters from Our Soldier Boys," *Troy Free Press*, June 28, 1918.

12. Rayburn, *History of Battery F, 342nd F.A., 89th Division*, 8.

13. Frazier Hunt, "'Fighting Sixty-Ninth,' First to Reach Camp Mills, L. I., Keeps Dominant Note That Gave It Fame," *New York Sun*, August 26, 1917.

14. "Letters from Our Soldier Boys," *Troy Free Press*, June 28, 1918.

15. Hunt, "'Fighting Sixty-Ninth.'"

16. Jack Laing, First in Sports, *Buffalo Courier Express*, May 3, 1952. Aimee Alexander later recalled that her husband had met her the night before his regiment left Camp Mills, but multiple newspaper accounts have them together earlier. It's unlikely the army would let any soldier, even a star pitcher, leave camp the night before he deployed.

17. "Alexander Here, Wants to Pitch against Giants," *New York Tribune*, June 11, 1918.

18. "Cubs Overwhelm Giants, 5–3," *New York Herald*, June 12, 1918.

19. Fred Van Ness, "Bombing the Sport Front," *New York Herald*, June 12, 1918.

20. "Aleck Watches Cubs Defeat Giants and Wants to Try Arm," *Chicago Tribune*, June 12, 1918.

21. "Baseball By-Plays," *The Sporting News*, July 4, 1918.

22. "Robins Are Idle Again," *New York Times*, June 13, 1918.

23. "Casey Stengel to Join Navy; Chuck Ward Now a Sergeant," *Brooklyn Eagle*, June 14, 1918.

24. "Soldier Player Bombs the Reds," *New York Herald*, June 14, 1918.

25. Bill Gottlieb, "War Year of 1918 Was Nightmare for Dodgers," *Brooklyn Eagle*, January 25, 1942.

26. "Casey Stengel to Join Navy."

27. "Ward Aids Dodgers in Defeating Reds," *Brooklyn Daily Standard Union*, June 14, 1918.

28. "Casey Stengel to Join Navy."

29. "Schmandt Called to Answer Draft," *Brooklyn Eagle*, June 16, 1918.

30. "Going Over," *Monett Times*, July 5, 1918.

9. Justicia

Epigraph: Grantland Rice, "A Pair of Parades," *New York Tribune*, May 4, 1919.

1. Rayburn, *History of Battery F, 342nd F.A., 89th Division*, 8.

2. Crowell and Wilson, *The Road to France*, 270.

3. Taylor, *Dazzle*, 27.

4. Witt, *Riding to War with "A,"* 53.

5. Chubb, *Regimental History, 342nd Field Artillery, 89th Division*, 15.

6. Rayburn, *History of Battery F, 342nd F.A., 89th Division*, 9.

7. "From Somewhere in France," *Franklin County Tribune*, August 30, 1918.

8. Chubb, *Regimental History, 342nd Field Artillery, 89th Division*, 14.

9. "Lambeth Writes from France," *The Sporting News*, October 3, 1918.

10. Chubb, *Regimental History, 342nd Field Artillery, 89th Division*, 15.

11. "Grover Cleveland Writes Killefer He May Be Back Soon as Huns are Losing," *Auburn Citizen*, September 26, 1918.

12. "Nine Day Veterans Sail Right Back," *Stars and Stripes*, December 6, 1918.

13. Witt, *Riding to War with "A,"* 69.

14. Col. Harold M. Bush commanded the 134th Field Artillery. A poem in the regimental history refers to it as "Colonel Bush's Travelling Show" (Kirtley, *The Liaison*, 67). Bush's grandnephew and great-grandnephew became presidents of the United States.

15. "Letter from Halley Ford," *Maryville Democrat-Forum*, September 2, 1918.

16. "From Somewhere in France."

17. John Alcock, "Aleck Welcomed Back to Chicago Under Heavy Fire of Camera Fleet," *Chicago Tribune*, April 18, 1919.

18. Rayburn, *History of Battery F, 342nd F.A., 89th Division*, 10.

19. "From Somewhere in France."

20. Chubb, *Regimental History, 342nd Field Artillery, 89th Division*, 18.

21. "Letter from 'Chuck' Ward Tells of Doings in Germany," *Brooklyn Eagle*, February 3, 1919.

22. Hinds, "The Training of Artillery in France," 376.

23. "Letter from 'Chuck' Ward."

24. Hinds, "The Training of Artillery in France," 383.

25. Alexander, *Memories of the World War*, 37–38.

26. English, *History of the 89th Division, U.S.A.*, 44.

27. "Alexander Has Been Promoted to Corporal in U.S. Army," *Syracuse Herald*, September 26, 1918.

28. Thomas S. Rice, "Mitchell Has Hopes of Early Reporting," *Brooklyn Eagle*, February 5, 1919.

29. "Bordeaux Great City for Sights," *El Paso Herald*, October 3, 1918.

30. Document no. 427, Box 1799, NARA-342.

31. "Letter from the Front," *Van Buren Current Local*, August 22, 1918.

32. "Harold Brisley Likes Military Life in France," *Prescott Weekly Journal-Miner*, August 28, 1918.

33. Rayburn, *History of Battery F, 342nd F.A., 89th Division*, 11.

34. "Alexander Has Been Promoted."

35. "Justicia Sunk in Fight with Eight U-Boats," *New York Sun*, July 25, 1918.

36. "The Justicia," editorial, *New York World*, July 25, 1918.

37. "Soldier Letters," *Sedalia Democrat*, August 21, 1918.

38. Item, *St. Paul Phonograph*, July 25, 1918.

39. "Alexander and Noyes Are on the Other Side," *Omaha Bee*, August 4, 1918.

40. "Huns Had Better Beware, for Grover Cleveland Alexander Is Somewhere in France," *Philadelphia Public Ledger*, August 19, 1918. The headline ran without an article below.

10. Camp de Souge

Epigraph: Grantland Rice, "Lines to a Howitzer," *New York Tribune*, July 31, 1918.

1. Witt, *Riding to War with "A,"* 84.

2. Rayburn, *History of Battery F, 342nd F.A., 89th Division*, 11.

3. Chubb, *Regimental History, 342nd Field Artillery, 89th Division*, 20.

4. Howard, *Autobiography of a Regiment*, 64.

5. Field and Richards, *The Battery Book*, 52.

6. Nash, "Gas-s-s-s," 470.

7. "From a Taney Boy 'Going Over,'" *Taney County Republican*, June 13, 1918.

8. *The Schneider Works in France*, 17.

9. *History of the 306th*, 72.

10. Howard, *Autobiography of a Regiment*, 60.

11. Randel, *Regimental History*, 67. The 134th Field Artillery had two men killed and several injured in a similar accident at about the same time while training at Camp de Souge.

12. Randel, *Regimental History*, 73.

13. "169,000 Horses Work for A.E.F.," *Stars and Stripes*, November 29, 1918.

14. Pershing, *My Experiences in the World War*, 2:358.

15. *The 302nd Field Artillery*, 62.

16. *History of the 306th*, 17.

17. Randel, *Regimental History*, 54–55.

18. "Letter from 'Chuck' Ward Tells of Doings in Germany," *Brooklyn Eagle*, February 3, 1919.

19. Chubb, *Regimental History, 342nd Field Artillery, 89th Division*, 19.

20. Junius B. Wood, "Players Anxious to Get Back Home," *Washington Star*, March 2, 1919.

21. Howard, *Autobiography of a Regiment*, 70.

22. *History of the 306th*, 74.

23. English, *History of the 89th Division, U.S.A.*, 50.

24. "History, 164th Field Artillery Brigade Headquarters," Box 44, NARA-164.

25. Document no. 411, Box 1797, NARA-342.

26. "He's a McGraw in Fighting," *Washington Times*, November 7, 1918.

27. Frank Finch, "'Old Pete': Intimate Details of Former Pitcher's Life Related by Alexander's Ex-Wife," *The Sporting News*, April 25, 1951. The army friend almost certainly was Potsy Clark.

28. "Grover Cleveland Writes Killefer He May Be Back Soon as Huns are Losing," *Auburn Citizen*, September 26, 1918.

11. Pauillac

Epigraph: Grantland Rice, "The Battle Line," The Sportlight, *Rome Sentinel*, August 24, 1923.

1. "Corporal Alexander Writes from France," *St. Paul Phonograph*, September 12, 1918.

2. "Alexander Arrives Safely Overseas," *Los Angeles Herald*, August 15, 1918.

3. "Alexander Now in France," *Schenectady Gazette*, August 16, 1918. The newspaper writer mistakenly assumes the artillerymen spent their nights in the trenches, which wasn't normally the case.

4. "2,000,000 Men Join Uncle Sam's League," *New York Times*, March 11, 1918.

5. "Alexander Has Been Promoted to Corporal in U.S. Army," *Syracuse Herald*, September 26, 1918.

6. "Sea and Sky Men Meet on Diamond," *Stars and Stripes*, April 19, 1918.

7. "German Soldiers Are Wise to 'Boners,'" *Washington Times*, January 14, 1919.

8. "Others May Have Class, But Look at This One," *The Sporting News*, September 26, 1918.

9. "Lambeth Writes from France," *The Sporting News*, October 3, 1918.

10. "Alexander Has Been Promoted."

11. "Grover Cleveland Writes Killefer He May Be Back Soon as Huns are Losing," *Auburn Citizen*, September 26, 1918. Hall of Fame second baseman Johnny Evers gave baseball lessons to French poilus (soldiers) during the war while serving overseas as a uniformed athletic director for the Knights of Columbus.

12. "Letter from 'Chuck' Ward Tells of Doings in Germany," *Brooklyn Eagle*, February 3, 1919.

13. "LaHarpe News," *Iola Register*, September 24, 1918.

14. "Stars and Stripes Is Hauled Down with This Issue," *Stars and Stripes*, June 13, 1919.

15. "The Sporting Page Goes Out," *Stars and Stripes*, July 26, 1918.

16. "Fans in Chicago Greet Alexander," *Washington Star*, April 19, 1919.

17. "Aleck, in France, Helps Army Men Defeat Navy Flyers," *Chicago Tribune*, October 21, 1918.

18. "Alexander Winning Abroad," *Schenectady Gazette*, October 10, 1918.

19. "Around the Bases," *Harrisburg Telegraph*, October 11, 1918.

20. "Notes of the Game," *Chicago Tribune*, October 21, 1918.

21. Foster, *Spalding's Official Base Ball Guide, 1919*, 264.

22. "Aleck, in France."

23. *Pauillac Pilot*, quoted in "Alexander Gets Name in Box Score as Hurler for Oversea Ball Team," *Omaha Bee*, September 26, 1918.

24. "Notes of the Game." Alexander recalled years later, incorrectly, that the final score had been 3–2 in ten innings.

25. "Yankees Clash Abroad," *Portland Oregonian*, October 2, 1918.

26. "Lambeth Writes."

27. "Looking 'Em Over in France," *Washington Herald*, November 1, 1918.

28. "Grover Cleveland Writes."

29. Grover Cleveland Alexander, "Reminiscences of Alexander," *Buffalo Evenings News*, June 26, 1930.

30. English, *History of the 89th Division, U.S.A.*, 276.

31. "Lambeth Writes."

32. Document no. 487, Box 1797, NARA-342. Colonel Biscoe listed the four Major Leaguers' army ranks and positions as of September 14, 1918: Sgt. Maj. Winfield C. Noyes, First Battalion; Sgt. Otis Lambeth, chief of section; Cpl. Grover C. Alexander, gas noncommissioned officer and substitute gunner; Cpl. C. W. Ward, gunner. Unaccountably, a shipyard in Superior, Wisconsin, had somehow expected Noyes to appear for a job and play on its industrial-league team when he was four thousand miles away at Camp de Souge. A local newspaper noted that he "failed to report to the Globe team of Superior yesterday on time to go on the hill against the Riverside team of Duluth" ("Globes Beat Riverside," *Duluth Herald*, September 2, 1918).

12. St. Mihiel

Epigraph: Grantland Rice, "The Six-Inch Speaks," *New York Tribune*, August 5, 1918.

1. Rayburn, *History of Battery F, 342nd F.A., 89th Division*, 11.

2. "Letter from George A. Nugent to the Commanding Officer of the 342nd Field Artillery," Missouri History Museum, https://www.sos.mo.gov/mdh/.

3. "Public Animals," letter from brigade to divisional headquarters, January 3, 1919, Box 291, Animals, NARA-16. Figures cited in brigade and regimental correspondence from August 1918 to January 1919 vary as animals died, were evacuated, or arrived as replacements.

4. Chubb, *Regimental History, 342nd Field Artillery, 89th Division*, 21.

5. "Corp. Dick Berry on Firing Line," *Jasper News*, November 14, 1918.

6. "Letter from 'Chuck' Ward Tells of Doings in Germany," *Brooklyn Eagle*, February 3, 1919. Ward refers to the 155-millimeter guns, which were nearly the same caliber as the U.S. 6-inch howitzers the regiment had used at Camp Funston.

7. English, *History of the 89th Division, U.S.A.*, 73.

8. Willis J. Abbot, "Abbot Says Pershing's Big Offensive Will Develop Into Campaign for Metz," *New York Times*, September 15, 1918.

9. Dalessandro and Wessels, "St. Mihiel Salient," in *World War I Battlefield Companion*.

10. Lt. Grantland Rice's 115th Field Artillery was part of the 55th Field Artillery Brigade, but Rice hadn't yet returned from his assignment at *Stars and Stripes*.

11. English, *History of the 89th Division, U.S.A.*, 134.

12. Pershing, *My Experiences*, 2:272.

13. Yockelson, *Forty-Seven Days*, 80.

14. Chubb, *Regimental History, 342nd Field Artillery, 89th Division*, 23.

15. Rayburn, *History of Battery F, 342nd F.A., 89th Division*, 12.

16. English, *History of the 89th Division, U.S.A.*, 92.

17. "Ben Reed Writes from France," *Hayti Herald*, January 23, 1919.

18. Chubb, *Regimental History, 342nd Field Artillery, 89th Division*, 23.

19. "From the Land of the Hun," *Taney County Republican*, January 30, 1919. Essey appears on modern maps as Essey-et-Maizerais.

20. Rayburn, *History of Battery F, 342nd F.A., 89th Division*, 12.

21. "Frank Wetzel Writes from Irrel, Germany," *Casconade County Republican*, January 31, 1919.

22. Chubb, *Regimental History, 342nd Field Artillery, 89th Division*, 25–26.

23. "Peace Proposals Warm from Guns Letter Describes," *Arizona Republican*, October 26, 1918.

24. Rayburn, *History of Battery F, 342nd F.A., 89th Division*, 12.

25. Embury, "Concealment," 304.

26. John Alcock, "Aleck Welcomed Back to Chicago Under Heavy Fire of Camera Fleet," *Chicago Tribune*, April 18, 1919.

27. "Fans in Chicago Greet Alexander," *Washington Star*, April 19, 1919.

28. "Grover Alexander and Bride Visit Home Folks," *St. Paul Phonograph*, April 24, 1919.

29. Rayburn, *History of Battery F, 342nd F.A., 89th Division*, 12. The village today is called Dommartin-la-Chaussée.

30. Chubb, *Regimental History, 342nd Field Artillery, 89th Division*, 26.

31. Rayburn, *History of Battery F, 342nd F.A., 89th Division*, 12.

13. Euvezin

Epigraph: Grantland Rice, "Voices of Ghosts," The Sportlight, *New York Tribune*, November 1, 1917.

1. Pershing, *My Experiences*, 2:294.

2. "Germans Have Three Lines," *New York Times*, September 12, 1918.

3. English, *History of the 89th Division, U.S.A.*, 134.

4. Yockelson, *Forty-Seven Days*, 46.

5. Chubb, *Regimental History, 342nd Field Artillery, 89th Division*, 29. Battery F alone, according to the battery history, fired nearly seven hundred shells into German positions along the Charey-St. Julien road on the night of September 25–26, seemingly contradicting the regimental history.

6. "Letter from Sgt. Carey J. Maupin to His Father, Rev. W. N. Maupin," *Troy Free Press*, January 3, 1919.

7. Ziehl and Zickrick, "Men Behind Opposing Guns," 39.

8. Wright and Ferrell, *Meuse-Argonne Diary*, 48.

9. Chubb, *Regimental History, 342nd Field Artillery, 89th Division*, 27.

10. English, *History of the 89th Division, U.S.A.*, 247.

11. Moorhead, *The Story of the 139th Field Artillery*, 203.

12. Harold Parrott, Both Sides, *Brooklyn Eagle*, March 29, 1941.

13. Editorial item, *Omaha Bee*, April 22, 1918.

14. Herbert E. Smith, *U.S. Army Recruiting News*, reprinted in "The Pinches Are Never Too Tight for Men Like Sgt. Grover C. Alexander," *Brooklyn Eagle*, October 24, 1926.

15. Jack Smith, "Indian Pitching Sensation of 25 Years Ago Still Is 'Fit and Able,'" *Arizona Republic*, February 14, 1942.

16. "Alexander Is Making Good War Promise," *Bridgeport Times*, February 5, 1920.

17. Junius B. Wood, "Players Anxious to Get Back Home," *Washington Star*, March 2, 1919.

18. "History, 164th Field Artillery Brigade Headquarters," Box 44, NARA-164.

19. "Memorandum to Regimental Commanders," October 5, 1918, G-3 Memos, NARA-164.

20. "Memorandum for Commanding Officer, 342nd F.A.," October 7, 1918, G-3 Memos, NARA-164.

21. English, *History of the 89th Division, U.S.A.*, 342.

22. Chubb, *Regimental History, 342nd Field Artillery, 89th Division*, 31.

23. Wright and Ferrell, *Meuse-Argonne Diary*, 49.

24. Cole and Howells, *Thirty-Seventh Division*, 2:345.

25. Wright and Ferrell, *Meuse-Argonne Diary*, 63.

26. Cole and Howells, *Thirty-Seventh Division*, 2:350.

27. Col. Harold Bush's 134th Field Artillery, which had crossed the English Channel with the 342nd Field Artillery, was attached to the 164th Field Artillery Brigade from October 28 to November 13. General Donnelly commended the regiment for executing missions "efficiently and with a display of cheerfulness and promptness that indicates a very high morale and state of training" (Kirtley, *The Liaison*, 64).

28. Pershing, *My Experiences*, 2:358.

29. Robert H. Ferrell, footnote in Wright and Ferrell, *Meuse-Argonne Diary*, 25.

30. English, *History of the 89th Division, U.S.A.*, 137.

31. English, *History of the 89th Division, U.S.A.*, 342.

32. English, *History of the 89th Division, U.S.A.*, 246.

33. Cole and Howells, *Thirty-Seventh Division*, 356.

34. *Pennsylvania in the World War*, 2:594.

35. English, *History of the 89th Division, U.S.A.*, 248.

36. Chubb, *Regimental History, 342nd Field Artillery, 89th Division*, 35–36.

37. "The Eagle's Two Pages of Special Military News of Brooklyn Boys in the American and European Camps," *Brooklyn Eagle*, December 22, 1918.

38. Albert-Paul Granier, "War Song," reprinted in Ruzich, *Behind Their Lines*.

39. English, *History of the 89th Division, U.S.A.*, 247. The 342nd Field Artillery war diary supplies the correct date, which the division history incorrectly lists as October 19 and the regimental history shows as October 15.

40. "Ex-Beaver in Front Line," *Portland Oregonian*, December 29, 1918.

41. "Otis Lambeth Has Been Decorated," *Oakland Tribune*, November 30, 1918.

42. "Operations Order Number 18, Headquarters, 164th F.A. Brigade, October 27, 1918," *Missouri Over There*, http://missourioverthere.org/.

43. "Sporting Squibs," *Lincoln Star*, November 12, 1918.

44. "Lambeth, Cleveland Pitcher, Gets a Medal," *Albany Journal*, October 31, 1918.

45. "Honors for Lambeth," *Schenectady Gazette*, November 6, 1918.

46. "News and Notes of Moran," *Iola Register*, November 7, 1918.

47. "The Lambeth Family," *Iola Register*, November 16, 1918.

48. "Otis Lambeth Has Been Decorated."

49. Wood, "Players Anxious."

50. Andrew Gordon Graham, "Forecasted a Quick Peace," unknown newspaper, n.d., Box 18, KHS-49.

51. "Arthur Wight Is Killed in France by Shrapnel," *Clifton Copper Era*, December 16, 1918. Wight's body was reinterred at Arlington National Cemetery following the war.

52. "Yanks Find Comforts of Home in Dugouts Taken from Germans," *Bellingham Herald*, October 31, 1918.

53. "Peace Proposals Warm from Guns Letter Describes," *Arizona Republican*, October 26, 1918.

54. "Yavapai Cowboy Knows How to Duck Shrapnel," *Prescott Weekly Journal-Miner*, November 15, 1918.

55. "Foot-Race—Not Fight," *Maryville Democrat-Forum*, November 20, 1918.

56. "Letters from Scott County Boys in the Service of the Big Uncle," *Benton Scott County Democrat*, December 19, 1918.

57. "Alexander May Be Missing Next Year," *Racine Journal-News*, December 3, 1918.

58. "Arthur Snyder Just Can't Like the German Air Planes," *Jasper News*, December 5, 1918.

59. "From Ira C. Stout," *Mansfield Mirror*, October 24, 1918.

60. "Letter from F. C. Krysher from His Nephew in France," *Carbondale Free Press*, November 15, 1918.

61. November 5, 1918, NARA-WD.

62. Chubb, *Regimental History, 342nd Field Artillery, 89th Division*, 36.

63. *The U.S. Army in the World War I Era*, 76.

64. English, *History of the 89th Division, U.S.A.*, 191.

65. English, *History of the 89th Division, U.S.A.*, 393. The citation permitted Dr. Withington to pin a tiny silver star to the ribbon of his World War I Victory Medal. In 1932 such citations were replaced by the Silver Star Medal, the third-highest American combat decoration.

66. Chubb, *Regimental History, 342nd Field Artillery, 89th Division*, 42.

67. "Was Fritzie Really Anxious to Quit the Fight? Read What He Says," *Omaha Bee*, December 21, 1918.

68. "Was Fritzie Really Anxious."

69. "Baseball Battery Last to Shoot," *The Sporting News*, December 26, 1918.

14. Armistice

Epigraph: Grantland Rice, "1919," *New York Tribune*, January 1, 1919.

1. Lowry, "Pershing and the Armistice," 284–85.

2. "Gave the Enemy Gas," *Sedalia Democrat*, December 19, 1918.

3. "Then and Now," *American Legion Monthly*, September 1927.

4. "Mike Menosky Back," *Washington Star*, April 15, 1919.

5. November 11, 1918, NARA-WD.

6. English, *History of the 89th Division, U.S.A.*, 351.

7. *89th Division Summary of Operations in the World War*, 44.

8. *War Expenditures: Hearings before Subcommittee No. 3*, 2:1740.

9. Persico, *Eleventh Month, Eleventh Day, Eleventh Hour*, 334.

10. "'French Poor Ball Players,' Says Matty," *Bucknell University Bucknellian*, February 25, 1919.

11. English, *History of the 89th Division, U.S.A.*, 250.

12. "From Over There," *Butler Weekly Times*, January 3, 1919.

13. Rayburn, *History of Battery F, 342nd F.A., 89th Division*, 16.

14. Chubb, *Regimental History, 342nd Field Artillery, 89th Division*, 47.

15. *Pennsylvania in the World War*, 2:594.

16. "From the Land of the Hun," *Taney County Republican*, January 30, 1919.

17. Ralph H. Hull, letter dated November 11, 1918, Box 23, KHS-49.

18. "Letter from 'Chuck' Ward Tells of Doings in Germany," *Brooklyn Eagle*, February 3, 1919.

19. "Seven American Divisions Called for Metz Attack," *Stars and Stripes*, February 14, 1919.

20. Rayburn, *History of Battery F, 342nd F.A., 89th Division*, 17.

21. "Ex-Beaver in Front Line," *Portland Oregonian*, December 29, 1918.

22. "Rigney Sends Christmas Greetings from France," *Brooklyn Daily Star*, December 24, 1918.

23. November 12, 1918, NARA-WD.

24. "An 'Old Home' Welcome," *Kansas City Times*, May 28, 1919.

25. English, *History of the 89th Division, U.S.A.*, 499.

26. English, *History of the 89th Division, U.S.A.*, 500.

27. English, *History of the 89th Division, U.S.A.*, 250–51.

28. "A Letter from Sgt. Carey J. Maupin to Home Folks," *Troy Free Press*, December 6, 1918.

29. "Letter from Sgt. Carey J. Maupin to His Father, Rev. W. N. Maupin," *Troy Free Press*, January 3, 1919.

30. "Baseball Battery Last to Shoot," *The Sporting News*, December 26, 1918.

31. "Captain Cobb and Johnny Evers Bring Tales of Adventure from Front Line Trenches," *New York Herald*, December 17, 1918. Various accounts had Evers meeting Alexander in France, but one sportswriter reported otherwise: "Johnny said he hadn't met Grover Alexander, but that he had heard plenty of him" (George B. Underwood, "Evers Here, Denies Libel on Baseball," *New York Sun*, December 17, 1918).

32. Junius B. Wood, "Players Anxious to Get Back Home," *Washington Star*, March 2, 1919.

33. Parrott, Both Sides.

34. "Send Christmas Greetings through Post," *Boston Post*, December 25, 1918.

35. "Ex-Beaver in Front Line."

36. "Letter from 'Chuck' Ward."

15. The March

Epigraph: Grantland Rice, "The Doughboys Speaks," *New York Tribune*, January 3, 1919.

1. Chubb, *Regimental History, 342nd Field Artillery, 89th Division*, 48.

2. "Frank Wetzel Writes from Irrel, Germany," *Casconade County Republican*, January 31, 1919.

3. "Baseball Sure to Be Back in Spring," *New York Times*, December 5, 1918.

4. English, *History of the 89th Division, U.S.A.*, 255.

5. "Then and Now," *American Legion Monthly*, September 1927.

6. Chubb, *Regimental History, 342nd Field Artillery, 89th Division*, 51.

7. Rayburn, *History of Battery F, 342nd F.A., 89th Division*, 17.

8. "Col. Wainwright Describes Army's March from Trenches to Rhine," *Brooklyn Standard Union*, May 18, 1919. The briefing officer was Lt. Col. James M. "Skinny" Wainwright. As a lieutenant general during World War II, he surrendered American forces in the Philippines to the Japanese. Wainwright later received the Medal of Honor.

9. "Tribute to Lieut. Jacobus," *Greenfield Recorder*, March 5, 1919.

10. "Interesting Letter from Germany Written by George Logue," *Edgefield Advertiser*, April 23, 1919.

11. Chubb, *Regimental History, 342nd Field Artillery, 89th Division*, 51.

12. "Will 'Alex' the Great Come Back," *South Bend News-Times*, January 30, 1919.

13. Chubb, *Regimental History, 342nd Field Artillery, 89th Division*, 52.

14. "Alexander Lost to Cubs," *New York Times*, December 4, 1918.

15. "May Play Ball in Berlin This Summer," *El Paso Herald*, December 16, 1918.

16. Rayburn, *History of Battery F, 342nd F.A., 89th Division*, 17.

17. "'Chuck' Ward on Rhine," *Portland Oregonian*, January 27, 1919.

18. Rayburn, *History of Battery F, 342nd F.A., 89th Division*, 18.

19. Chubb, *Regimental History, 342nd Field Artillery, 89th Division*, 54–55.

20. "Will 'Alex' the Great Come Back."

21. "To the Third Army," *Stars and Stripes*, December 13, 1918.

22. English, *History of the 89th Division, U.S.A.*, 263.

23. Rayburn, *History of Battery F, 342nd F.A., 89th Division*, 18.

24. "Will 'Alex' the Great Come Back."

25. Chubb, *Regimental History, 342nd Field Artillery, 89th Division*, 56.

26. "Frank Wetzel Writes."

27. Chubb, *Regimental History, 342nd Field Artillery, 89th Division*, 56.

28. Rayburn, *History of Battery F, 342nd F.A., 89th Division*, 18.

29. "Await Word from Alex," *Ogden Standard*, December 21, 1918.

30. "Send Christmas Greetings through Post," *Boston Post*, December 25, 1918.

31. "Soldiers' Letters," *Benton Scott County Democrat*, February 13, 1919.

32. "Letters from Our Boys 'Over There,'" *Clifton Copper Era*, February 7, 1919.

33. "Tribute to Lieut. Jacobus."

34. Chubb, *Regimental History, 342nd Field Artillery, 89th Division*, 59.

16. Occupied Germany

Epigraph: Grantland Rice, "Then—and Now," *New York Tribune*, March 5, 1919.

1. "Soldiers' Letters," *Hutchinson News*, February 17, 1919.

2. Chubb, *Regimental History, 342nd Field Artillery, 89th Division*, 61.

3. "Roy Snyder in Germany," *Jasper News*, February 20, 1919.

4. Chubb, *Regimental History, 342nd Field Artillery, 89th Division*, 56.

5. "Frank Wetzel Writes from Irrel, Germany," *Casconade County Republican*, January 31, 1919.

6. Rayburn, *History of Battery F, 342nd F.A., 89th Division*, 19.

7. "Then and Now," *American Legion Monthly*, September 1927.

8. Grover C. Alexander, "Pitched Three Games for Cubs, Then to War," *Boston Globe*, June 16, 1930.

9. Rayburn, *History of Battery F, 342nd F.A., 89th Division*, 19.

10. "Letter from 'Chuck' Ward Tells of Doings in Germany," *Brooklyn Eagle*, February 3, 1919.

11. "Outlook Bright for Sports in 1919," *Stars and Stripes*, January 3, 1919. The army newspaper had resumed its sports coverage with the December 27 weekly issue.

12. "Battery Work!," *Chicago Tribune*, December 15, 1918.

13. James Crusinberry, "Catcher Killefer Will Report for Cubs' Trip to California," *Chicago Tribune*, December 27, 1918.

14. Caught on the Fly, *The Sporting News*, December 26, 1918.

15. "Alex Finds Star for Bruin Club on French Lot," *Duluth Herald*, December 25, 1918.

16. Chubb, *Regimental History, 342nd Field Artillery, 89th Division*, 59.

17. Rayburn, *History of Battery F, 342nd F.A., 89th Division*, 20.

18. Chubb, *Regimental History, 342nd Field Artillery, 89th Division*, 61.

19. "A Letter from France," *Iron Country Register*, December 26, 1918.

20. Chubb, *Regimental History, 342nd Field Artillery, 89th Division*, 63–64.

21. Rayburn, *History of Battery F, 342nd F.A., 89th Division*, 20.

22. "Letters from Soldier Boys," *Akron Register-Tribune*, May 1, 1919.

23. "Will 'Alex' the Great Come Back," *South Bend News-Times*, January 30, 1919.

24. "Mitchell Soon to Return," *Brooklyn Eagle*, January 22, 1919.

25. Junius B. Wood, "Players Anxious to Get Back Home," *Washington Star*, March 2, 1919.

26. "Bigger and Better Baseball in 1919," *Wilmington Journal*, November 21, 1918.

27. "Great Pitchers in Service Believed Lost to the Game," *El Paso Herald*, December 21, 1918.

28. "Fans Will Find Baseball Line-up Badly Scrambled When They Return Home," *Stars and Stripes*, April 18, 1919.

29. Johnson and Brown, *Official Athletic Almanac*, 23.

30. English, *History of the 89th Division, U.S.A.*, 270.

31. Camp, *Spalding's Official Foot Ball Guide 1919*, 245.

32. English, *History of the 89th Division, U.S.A.*, 270.

33. Camp, *Spalding's Official Foot Ball Guide 1919*, 243.

34. Johnson and Brown, *Official Athletic Almanac*, 25.

35. English, *History of the 89th Division, U.S.A.*, 272.

36. "Husky Third Army Football Team," *Stars and Stripes*, March 28, 1919.

37. "'Abe, the Cobbler,'" *Troy Times*, December 15, 1919. Harvard later wore Withington shoes during its 1920 victory over the University of Oregon in a game today called the Rose Bowl.

38. "89th Division Wins Football Palm in France," *Washington Herald*, March 31, 1919.

39. Clark, "Our Other National Game," 52.

40. "89th Division in the Great War," *St. Louis Post-Dispatch*, May 25, 1919.

41. "89th Division Wins Gridiron Title from 36th," *Stars and Stripes*, April 4, 1919.

42. *New York Herald*, overseas edition, quoted in "Athletics," *Alumni Quarterly*, May 1, 1919, 300.

43. Camp, *Spalding's Official Foot Ball Guide 1919*, 245.

44. Johnson and Brown, *Official Athletic Almanac*, 21.

45. Wood, "Players Anxious."

46. Hugh S. Fullerton, "National League Imbued with New Life Since Heydler Took Reins," *New York World*, December 23, 1918.

47. "Cubs Issue Complete Denial of Alexander Rumor," *Bridgeport Times*, December 26, 1918.

48. Parke Brown, "Alexander Slated to Start Home from Germany Today," *Chicago Tribune*, March 6, 1919.

49. Grantland Rice, The Sportlight, *New York Tribune*, March 8, 1919.

50. Frederick G. Lieb, "Mathewson Again Becomes a Giant," *New York Sun*, March 8, 1919.

51. Document no. 827, Box 1798, NARA-342.

52. "Alexander on Way Home," *New York Sun*, March 19, 1919.

53. I. E. Sanborn, "Hollocher and Aleck the Great at Assured to Cubs," *Chicago Tribune*, March 19, 1919.

54. "Cubs Leave for Pasadena Tonight," *Dubuque Herald-Telegram*, March 19, 1919.

55. Alexander, "Pitched Three Games."

56. "Grover Cleveland Alexander Homeward Bound," *St. Paul Phonograph*, March 20, 1919.

17. Safe at Home

Epigraph: Grantland Rice, "The A.E F.," *Stars and Stripes*, July 26, 1918.

1. King and Elliot, "There's a Long, Long Trail."

2. "Colorful Soldier of Fortune, Friend of Pershing, Dead," *Washington Star*, March 16, 1925.

3. "Chicago Cubs' Great Pitching Star Wins Last Game in France," *Stars and Stripes*, April 11, 1919.

4. "Then and Now," *American Legion Monthly*, June 1927. The article misidentifies the site of the game as near Camp Genicart, which was situated near Bordeaux.

5. "Blue Denim Suits for All Homegoers," *Stars and Stripes*, April 11, 1919.

6. Louis A. Dougher, "Mike Menosky in America Eager to Report to Washington Outfit," *Washington Times*, April 15, 1919.

7. Alexander's dog had been on an adventure too. The bulldog apparently had run off from Aimee in Newport. A woman in nearby Fort Thomas found the runaway and wrote to the Omaha city clerk with the license number. "Her description of the dog corresponds to the animal for which tag 3,019 was issued to Alexander." ("Big League Pitcher's Dog, Licensed Here, Is Lost in Kentucky," *Omaha Bee*, April 6, 1919.)

8. C. V. Julian, "Alexander the Great Back from War Service in France," *Chicago Tribune*, April 15, 1919. Boston Braves shortstop Walter Maranville reached New York the same day on the battleship USS *Pennsylvania* with a parrot on his shoulder and a monkey on his arm. "Rabbit" was soon on his way home to Massachusetts.

9. "Alex Home Again," *Reading Eagle*, April 15, 1919.

10. "Sergeant Alexander Returns to Join Cubs Pitching Staff," *New York Herald*, April 15, 1919.

11. "Ready for His Turn May 1," *Kansas City Times*, April 17, 1919.

12. "Alexander, Back From France, to Play Ball," *New York Tribune*, April 15, 1919.

13. Julian, "Alexander the Great Back."

14. "Then and Now," *American Legion Monthly*, April 1927.

15. John Alcock, "Aleck Welcomed Back to Chicago Under Heavy Fire of Camera Fleet," *Chicago Tribune*, April 18, 1919.

16. "Aleck the Great Arrives Today with Wrigley," *Chicago Tribune*, April 17, 1919.

17. Alcock, "Aleck Welcomed Back."

18. "Fans in Chicago Greet Alexander," *Washington Star*, April 19, 1919.

19. Ring W. Lardner, In the Wake of the News, *Chicago Tribune*, April 18, 1919.

20. "Grover Alexander and Bride Visit Home Folks," *St. Paul Phonograph*, April 24, 1919.

21. Alexander, "The Shock of War," 59–60.

22. Hugh S. Fullerton, "Baseball Fighters Recite Experiences of Great Conflict," *Atlanta Constitution*, May 6, 1919. The unnamed former player almost certainly was Harry McCormick.

23. Yale University, *Obituary Record of Yale Graduates*, 497.

24. "Lieut. Joe Jenkins and Sergt. Aleck Meet Up in the Loop," *Chicago Tribune*, April 23, 1919.

25. James Crusinberry, "Cubs Champ at Bit as Leaking Skies Defer Start," *Chicago Tribune*, April 24, 1919.

26. "Cold Weather Mars Chicago Prospects," *Boise Capital News*, April 24, 1919.

27. James Crusinberry, "One Hot Rally in Frigid Air Means Victory for Cubs, 5–1," *Chicago Tribune*, April 25, 1919.

28. Notes, *Chicago Tribune*, May 5, 1919.

29. "Lieut. Joe Jenkins and Sergt. Aleck."

30. "Alec Defeated by Cincy, 1 to 0," *Rock Island Argus*, May 10, 1919.

31. James Crusinberry, "Alexander Shows He's Great as Ever, but Reds Beat Him," *Chicago Tribune*, May 10, 1919.

32. H. C. Hamilton, "Alexander Back in Game," *Keokuk Daily Gate City*, May 10, 1919.

33. Jack Sher, "Old Pete," in Heyn, *Twelve More Sport Immortals*, 155.

34. Robert W. Maxwell, "Jacobs and Gravath Combine to Humble Bezdekless Pirates," *Philadelphia Public Ledger*, May 14, 1919.

35. Grantland Rice, The Sportlight, *New York Tribune*, May 21, 1919.

36. Robert W. Maxwell, "Alex Gets Present, Then Gets Walloped for Third Defeat," *Philadelphia Public Ledger*, May 24, 1919.

37. I. E. Sanborn, "Sergt. Aleck 'Over the Top' for Season's First Victory," *Chicago Tribune*, June 3, 1919.

38. "Blame Result on Army Life," *Chicago Eagle*, December 20, 1919.

18. Postwar

Epigraph: Grantland Rice, "The Eternal Drift," *New York Tribune*, July 29, 1918.

1. George B. Underwood, "Schmandt Badly Spiked in Practice," *New York Sun*, April 1, 1919.

2. Thomas S. Rice, "Cardinals Slaughter Mitchell and Grimes," *Brooklyn Eagle*, July 13, 1919.

3. "Hosts of Candidates," editorial, *New York Sun*, August 14, 1934.

4. "Clarence Mitchell Is Dead at 72; One of the Last Spitball Pitchers," *New York Times*, November 7, 1963.

5. Sport Shrapnel, *Memphis News Scimitar*, March 31, 1919.

6. Rayburn, *History of Battery F, 342nd F.A., 89th Division*, 22.

7. "Another Changes Uniform," *The Sporting News*, June 12, 1919.

8. "Majors Pass Up Lambeth," *Lockport Union-Sun and Journal*, July 19, 1919.

9. Item, *Iola Register*, July 18, 1919.

10. "Release to Lambeth," *Topeka State Journal*, July 16, 1919.

11. "His Debut Was a Success," *Columbus Dispatch*, July 20, 1919. Lambeth later faced the Washington Senators' great hurler on Walter Johnson Day at Humboldt, Kansas, October 24, 1919. Johnson and the Humboldt Grays beat Lambeth and the Moran, Kansas, team, 12–5.

12. "Lambeth to Aid Hurley," *Iola Register*, December 9, 1930.

13. "Looks As If the Only Win Connie Mack Can Get in the American League Is Win Noyes," *Philadelphia Public Ledger*, July 21, 1919.

14. "Macks Again Share Bill with Leaders," *Philadelphia Inquirer*, August 9, 1919.

15. "Alexander Is Making Good War Promise," *Bridgeport Times*, February 5, 1920.

16. "Greatest Pitcher in World Tutors Potsy's Twirlers," *Daily Illini*, January 28, 1920.

17. John Kieran, Sports of the Times, *New York Times*, June 29, 1942.

18. Elmont Waite, "Ad Lindsey Is Coaching Again," *Ardmore Ardmoreite*, November 2, 1944.

19. "Paul Withington Favors General Military Training," *Boston Globe*, August 9, 1919.

20. "Gridiron Star Is Back," *Lawrence Journal-World*, June 25, 1919.

21. Item, *Hutchinson News*, October 26, 1920.

22. Frank Finch, "'Old Pete': Intimate Details of Former Pitcher's Life Related by Alexander's Ex-Wife," *The Sporting News*, April 25, 1951.

23. "Snug Harbor for the Shell-Shocked," *New York Times Book Review and Magazine*, January 2, 1921.

24. Hayden, "Shell-Shocked—and After."

25. *Baseball Magazine*, quoted in Kavanagh, *Ol' Pete*, 72.

26. "Alexander, the Great, Gets in 'Dutch,'" *St. Paul Phonograph*, June 23, 1926, largely reprinted from the *Omaha Daily News*.

27. Weatherby, "Bill Killefer."

28. Finkel, "Pete Alexander."

29. James B. Harrison, "Cards Win World Series, Taking Final Game, 3 to 2; $1,207,864 Is Record Gate," *New York Times*, October 11, 1926.

30. George Kirksey, "Grover Cleveland Alexander Is Added to 'Hall of Fame,'" *Wisconsin State Journal*, January 19, 1938.

31. "Greatest Feat Since Matty's, Is McGraw's Praise for Alex," *New York Times*, October 11, 1926.

32. Harry Grayson, "Effortless, Matchless for Nineteen Years, Alex Picked Up Where Young Left Off," *Ogden Standard-Examiner*, May 5, 1943.

33. Frederick G. Lieb, "Bob Meusel Only Player Who Crossed Dope Badly," *Washington Star*, October 12, 1926.

34. "'Alexander the Greater' and Wife Home," *St. Paul Phonograph*, October 27, 1926.

35. "Alexander Movie Will Show Here This Week," *St. Paul Phonograph*, June 11, 1952.

36. "Fear's Sense of Duty Is Equal to Shellshock," *Bemidji Pioneer*, November 18, 1918.

37. Honig, *Baseball America*, 93. Biographer John C. Skipper suggests that Alexander perhaps was too hard of hearing to notice the fireworks. But had he been so nearly deaf, the pitcher likely still would have noticed the others jump. Hallahan's description makes shell shock the more probable reason for Alexander's odd reaction.

38. Bob Broeg, "Spunky Aimee Still Loyal To Alexander the Great," *St. Louis Post-Dispatch*, February 6, 1977.

39. Roscoe McGowen, "Alexander Equals Mathewson's Feat," *New York Times*, August 2, 1929.

40. "Alexander Victor, Sets League Mark," *New York Times*, August 11, 1929.

41. "Alex 'On Carpet' as Rule Breaker," *Washington Star*, August 20, 1929.

42. "Alexander's Big League Days Are All Over," *St. Paul Phonograph Star*, June 11, 1930.

43. "A Sad Case," editorial, *The Sporting News*, August 7, 1930.

44. Harry Robert, "Major Days Over, 'Old' Alex Admits," *Washington Star*, June 4, 1930.

45. "Cops Seek Alexander! (As Base Ball Pitcher)," *Washington Star*, June 7, 1930.

46. "Alexander, 'Wouldn't Touch a Drop,' If Starting Now," *Brooklyn Standard Union*, August 8, 1930.

47. Finkel, "Pete Alexander."

19. The Long, Long Trail

Epigraph: Grantland Rice, The Sportlight, *New York Tribune*, June 3, 1919.

1. "Old Aleck Climbs on Wagon; Wife Returns to Him," *Beatrice Sun*, November 2, 1931.

2. John Kieran, Sports of the Times, *New York Times*, August 27, 1932.

3. Jack Sher, in Heyn, *Twelve More Sport Immortals*, 163.

4. Aimee revealed after Alexander's death that a payment of one hundred dollars per month, which he believed was a small National League pension, came from Cardinals president Sam Breadon. The club later clarified that although Breadon had suggested it, payment came from league funds.

5. "Grover C. Alexander to Louisville, Ky.," *St. Paul Phonograph*, January 29, 1936.

6. "Grover C. Alexander Is Able to Leave Hospital," *Lincoln Star*, August 8, 1936.

7. "Alexander on His Election," *Otsego Farmer*, January 28, 1938.

8. "Baseball Immortals Who Took Part in Centennial Celebration," *New York Sun*, June 13, 1939.

9. "Judge Landis Takes Over," *New York Sun*, June 12, 1939.

10. Jack Miley, "First Hundred Years Easiest the Best Show," *New York Post*, June 13, 1939.

11. Fred Lieb, "Heart-Break Story of Alex the Great Ends," *The Sporting News*, November 15, 1950.

12. "Request for Army Information," Bronx, New York, Veterans Administration Form 3101, November 15, 1940, NARA-GCA.

13. Rehman, "Characteristics of Veterans Diagnosed with Seizures," 758.

14. "Broke, Ill, Alexander in Veterans' Hospital," *Albany Times-Union*, March 22, 1941.

15. J. G. Taylor Spink, "'No Regrets—I Got My Memories,' Says Old Alex, Leaving Hospital and Hoping for Cooperstown Job," *The Sporting News*, April 3, 1941.

16. "Alexander Is Dead; Noted Pitcher, 63," *New York Times*, November 5, 1950.

17. Roundy Says, *Madison Wisconsin State Journal*, September 18, 1944. Rogers Hornsby had brought Alexander to East St. Louis for a job on his radio program.

18. "Alexander Injured; Leaves Hospital Bed," *Philadelphia Inquirer*, May 14, 1948.

19. Bill Becker, "Ol' Pete Will Need All His Stuff," *Albany Knickerbocker News*, December 28, 1949.

20. "Alexander Day Did Not Attract Many," *St. Paul Howard County Herald*, May 31, 1950.

21. Robert G. Phipps, "Ol' Alex Laid to Rest with Military Rites," *The Sporting News*, November 15, 1950.

22. "Ol' Alex Day Is Big Success Wednesday," *St. Paul Phonograph*, May 24, 1950. The *Phonograph* apparently refers to the local celebration following the 1926 World Series, which was twenty-four years earlier. The newspaper considered the 1950 event a success because of the presence of "a host of well known personalities" who wouldn't have visited St. Paul otherwise.

23. Aimee Alexander, letters to the editor, *St. Paul Phonograph*, June 20, 1951.

24. Will Grimsley, "'Old Pete' Finally Gets to World Series, Has Trouble Getting Past Man at Gate," *Buffalo Evening News*, October 7, 1950.

25. "Alexander, Famed Hurler, Dies at 63 in Rented Room," *Philadelphia Inquirer*, November 5, 1950.

26. Louis Effrat, "Old Pete Standee; Sic Transit Gloria," *New York Times*, October 7, 1950.

27. "'Alex' Wonders How Whiz Kids Ever Won Flag," *Brooklyn Eagle*, October 7, 1950.

28. "Old Pete in His Glory At 1950 World Series," *Washington Star*, November 5, 1950.

29. "Grover Alexander Dies at 63; One of Baseball's Immortals," *Rochester Democrat and Chronicle*, November 5, 1950.

30. Frank Finch, "'Old Pete': Intimate Details of Former Pitcher's Life Related by Alexander's Ex-Wife," *The Sporting News*, April 25, 1951.

31. "Balldom's Immortal Dies of Heart Attack Saturday," *Howard County Herald*, November 8, 1950.

32. "Alexander, Famed Hurler."

33. "Old Pete Alexander Was Known as One of the Diamond's Greatest Figures," *Ogdensburg Journal*, November 11, 1950.

34. Arthur Daley, Sports of the Times, *New York Times*, November 6, 1950.

35. "Grover Cleveland Alexander Ended Days In Bitterness towards St. Paul, Writer In Sporting News Says in Feature Story," *St. Paul Phonograph*, May 16, 1951.

36. "All-Time Pitching Great Is Buried," *Long Beach Independent*, November 7, 1950.

37. "Cards Pay for Funeral Of Alex; Ex-Wife Says Breadon Paid Pension," *Washington Star*, November 7, 1950.

38. "Rogers Hornsby to Start a Memorial for Alexander Here," *St. Paul Phonograph*, January 31, 1951.

39. "Alexander Film Interests," *St. Paul Phonograph*, June 18, 1952.

40. Edelman, "The Winning Team," 76.

41. Josh Salmon, "Former MLB Players Take Part in Grover Cleveland Alexander Days," *Grand Island Independent*, July 9, 2016.

42. Jim Murray, "The Big Leaguer," *Los Angeles Times*, April 21, 1974.

43. "Alex's Widow Faces Eviction from Home," *Orange County Register*, February 3, 1977.

BIBLIOGRAPHY

Alexander, Caroline. "The Shock of War." *Smithsonian* 41, no. 5 (September 2010): 58–66.

Alexander, Grover Cleveland. "King Baseball." *American Legion Magazine*, June 1938.

Alexander, Robert. *Memories of the World War, 1917–1918*. New York: Macmillan Company, 1931.

Allerdice, Bruce. "Win Noyes." SABR BioProject, sabr.org/bioproject.

American Battle Monuments Commission. *American Armies and Battlefields in Europe: A History, Guide, and Reference Book*. Washington DC: Center of Military History, U.S. Army, 2018 [reprint]. https://history.army.mil.

———. *89th Division Summary of Operations in the World War*. Washington DC: Government Printing Office, 1944.

———. *37th Division Summary of Operations in the World War*. Washington DC: Government Printing Office, 1944.

———. *28th Division Summary of Operations in the World War*. Washington DC: Government Printing Office, 1944.

Andruss, Malcolm P. "Baseball Champions American Expeditionary Forces." *Liaison: The Courier of the Big Guns* 1, no. 27 (June 29, 1919): 267–68.

———. "A Corner in Horsehide." *American Legion Magazine*, April 1938.

Association of the 110th Infantry. *History of the 110th Infantry (10th Pa.) of the 28th Division, U.S.A., 191–1919: A Compilation of Orders, Citations, Maps, Records and Illustrations Relating to the 3rd Pa. Inf., 10th Pa. Inf., and 110th U.S. Inf.* Pittsburgh: The Association, 1920.

"Athletics." *The Alumni Quarterly and Fortnightly Notes* 1, no. 17 (June 1, 1916): 376–78.

"Athletics." *The Alumni Quarterly and Fortnightly Notes* 4, no. 15 (May 1, 1919): 300.

Bacon, William. *History of the Fifty-Fifth Field Artillery Brigade, 1917, 1918, 1919*. Memphis: Benson Printing, 1920.

Barry, John M. "How the Horrific 1918 Flu Spread across America." *Smithsonian*, November 2017. https://www.smithsonianmag.com/.

Baseball: The National Pastime in the National Archives. Washington DC: National Archives and Records Administration, 2014.

Battery "B," 340th Field Artillery, 89th Division. Undated. http://cdm.sos.mo.gov/cdm/.

Beers, Henry P. *U.S. Naval Port Officers in the Bordeaux Region, 1917–1919.* Washington DC: Navy Department, 1943.

Berglund, Abraham. "The Iron-Ore Problem of Lorraine." *Quarterly Journal of Economics* 33, no. 3 (May 1919): 531–54.

Bowen, Albert S. *The Medical Department of the U.S. Army in the World War, Volume IV: Activities Concerning Mobilization Camps and Ports of Embarkation.* Washington DC: Government Printing Office, 1928.

Camp, Walter, ed. *Spalding's Official Foot Ball Guide 1918, 1919.* New York: American Sports Publishing, 1918–19.

Camp Funston Photograms. Ogdensburg KS: Lyle Webb, 1917. http://cdm.sos.mo.gov/cdm/.

Cantonment Life: Camp Funston Illustrated. Kansas City: Baird Company, 1918.

Capozzola, Christopher. *Uncle Sam Wants You: World War I and the Making of the Modern American Citizen.* New York: Oxford University Press, 2008.

Cart, Doran L. "Kansas Football 'Over There.'" *Kansas History: A Journal of the Central Plains* 29 (Autumn 2006): 194–99.

Carter, Donald A. *St. Mihiel: 12–26 September 1918.* Washington DC: Center of Military History, 2018.

Cava, Pete. *Indiana-Born Major League Baseball Players: A Biographical Dictionary, 1871–2014.* Jefferson NC: McFarland, 2015.

Chen, Yu-Hsiung, Han-Ting Wei, Ya-Mei Bai, Ju-Wei Hus, Kai-Lin Huang, Tung-Ping Su, Cheng-Ta Li, et al. "Risk of Epilepsy in Individuals with Posttraumatic Stress Disorder: A Nationwide Longitudinal Study." *Psychosomatic Medicine* 79, no. 6 (July–August 2017): 664–69.

Chubb, Walston. *Regimental History, 342nd Field Artillery, 89th Division.* New York: Regimental Historian, 1921.

Clark, George. "Our Other National Game." *American Legion Magazine*, October 1934.

Cole, Ralph D., and W. C. Howells. *The Thirty-Seventh Division in the World War, 1917–1918.* 2 vols. Columbus OH: Thirty-Seventh Division Veterans Association, 1926, 1929.

Crawford, Russ. *Le Football: A History of American Football in France.* Lincoln: University of Nebraska Press, 2016.

Crowell, Benedict, and Robert Forrest Wilson. *The Road to France: I. The Transportation of Troops and Military Supplies, 1917–1918.* New Haven: Yale University, 1921.

Crowell, Thomas Irving, ed. *A History of the 313th Field Artillery, U.S.A.* New York: Thomas Y. Crowell Company, 1920.

Dalessandro, Robert, and John Wessels. *World War I Battlefield Companion.* Arlington VA: American Battle Monuments Commission, 2018. https://www.abmc.gov/sites/default/files/publications/ABMC_WWI%2520Battlefield%2520Companion%2520Book_20180904.pdf.

Doutrich, Paul E. "October 10, 1926: Pete Alexander Saves the Day." SABR Baseball Games Project, sabr.org/content/sabr-games-project.

Edelman, Rob. "The Winning Team: Fact and Fiction in Celluloid Biographies." *National Pastime* 26 (2006): 72–76.

Eggers, Harold E., and Ellis H. Kerr. "Communicable Disease at Camp Funston and the Medical Officers' Training Camp, Fort Riley, Kansas, October 15th, 1917, to January 15th, 1918." *The Military Surgeon* 43, no. 1 (July 1918): 17–44.

The 88th Division in the World War. New York: Wynkoop Hallenbeck Crawford Company, 1919.

Eisenhower, John S. D. *Teddy Roosevelt and Leonard Wood.* Columbia: University of Missouri Press, 2014.

Embury, Aymar, II. "Concealment of Artillery Positions." *Field Artillery Journal* 12, no. 4 (July–August 1923): 297–304.

Emerson, William K. "The Army's Last Set of Confusing Chevrons." *Military Collector & Historian* 56, no. 4 (Winter 2004): 219–33.

English, George H., Jr. *History of the 89th Division, U.S.A.* Denver: War Society of the 89th Division, 1920.

Faber, Charles F. "Clarence Mitchell." SABR BioProject, sabr.org/bioproject.

Faulkner, Richard S. *Meuse–Argonne: 26 September–11 November 1918.* Washington DC: Center of Military History, 2018.

Field, Francis L., and Guy H. Richards, eds. *The Battery Book: A History of Battery "A," 306 F.A.* New York: DeVinne Press, 1921.

Finkel, Jan. "Pete Alexander." SABR BioProject, sabr.org/bioproject.

Foster, John B., ed. *Spalding's Official Base Ball Guide, 1919.* New York: American Sports Publishing, 1919.

Frankau, Gilbert. *A Song of the Guns in Flanders.* Boston: Houghton Mifflin, 1916.

Gates, Frederick L. "A Report on Antimeningitis Vaccination and Observations on Agglutinins in the Blood of Chronic Meningococcus Carriers." *Journal of Experimental Medicine* 28, no. 4 (October 1, 1918): 449–74.

"George M. 'Potsy' Clark." In "Michigan People of the Great War." United States World War One Centennial Commission. http://www.worldwar1centennial.org.

Gibson, Eugène. *The 28th Division in France.* Philadelphia, 1919.

Handbook of Artillery: Including Mobile, Anti-Aircraft and Trench Matériel. Washington DC: U.S. Government Printing Office, 1920.

The Hatchet: Being the Washington University Year Book, Volume 14. St. Louis: Washington University Class of 1917, 1916.

Hayden, Herbert B. (published anonymously). "Shell-Shocked—and After." *Atlantic Monthly*, December 1921.

Heyn, Ernest V., ed. *Twelve More Sport Immortals.* New York: Bartholomew House, 1951.

Hinds, Ernest. "The Training of Artillery in France." *Field Artillery Journal* 9, no. 4 (September–October 1919): 373–90.

History of Battery "A," 340th Field Artillery, 89th Division, U.S.A. Trier, Germany: J. Lintz, 1919.

History of the Fifty-Fifth Field Artillery Brigade, 1917–1918–1919. Nashville: Benson Printing, 1920.

The History of the 306th Field Artillery: Compiled by the Men Who Participated in the Events Described. New York: Knickerbocker Press, 1920.

Honig, Donald. *Baseball America: The Heroes of the Game and the Times of Their Glory.* New York: Simon & Schuster, 2001.

Howard, James M. *The Autobiography of a Regiment: A History of the 304th Field Artillery in the World War.* New York, 1920.

Howe, M. A. DeWolfe, ed. *The Harvard Volunteers in Europe: Personal Records of Experience in Military, Ambulance, and Hospital Service.* Cambridge MA: Harvard University Press, 1916.

Hunt, Edward Livingston. "Shell Shock and Other War Neuroses." *Medical Record* 94, no. 3 (July 20, 1918): 91–97.

Johnson, Wait C., and Elwood S. Brown, eds. *Official Athletic Almanac of the American Expeditionary Forces 1919: A.E.F. Championships, Inter-Allied Games.* New York: American Sports Publishing, 1919.

Jones, Carlisle L., ed. *History and Roster of the 355th Infantry, 89th Division.* Lincoln: Society of the 355th Infantry, 1919.

Kavanagh, Jack. *Ol' Pete: The Grover Cleveland Alexander Story.* South Bend IN: Diamond Communications, 1996.

King, Stoddard, and Zo Elliot. "There's a Long, Long Trail." M. Witmark & Sons, 1914.

Kirtley, Lorin, ed. *The Liaison: A History of Regimental Headquarters Company, One Hundred Thirty-Fourth U.S. Field Artillery.* Dayton OH: Otterbein Press, 1919.

Lane, F. C. "Baseball's Bit in the World War." *Baseball Magazine,* March 1918.

Lane, Jack C. *Armed Progressive: General Leonard Wood.* Lincoln: University of Nebraska Press, 2009.

Leeke, Jim. *Ballplayers in the Great War: Newspaper Accounts of Major Leaguers in World War I Military Service.* Jefferson NC: McFarland, 2013.

———. *From the Dugouts to the Trenches: Baseball during the Great War.* Lincoln: University of Nebraska Press, 2017.

Lindsey, Adrian. "Ad Lindsey 89th Division vs. 36th Division Football Game Notes—March 1959." Charles S. Stevenson Collection, Missouri Over There. http://missourioverthere.org/.

Lowry, Bullitt. "Pershing and the Armistice." *Journal of American History* 55, no. 2 (September 1968): 281–91.

McCallum, Jack. *Leonard Wood: Rough Rider, Surgeon, Architect of American Imperialism.* New York: New York University, 2006.

Mead, Frederick S., ed. *Harvard's Military Record in the World War.* Boston: Harvard Alumni Association, 1921.

Meany, Tom. *Baseball's Greatest Pitchers.* New York: A. S. Barnes, 1951.

Moorhead, Robert L. *The Story of the 139th Field Artillery, American Expeditionary Forces.* Indianapolis: Bobbs-Merrill, 1920.

Moretti, Onorio, and Robert M. Danford. *Notes on Training Field Artillery Details.* New Haven: Yale University, 1918.

Nash, John. "Gas-s-s-s-s." *Field Artillery Journal* 9, no. 4 (September–October 1919): 469–72.

Palmer, Frederick. *Our Greatest Battle (The Meuse-Argonne)*. New York: Dodd, Mead, 1919.

Paul, Andrea I. "His Own Worst Enemy: The Rise and Fall of Grover Cleveland Alexander." *Nebraska History* 71 (1990): 2–12.

———. "The Life and Times of Clarence Mitchell." NEBRASKA*land*, August 1993.

Pennsylvania in the World War: An Illustrated History of the Twenty-Eighth Division. Pittsburgh: States Publication Society, 1921.

Pershing, John J. *My Experiences in the World War*. 2 vols. New York: Frederick A. Stokes, 1931.

Persico, Joseph E. *Eleventh Month, Eleventh Day, Eleventh Hour: Armistice Day, 1918, World War I and Its Violent Climax*. New York: Random House, 2005.

Prince, Justin G. "They Surely Had Men at Those Guns: The Development of United States Field Artillery 1907–1923." PhD diss., Oklahoma State University, 2010.

Randel, Harry E., ed. *Regimental History, Three Hundred and Forty-First Field Artillery, Eighty-Ninth Division of the National Army*. Kansas City MO: Union Bank Note Co., 1920.

Ray, Harold, and Peter Norcross. "From Lion Tamer to Bulls and Bears: The Story of George (Potsy) Clark." *Proceedings and Newsletter*, North American Society for Sport History, 1980.

Rayburn, Charles W. *History of Battery F, 342nd F.A., 89th Division, A.E.F., 1917–1919*. U.S. government publication, [1919?].

Rehman, Rizwana, Pamela R. Kelly, Aatif M. Husain, Tung T. Tran. "Characteristics of Veterans Diagnosed with Seizures within Veterans Health Administration." *Journal of Rehabilitation Research and Development* 52, no. 7 (January 2015): 751–62.

Rice, Grantland. *The Tumult and the Shouting: My Life in Sports*. New York: A. S. Barnes, 1954.

Ritter, Lawrence S. *The Glory of Their Times: The Story of the Early Days of Baseball Told by the Men Who Played It*. New York: Harper Perennial, 2010.

Ruzich, Connie. *Behind Their Lines: Poetry of the Great War*. https://behindtheirlines.blogspot.com/.

The Schneider Works in France. Paris: Schneider and Cie, 1919.

Serb, Chris. *War Football: World War I and the Birth of the* NFL. Lanham MD: Rowman & Littlefield, 2019.

Service Handbook of the 155-MM Howitzer Matériel Model of 1918 (Schneider) Motorized, with Instructions for Its Care. Washington DC: Government Printing Office, 1920.

Showalter, William Joseph. "America's New Soldier Cities." *National Geographic* 32, nos. 5–6 (November–December 1917): 439–76.

Skipper, John C. *Wicked Curve: The Life and Troubled Times of Grover Cleveland Alexander*. Jefferson NC: McFarland, 2006.

Taylor, James. *Dazzle: Disguise and Disruption in War and Art*. Annapolis MD: Naval Institute Press, 2016.

The 302nd Field Artillery, United States Army. Cambridge MA: 302nd Field Artillery Association, 1919.

Tuchman, Barbara. *The Guns of August*. New York: Ballantine Books, 2009.

The U.S. Army in the World War I Era. Washington DC: Center of Military History, 2017.

Verdun, Argonne-Metz, 1914–1918. Paris: Michelin & Cie., 1919.

War Expenditures: Hearings before Subcommittee No. 3 (Foreign Expenditures) of the Select Committee on Expenditures in the War Department, House of Representatives. Washington DC: Government Printing Office, 1920.

Weatherby, Charlie. "Bill Killefer." SABR BioProject, sabr.org/bioproject.

———. "Red Killefer." SABR BioProject, sabr.org/bioproject.

Wilson, T. P. Cameron. *Magpies in Picardy.* London: Poetry Bookshop, 1919.

Withington, Paul, ed. *The Book of Athletics.* Boston: Lothrop, Lee & Shepard, 1914.

Witt, Fred Ralph. *Riding to War with "A": A History of Battery "A" of the 135th Field Artillery.* Cleveland: Cleveland Evangelical Press, 1919.

Wright, William M., and Robert H. Ferrell, eds. *Meuse-Argonne Diary: A Division Commander in World War I.* Columbia: University of Missouri, 2004.

Yale University. *Obituary Record of Yale Graduates.* Series 18, no. 22, August 1, 1922.

Yockelson, Mitchell. *Forty-Seven Days: How Pershing's Warriors Came of Age to Defeat the German Army in World War I.* New York: NAL Caliber, 2016.

Zardetto, Ray, *'30: Major League Baseball's Year of the Batter.* Jefferson NC: McFarland, 2008.

Ziehl, John, and Ernest Zickrick, interviewed by Kenneth P. Czech. "Men behind Opposing Guns." *MHQ: The Quarterly Journal of Military History* (2002): 36–40.

INDEX

55th Field Artillery Brigade, 121, 225n10

134th Field Artillery Regiment, 93, 221n14, 222n11, 226n27

164th Field Artillery Brigade: and artillerymen, 74; departure of, from Camp Mills, 89; doughboys in, 19; and Eighty-Ninth Division, 127–28, 133, 153–54; firing schedule of, 130; first fatality suffered by, 103; fully equipped, 119–20; high opinion of, 146; and Hindenburg Line, 144; and John Pershing, 133; units of, 19

314th Ammunition Train, 19, 95, 104, 129

317th Ammunition Train, 75

340th Field Artillery Regiment, 19, 73–74, 81, 98, 124, 159; and Battery A, 74, 123, 134, 151; and Battery D, 137

341st Field Artillery Regiment, 89, 103, 104, 120, 139, 160; and Battery C, 103, 135, 144, 145, 151

342nd Field Artillery Regiment: about, 80, 81; at Alsdorf, 158, 160, 161; and animals' deaths, 122; and artillerymen, 74; athlete distribution by, 80–81; and barrages, 128–29; baseball team of, 19–20, 114, 118; and Battery B, 71, 88, 99, 151; and Battery D, 92, 123–24, 135, 145; and Battery E, 83, 86, 102, 123, 129, 147; in Belgium, 155; at Camp Mills, 83–84; casualties suffered by, 66, 147; Christmas party of, 161–62; comfortable quarters for, 151–52; command post of, 123; and deficiencies in material, 95; drill schedule of, 158; establishment of, 17; in Ettlebruck, 156; field officers of, 18; firing by, 135, 226n5; and gas attacks, 125; gathering around fire, 89; in Germany, 153–54, 156, 157; heavy firepower provided by, 96–97; history of, 94; in Hoboken, 184; in Holsthum, 164; and howitzers, 101–2, 120; and life under fire, 124; in Meckel, 163–64; new insignia for, 106–7; organization of, 17–18; Pete Alexander as member of, 82; in Pickliessem, 157; Potsy Clark in, 80; and shelling, 123, 125; and Sunday games, 113–15; test of endurance of, 126; at Toul station, 122; training of, 97; undergoing transformation, 164–65; war diary of, 146. *See also* Camp Funston

355th Infantry Regiment, 73, 76

Alexander, Aimee, 78–79, 108, 176–78, 190, 202–3, 220n16

Alexander, Esther Elizabeth, 109

Alexander, George, 41

Alexander, Grover Cleveland: American Legion job of, 198–99, 201; army training of, 66, 77; arrival of, in the United States, 174–75; and Base Champs, 115–16; and Bill Killefer, 32–34, 113, 117, 162; casual steeliness of, 131; and Charles Ward, 110, 148, 149; and Charles Wrigley, 175, 176; in Chicago, 176–77; Christmas greetings from, 158; civilian life of, 188; and Clarence Mitchell, 67, 79, 183, 201; in Class 1-A, 35, 36, 40; and combat dangers and effects, 148–49, 177; and contract signing, 175, 176; death of, 1, 200; in deep trouble, 192, 196–98;

Alexander, Grover Cleveland (*cont.*)
  at detention camp, 63, 65, 84; discharge of,
  171–72, 175–76; divorce of, 190, 198; dog of,
  232n7; draft number of, 12; draft status of, 39,
  44, 48–49, 60, 112; duty assignment of, 68; earlobe issue of, 197; to Eighty-Ninth Division,
  68; epitaph for, 2; fan letters for, 199; festival in
  honor of, 202; final appearance of the season
  of, 60–61; final gift from, 192; and Fred Mitchell, 46, 155, 158; funeral of, 201; on furlough,
  85; and Hall of Fame, 195–96, 201, 203; hearing problems of, 234n37; heavy drinking by,
  35, 161, 177, 188–89; and hope of pitching, 69–
  70; and horse riding, 105–6; hospitalization of,
  195, 196, 197; and House of David team, 194,
  195; and Johnny Evers, 148; medical and psy-
  chological examination of, 64–65; as member
  of Battery F, 82; memorable moment of, 85–
  86; monument of, 202; and Nick Alexander,
  200, 201; nickname of, 1, 112; as overseas scout
  for Cubs, 117, 163; pension for, 235n4; performance in baseball of, 188; pitching for the Cardinals, 191–92; and Potsy Clark, 131, 163, 201;
  preference of, for navy, 46, 47, 116; promotion
  of, 67–68, 107–8, 130–31, 223n5; remarriage of,
  194; season of (1917), 8; season of (1918), 39–
  40; seizures experienced by, 37–39, 65, 107–8,
  196; and shell shock disorder, 147, 177–78, 188,
  196–97, 203, 234n37; skin cancer issue of, 197;
  sobriety issue of, 194–95; speculation about
  return of, 170–71; superlatives to describe,
  16; suspension of, 193; and test of endurance,
  126; as tragic figure, 200–201; traveling of, as
  a casual, 173–74; unhappy letters written by,
  200; victories and losses for, 180–81; on waivers, 188–89; war experiences of, 148–49; wedding of, 78–79; wristwatch for, 61; at Yankee
  Stadium, 199, 200
Alexander, Nick, 200, 201
Alexander, Pete. *See* Alexander, Grover
  Cleveland
allied armed forces, 104, 152
American Expeditionary Forces. *See* U.S. Army
American League, 7, 11, 13, 152, 162, 185
American Red Cross, 21, 83, 89, 111
ammunition, 123–24, 126, 127, 129, 137, 144

Andruss, Malcolm P., 18, 20–21
animals: availability of, 96, 104; death of, 104,
  122, 126, 148, 152, 158; gas masks for, 102;
  grooming of, 74, 153; handling of, 105, 106; of
  inferior quality, 104; lack of, 133; price of, 165;
  surrendering of, 164
armistice terms, 141–51
Army City, 55, 56, 57, 58
artillerymen: and 164th FA, 74; and 342nd FA,
  74; about, 55, 69; discharge of, 184; and German dugouts, 138; large crowds welcoming,
  82; and readiness issue, 74–75; training of, 84.
  See also soldiers

ballplayers: about, 1, 7, 9; anxiety of, about voyage home, 165–66; conflicting information to,
  7; draft eligible, 10, 15; draft status of, 54; early
  release of, 155; regimental, 114, 118; and Selective Service, 15; and St. Louis Cardinals, 55;
  at Topeka clubs, 57–58; wait-and-see situation for, 163
Barry, Jack, 14, 46, 165
baseball immortals, 196, 200
basketball, 51
Bat and Ball Fund game, 86, 87, 88
Biscoe, Earl, 118, 119, 132, 224n32
bombardment, 126, 129, 135, 147
Bordeaux, France, 94, 97, 98, 110, 115, 117–18
Boston Braves, 10, 14, 112, 163, 232n8
Boston Red Sox, 14, 23, 46, 52, 118, 165
British Army, 42, 96, 136
Brooklyn Dodgers: about, 8, 11, 15; and Charles
  Ward, 184; and Chicago Cubs, 67; and Clar-
  ence Mitchell, 62, 86–88, 165, 182

Camp Cody, 41, 42, 43, 46, 49
Camp de Souge, 95, 100–101, 103–4, 107, 108,
  113–14
Camp Devens, 75–76
Camp Dodge, 29–30, 51, 58, 69
Camp Doniphan, 28, 29, 51
Camp Funston: about, 17; ball club at, 20;
  Charles Ward at, 56; under construction, 71–
  72; detention camps at, 63, 65–68, 76, 84; dif-
  ficulties encountered at, 74; enormous size
  of, 73; and gridiron season, 25–31; Leonard
  Wood at, 57; Major Leaguers at, 53; meningi-

tis outbreak at, 66; Otis Lambeth at, 62; rail trip to, 63; sports training at, 51

Camp MacArthur, 30, 214n24

Camp Mills, 76, 77, 80–89

Casual Company 2950, 173, 174

casuals, 90, 173, 174

casualties, 66, 139, 142–43

censorship, 9, 83, 111

Chicago Cubs: and Bill Killefer, 48; and Dodgers, 67; game of, with Brooklyn, 88; gift from, 61; home opener game of, 178–79; and Santa Rita game, 41–42; season of (1919), 179–80; and spring training, 40; and star battery exchange, 32–34; and St. Louis Cardinals, 47; unwise move by, 170; winless streak for, 180; and World Series, 118, 175

Chicago White Sox, 14, 56, 174, 178, 185

Clark, George "Potsy": about, 25–26; in Battery F, 80; and Clarence Rowland, 57; as coach, 51, 186; and Lloyd Wait, 107; and Pete Alexander, 163, 201; touchdown made by, 28; in World War II, 186

Cleveland Indians, 53, 184

Coast Artillery Corps. See U.S. Army

Cobb, Ty, 7, 143, 163, 196, 229n31

conscription plan, 6–7, 9–10, 34, 36, 38, 59

Donnelly, Edward T., 131, 132, 146, 226n27

doughboys: in 164th FA, 19; in 340th FA, 19; about, 17; adjustment of, to military life, 18; at camps, 68, 93; casualties suffered by, 66, 139; difficulties faced by, 72; gas masks worn by, 101–2; and grape-growing region, 97–98; lessons learned by, 67; loss for, 44; passes for, 97; popularity of baseball with, 111; and travel by train, 120

draft system: and draft boards, 12–13, 35, 38–39, 47, 49, 59; and draftees, 19, 42, 56, 64–66, 71, 73; and draft numbers, 12–13, 39; exemption from, 13, 39, 45; and Registration Day, 9, 10; and Selective Service, 9, 13, 15, 59, 64; and slackers, 11, 35, 45, 112; and young players, 15

Ebbets, Charles, Jr., 86, 94, 97, 145, 162, 165

Ebbets Field, 8, 15, 83, 84, 86–88

Eighty-Ninth Division: and 164th FA, 127–28, 133, 153–54; about, 19; athletic director of, 20–21; and Euvezin Sector, 147; as "Fight-
ing Farmers," 77, 127, 133, 139–40, 142–43, 152–53; gridiron season of, 25–31; and gunnery standards, 131–32; leaving for France, 69; and Leonard Wood, 23, 50, 74; and Meuse-Argonne offensive, 132, 139, 142; new insignia for, 106–7; and Paul Withington, 54–57; Pete Alexander transferred to, 68; and regimental players, 118; rematches for, 58; and Salina club, 58; and St. Louis Cardinals, 55, 56; and St. Mihiel offensive, 121–22; team of, 51; and William Wright, 129–30, 142

Eller, Horace, 87, 88

English Channel, 91, 93, 94, 99, 174, 226n27

epilepsy, 37–39, 65, 177, 196, 203

Euvezin Sector, 127–40, 143, 147, 151

Evers, Johnny, 148, 188, 223n11, 229n31

exhibition games, 6, 41, 55, 116

farmers, exemption by, 45, 59

Fast, John C. "Jick," 26, 80, 131, 187

Fighting Farmers. See Eighty-Ninth Division

First Army, 120, 122, 127, 139

Fitzpatrick, Francis X., 153, 161

football: AEF championship of, 166–69; players, 25, 28, 66; stars, 20, 28, 185

Forty-Second Division, 112, 132, 152

gas attacks, 101, 121, 125

gas masks, 43, 97, 101, 102, 103, 125

Germany and Germans: and 342nd FA, 154, 156; about, 3; American raid on, 135; anger at, 3–4; and armistice terms, 141–50; casualties suffered by, 139; dangerous offensives launched by, 82; and dugouts and shelters, 137–38; and Hindenburg Line, 128; spymasters of, 6; and St. Mihiel offensive, 121; submarines of, 98; troops of, 111, 137; and Zimmermann Telegram, 4

Grant, Eddie, 8, 9, 147

Grey, Sir Edward, 4, 8

Griffith, Clark, 4, 5, 11, 86, 174

Hindenburg Line, 128, 134, 139, 144

horses. See animals

House of David baseball team, 194, 195

howitzers, 95–96, 101–3, 105–6, 120, 130, 135

Huston, T. L., 23, 163

influenza, 158, 159

Jacobus, Harold, 18, 72, 97, 154, 159, 213n4
Jenkins, Joe, 174, 178
Johnson, Ban, 7, 23, 152
Johnson, Walter, 1, 5, 6, 195
Justicia, 89–99

Killefer, Bill: and Chicago Cubs, 48; as coach, 189; and Pete Alexander, 32, 113, 117, 162; as player-manager, 188–89; and star battery exchange, 32–34
Kling, Johnny, 54, 55

Lafitte, Ed, 8, 147
Lambeth, Otis: account of voyage of, 92; at Camp Funston, 62; and Charles Ward, 165, 183–84; early life of, 53–54; first game won by, 69; and Johnny Evers, 148; as mail carrier, 185; and mistaken identity issue, 135; return of, to the Indians, 184; and Win Noyes, 116–18
Lazzeri, Tony, 189, 190
Le Taillan, 95, 96, 97, 99, 113
Lewis, Monroe C., 26, 52, 55–56, 115–16, 166
Liberty war bonds, 60, 61, 63
Lindsey, Adrian, 25–26, 29, 52, 55, 58, 116–17, 166, 168–69, 186–87
live-fire exercise, 51, 75

Mack, Connie, 8, 13–14, 53, 115, 185
Major Leaguers: at Camp Funston, 53; enlistment of, 14, 46; gathering of, 156; hard war fought by, 147–48; and league standings, 113; in navy, 46; at Nugent regiment, 68–69; and Paul Withington, 22; ready to rejoin baseball, 162; and Sunday games, 110–11
Marquard, Rube, 87
Mathewson, Christy, 143, 163, 188, 190, 192–93, 195
Maupin, Carey J., 74, 83, 129, 147
McCormick, Harry, 8, 9, 147, 232n22
Merkle, Fred, 43, 162, 178
Metz, 128, 130, 140, 144
Meuse-Argonne offensive, 132, 139, 142–43
Miller, Hugh, 8, 148
Minor Leaguers, 54, 124, 184
Mitchell, Clarence: about, 54; and Charles Ward, 86–88; and crossing English Channel, 94; discharge of, 182–83; and Dodgers, 62, 86–88, 165, 182; heading for army, 62; and Johnny Evers, 148; and Pete Alexander, 67, 79, 183, 201
Mitchell, Fred, 40, 46, 155, 158
Monplaisir Farm, 130, 135
Moran, Pat, 4–5, 7, 10, 15, 114
mules. *See* animals
mumps and measles, 27, 65

National Baseball Hall of Fame, 195–96, 201, 203
National Guard, 9, 10, 24, 28, 42, 93, 107, 134, 152
National League, 6–8, 11
Naval Air Station Pauillac, 109–18
New York Giants, 8, 85–86, 143, 147, 165, 171
Noyes, Win: about, 8, 224n32; at Bordelais stadium, 117; and Charles Ward, 58; draft notice of, 53; and hope of pitching, 69; and Otis Lambeth, 116–18; at Pauillac, 116; return of, 185
Nugent, George, 53, 68–69, 119
Nugent Field, 54, 55

Paskert, Dode, 33, 42, 178
Pershing, John J.: about, 76, 96, 104; on lack of artillery horses, 133; morale booster for, 122; strict orders by, 157; and Third Army, 152; and William Wright, 142
Philadelphia Phillies: about, 3; interleague exhibition by, 4, 6; and Registration Day, 10; season of (1917), 8, 14, 15, 23, 30, 131; and spring training, 5; star battery exchange by, 32–34
Pittsburgh Pirates, 24, 30, 178, 179
pneumonia, 66, 124, 159, 193, 200
poison gas, 143, 166
Polo Grounds, 23, 84, 85, 86
post-traumatic stress disorder (PTSD), 177, 196, 205

Registration Day, 9–11
Rice, Grantland, 19, 114, 171, 173, 180, 205
Robinson, Wilbert, 53, 62, 182
Roosevelt, Theodore, 22, 23
Ruth, Babe, 189, 196

seizures, 37–39, 65, 107–8, 196
shell shock, 147, 177–78, 188, 196–97, 203, 234n37

slackers, 11, 35, 45, 112

soldiers: about, 10, 18, 20; as casuals, 90, 173, 174; at detention camp, 67; and Fourth of July celebration, 92; game won by, 57–58; and Johnny Kling, 55; lodging for, 95; strict orders to, 157; training of, 42; train travel by, 94–95

Spanish influenza, 158, 159

spring training, 5, 23, 81, 152, 156, 191

Stankowski, Anton, 26, 27, 29

St. Louis Browns, 14, 32, 56, 62, 124, 185

St. Louis Cardinals, 15, 24, 47, 55, 56, 189

St. Mihiel, 119–26

submarines, 4, 41, 46, 90, 92, 98

Sunday baseball games, 110–11, 114–15

Third Army, 152, 153, 157, 163

Thirty-Fourth Division, 41, 42

Thirty-Seventh Division, 93, 132, 133, 134, 152

Thompson, T. B., 80, 102, 123, 144

traumatic brain injury (TBI), 37, 38, 197

Twenty-Eighth Division, 133–34, 140, 143–44, 146, 156, 167

U-boats, 3, 90, 91, 98

Union Pacific Railroad, 29, 63, 66, 73

University of Illinois football team, 28, 29

U.S. armed forces, 10, 41, 162, 170, 179, 188

U.S. Army, 104, 115; American Expeditionary Forces, 76, 90, 95, 141, 164, 185; Coast Artillery Corps, 18, 96, 117; life in, 41, 66, 68, 84, 181; as occupation army, 153, 163; service in, 38, 42, 47, 180, 185; troops, 86, 96, 111, 115, 137–39, 142, 173

USS Huntington, 91, 92

Wait, Lloyd L., 24, 27, 52, 55, 82, 107, 111, 116

Ward, Charles: about, 53; at Camp Funston, 56; and Charles Ebbets, 145, 162; and Clarence Mitchell, 86–88; as coach, 184; and Dodgers, 184; marching toward Germany, 154; and Otis Lambeth, 165, 183–84; and Pete Alexander, 110, 148, 149; and reception from Germans, 157; war experiences of, 137, 149, 225n6; and Win Noyes, 58

warfare methods, 96, 132

Weeghman, Charles N., 35, 40, 44–46, 61

Wetzel, Franklin, 24, 52–53, 152, 157, 185, 213n17

Wight, Arthur A., 137, 227n51

Wilson, Woodrow, 3, 4, 6, 9, 76

Winn, Frank L., 77, 168, 169

Winning Team (movie), 202

Withington, Paul: about, 20, 228n65; in army, 21–22; as coach, 21, 187; education of, 21; and Eighty-Ninth Division, 54–57; exceptional gallantry of, 140; and gridiron season, 25–27; heading to Camp Devens, 75–76; and Major Leaguers, 22; as medical officer, 120–21; in World War II, 187

Witt, Lawton "Whitey," 13, 14, 47

Wood, Leonard, 22–23, 50–51, 57, 74, 76–77

World Series: about, 2, 9, 14; and Chicago Cubs, 118, 175; and Major League baseball, 152; in 1917, 24; in 1919, 185; in 1920, 183; in 1926, 189

World War II, 186, 187, 197

Wright, William, 129, 131–33, 142

Wright-Wood-Winn, 77, 167

Wrigley, Charles, 171, 175, 176, 177